First World War
and Army of Occupation
War Diary
France, Belgium and Germany

17 DIVISION
Divisional Troops
Divisional Signal Company
1 June 1915 - 28 February 1918

WO95/1994

The Naval & Military Press Ltd
www.nmarchive.com
Published in association with The National Archives

Published by

The Naval & Military Press Ltd

Unit 10 Ridgewood Industrial Park,
Uckfield, East Sussex,
TN22 5QE England
Tel: +44 (0) 1825 749494

www.naval-military-press.com

www.nmarchive.com

This diary has been reprinted in facsimile from the original. Any imperfections are inevitably reproduced and the quality may fall short of modern type and cartographic standards.

© **Crown Copyright**
Images reproduced by permission of The National Archives, London, England, 2015.

Contents

Document type	Place/Title	Date From	Date To
Heading	17th Division 17th Divl Sig. Coy R.E. Jly 1915-Feb 1919		
Heading	17th. Division. 17th Signal Coy. RE Vol I 12-31.7.15		
War Diary	Southampton	12/07/1915	12/07/1915
War Diary	Havre	13/07/1915	14/07/1915
War Diary	Lumbres	15/07/1915	15/07/1915
War Diary	Renescure	18/07/1915	18/07/1915
War Diary	Steenvoorde	19/07/1915	19/07/1915
War Diary	Renninghelst (Zevecolen)	24/07/1915	24/07/1915
War Diary	Zevecoten	25/07/1915	31/07/1915
War Diary	Southampton	12/07/1915	12/07/1915
War Diary	Harve	13/07/1915	14/07/1915
War Diary	Lumbres	15/07/1915	15/07/1915
War Diary	Renescure	18/07/1915	18/07/1915
War Diary	Steenvoorde	19/07/1915	19/07/1915
War Diary	Renninghelst (Zevecolen)	24/07/1915	24/07/1915
War Diary	Zevecoten	25/07/1915	31/07/1915
War Diary	Renninghelst	04/08/1915	31/08/1915
Diagram etc	Diagram of Communication from 17th Divl Signal Office		
Heading	17th Division. 17th Signal Coy. RE. Vol. II From 4-31.8.15		
War Diary	Renninghelst	04/08/1915	31/08/1915
Diagram etc			
Miscellaneous	50th, Infantry Brigade.	02/10/1915	02/10/1915
Miscellaneous			
Operation(al) Order(s)	17th Div. Op Order No. 19 (Extracts)		
Miscellaneous			
Miscellaneous	17th. Division Operation Order No. 20	05/10/1915	05/10/1915
Operation(al) Order(s)	17th Division Order No. 7	01/08/1915	01/08/1915
Diagram etc			
Heading	17th Division. 17th Signal Company RE. Vol. 3 Sept. 15		
War Diary	Reninghelst	03/09/1915	05/10/1915
War Diary	Steenvoorde	06/10/1915	22/10/1915
War Diary	Renninghelst	23/10/1915	31/10/1915
Heading	17th Division 17th Signal Coy RE. Vol 4 Oct 15		
War Diary	Reninghelst	01/10/1915	06/10/1915
War Diary	Steenvoorde	06/10/1915	22/10/1915
War Diary	Reninghelst	23/10/1915	31/10/1915
Operation(al) Order(s)	Operation Order No. 21	20/10/1915	20/10/1915
Miscellaneous	Reliefs Of 3rd Division By 17th Division.		
Operation(al) Order(s)	17th Division Operation Order No. 23	07/11/1915	07/11/1915
War Diary	Reninghelst	01/11/1915	27/11/1915
Heading	17th Division 17th Signal Coy. RE. Vol. 5 Nov. 15		
War Diary	Reninghelst	01/11/1915	27/11/1915
Heading	1915		
War Diary	Reninghelst	01/12/1915	31/12/1915
Heading	17th Signal Coy. RE. Vol. 6		
War Diary	Reninghelst	01/12/1915	31/12/1915

Type	Description	Start	End
War Diary	Reninghelst	01/01/1916	10/01/1916
War Diary	Tilques	11/01/1916	31/01/1916
Heading	17th Signals Vol. 7 Jan 16		
War Diary	Reninghelst	01/01/1916	10/01/1916
War Diary	Tilques	11/01/1916	29/02/1916
Heading	17th Signals Vol. 8		
War Diary		01/02/1916	29/02/1916
Diagram etc	Diagram of Connections 17th Signal Coy		
War Diary		01/03/1916	31/03/1916
Heading	17 Sig Coy RE Vol 9		
War Diary		01/03/1916	12/04/1916
War Diary	??	12/04/1916	31/05/1916
Diagram etc	Plan of CME with Artillery 52nd Brigade Lines		
War Diary		01/06/1915	30/06/1915
Heading	War Diary Of 17th Divisional Signal Coy. July 1st-31st 1916 Volume 13		
War Diary		01/07/1916	31/07/1916
Heading	17 Divisional Engineers 17th Divisional Signal Company R.E. August 1916		
War Diary		01/08/1916	31/08/1916
Heading	War Diary of 17 Signal Coy L.E. Aug 1-31 1916 Volume 14		
War Diary		01/08/1916	31/08/1916
Heading	War Diary 17 Signal Coy Aug 1-31 1916		
Map			
Heading	War Diary of 17th Divisional Signal Company R.E. September1-30th 1916. Volume 15		
War Diary		01/09/1915	06/09/1915
War Diary	In The Field	06/09/1916	30/09/1916
War Diary		01/09/1915	06/09/1915
War Diary	In The Field	06/09/1916	30/09/1916
War Diary	In The Field	01/10/1916	31/10/1916
Heading	War Diary 17th Signal Company, R.E. Volume No 16		
War Diary	In the Field	01/10/1916	03/11/1916
War Diary	Night	04/11/1916	30/11/1916
War Diary	War Diary 17th Divl Signal Coy November 1916 Vol 17		
War Diary	In The Field	01/11/1916	03/11/1916
War Diary	Night	04/11/1916	30/11/1916
War Diary	In the field	01/12/1916	31/12/1916
Heading	War Diary 17th Divisional Signal Company R.E. January 1917. Volume 19		
War Diary	In The Field	01/01/1917	31/01/1917
Diagram etc	17th Division Communications.		
Diagram etc	Communications. 17th Signal Coy R.E.		
War Diary	In The Field	01/01/1917	08/02/1917
War Diary	Field	08/02/1917	16/02/1917
War Diary	Action Head Copse	17/02/1917	20/02/1917
War Diary	Heilly	21/02/1917	28/02/1917
Diagram etc	Circuit Diagram 17th Signals		
Heading	War Diary of 17th Signal Company R.E. Vol. 20-February 1917		
War Diary	In The Field	01/02/1917	08/02/1917
Diagram etc	Route Diagram		
War Diary	Field	08/02/1917	16/02/1917
Diagram etc	Circuit Diagram 17th Signals Feb 21st-March 2nd 1916		

War Diary	Arrow Head Copse	17/02/1917	28/02/1917
War Diary	Heilly Contay	01/03/1917	12/03/1917
Diagram etc	17th Division Circuit Diagram Of Commns Willeman		
War Diary	Contay	13/03/1917	14/03/1917
War Diary	Willeman	15/03/1917	22/03/1917
War Diary	Lecauroy	23/03/1917	31/03/1917
Diagram etc	17th Division Circuit Diagram Of Communications Le Cauroy		
Diagram etc	17th Division Circuit Diagram Of Communications. Contay		
Heading	War Diary of 17th Divn'l Signal Coy R.E. Vol 21 March 1917		
Heading	War Diary Of 17th Divn'l Signal Coy RE Vol 21-March 1917		
War Diary	Heilly	01/03/1917	01/03/1917
War Diary	Contay	02/03/1917	12/03/1917
Diagram etc	17th Division Circuit Diagram Of Communications. Contay		
Heading	17th Division Circuit Diagram Of Commns Willeman		
War Diary	Contay	13/03/1917	14/03/1917
War Diary	Willeman	15/03/1917	22/03/1917
War Diary	Le Cauroy	23/03/1917	23/03/1917
Diagram etc	17th Division Circuit Diagram Of Communication Le Cauroy		
War Diary	Le Cauroy	24/03/1917	31/03/1917
Heading	War Diary 17th Signal Coy. R.E. Vol 22-April 1917		
War Diary	Le Cauroy	01/04/1917	05/04/1917
War Diary	Haute Avesnes	06/04/1917	08/04/1917
War Diary	Arras	09/04/1917	25/04/1917
War Diary	Le Cauroy	26/04/1917	30/04/1917
Diagram etc	17th Division Lines		
Diagram etc	17th Division Signals		
Heading	File 1st copy to war diary 1st copy com file		
Diagram etc	17th Division Lines		
War Diary	Le Cauroy	01/04/1917	05/04/1917
War Diary	Haute Avesnes	06/04/1917	10/04/1917
War Diary	Arras	11/04/1917	25/04/1917
War Diary	Le Cauroy	26/04/1917	30/04/1917
Heading	War Diary Of 17th Divl Signal Coy R.E. Vol 23-May 1917		
War Diary	Hermaville	01/05/1917	13/05/1917
War Diary	St Nicholas (Arras)	14/05/1917	31/05/1917
Miscellaneous	War Diary 17th Divn'l Signal Company Vol 23-May 1917		
War Diary	Hermaville	01/05/1917	09/05/1917
War Diary	Railway Cutting	10/05/1917	13/05/1917
Diagram etc	Hermaville		
War Diary	St Nicholas (Arras)	14/05/1917	31/05/1917
Diagram etc	C H 17th Division Wires		
Diagram etc	17th Division Wires		
Miscellaneous			
Miscellaneous	Summary of Events and Information		
Heading	17th Signal Company R.E. Secret And Confidential War Diary Vol 24-June 1917		
Miscellaneous	War Diary 17th Divn'l Signal Coy Vol 24-June 1917		
War Diary	Couterelle	01/06/1917	21/06/1917

War Diary	St Nicholas	22/06/1917	30/06/1917
Diagram etc	C H 17th Division Wire S		
Map	7th Division Wires. Map. No. 4		
War Diary	Couterelle	01/06/1917	21/06/1917
War Diary	St. Nicholas	22/06/1917	31/07/1917
Miscellaneous	War Diary Of 17th Divnl Signal Coy R.E. Vol 25-July 1917		
War Diary	St Nicholas	01/07/1917	20/07/1917
Diagram etc	17th Div. Communications		
Miscellaneous	Signal Communications-17th Division		
Diagram etc	17th Div Arty Comns		
War Diary	St. Nicholas	10/07/1917	31/07/1917
Diagram etc	Circuit Diagram Lines Left Brigade Sector		
War Diary	St Nicholas	23/07/1917	31/07/1917
Miscellaneous	Instructions Regarding Communication By Buzzer and Telephone in the Danger Zone		
Miscellaneous	Position Calls		
Miscellaneous	Artillery Wagon Lines		
Miscellaneous	Left Brigade		
War Diary	St. Nicholas	01/08/1917	31/08/1917
Heading	War Diary 17th Divn'l Signal Coy Vol 26 August 1917		
Miscellaneous	War Diary 17th Divnl Signal Coy August 1917 Vol 26		
War Diary	St. Nicholas	01/08/1917	31/08/1917
Heading	War Diary Of 17th Divn'l Signal Coy R.E. Vol 27. September 1917		
War Diary	St Nicholas	01/09/1917	25/09/1917
War Diary	La Cauroy	26/09/1917	30/09/1917
Heading	War Diary Of 17th Divn'l Signal Coy. R.E. Vol 27 September 1917		
War Diary	St Nicholas	01/09/1917	08/09/1917
Map	17th Division Map. T. 13. Fampoux		
Map	Brigade Head Quarters Shewn Thus		
War Diary	St Nicholas	01/09/1917	25/09/1917
War Diary	La Cauroy	26/09/1917	30/09/1917
Diagram etc	Details of Raid September 16th 1917		
War Diary	La Cauroy	26/09/1917	03/10/1917
War Diary	Proven	04/10/1917	10/10/1917
War Diary	Elverdinghe	11/10/1917	17/10/1917
War Diary	Proven	18/10/1917	20/10/1917
War Diary	Zutkerque	21/10/1917	31/10/1917
Miscellaneous			
Heading	War Diary 17th Divn'l Signal Coy RE. Vol 28-October 1917		
War Diary	Lecauroy	01/10/1917	03/10/1917
War Diary	Proven	04/10/1917	10/10/1917
War Diary	Elverdinghe	11/10/1917	17/10/1917
War Diary	Proven	18/10/1917	20/10/1917
War Diary	Zutkerque	21/10/1917	31/10/1917
Diagram etc	Diagram of Communications Proven 17th Divisional Signal Co. R.E.		
Diagram etc	Diagram of Communications Zutekerque 17th Divisional Signal Co. R.E.		
Diagram etc	Route Diagram 17th Divisional R.E. Signal Company Elverdinghe		
Diagram etc	Circuit Diagram 17th Divisional R.E. Signal Coy.		

Miscellaneous	Offensive Operations. G.S. Instructions No. 4 Signals And Communications.	08/10/1917	08/10/1917
Diagram etc	Stage 2. Consolidation Of Advance Position		
Diagram etc	Forecast Diagram 17th Divisional Coy R.E. Signals		
Diagram etc	Stage 1. Immediately After Advance		
Heading	War Diary of 17th Divisional Signal Co R.E. November 1917 Vol 29		
Miscellaneous	Summary of Events and Information		
War Diary	Zutkerque	01/10/1917	06/10/1917
War Diary	Proven	07/11/1917	07/11/1917
War Diary	Welsh Farm Elverdinghe	08/11/1917	30/11/1917
War Diary	Welsh Farm Elverdinghe	09/10/1917	25/10/1917
Heading	War Diary Of 17th Divnl Signal Coy R.E. Vol 29 November 1917		
Miscellaneous	Summary of Events and Information		
Diagram etc	Circuit Diagram 17th Divisional Signal Company. R.E. 19th Corps.		
War Diary	Welsh Farm Elverdinghe	16/10/1917	30/10/1917
Diagram etc	Circuit Diagram Right Artillery 17th Division 19th Corps.		
Diagram etc	17th Division Forward Signal Communications		
Diagram etc			
War Diary	Zutkerque	01/10/1917	06/10/1917
War Diary	Proven	07/10/1917	07/10/1917
War Diary	Welsh Farm Elverdinghe	08/10/1917	08/10/1917
Heading	War Diary 17th Divn'l Signal Coy R.E. Vol 29 November 1917		
Miscellaneous	17th. Division G. 246	21/10/1917	21/10/1917
Miscellaneous	Return Of Officers-17th Signal Coy. R.E.	28/11/1917	28/11/1917
Miscellaneous	Report According To XIX Corps No. G. 61/1/1. Signals And Communications.	20/11/1917	20/11/1917
Miscellaneous	Report According To XIX Corps No. G. 61/1/1	23/11/1917	23/11/1917
Miscellaneous	Report According To XIX Corps No. G. 61/1/1	30/11/1917	30/11/1917
Heading	War Diary Of 17th Divisional Signal Company. R.E. December 1917 Vol 30		
War Diary	In The Field	01/12/1917	31/12/1917
Heading	War Diary Of 17th Divl Signal Coy R.E. January 1918 Vol. 31		
War Diary	In The Field	01/01/1918	31/01/1918
War Diary	In The Field	01/01/1918	28/02/1918
Heading	17th Signal Coy, Royal Engineers. War Diary Vol. 32. February 1918		
War Diary		01/02/1918	28/02/1918

17TH DIVISION

17TH DIVL SIG. COY R.E.
JLY 1915 - FEB 1919

17TH DIVISION

17/6/19

17th Signal Coy. R.E.

Vol. I. 12 — 31.7.15.

Army Form C. 2118.

WAR DIARY
of
INTELLIGENCE SUMMARY. of 17th Signal Co R.E. Signal Company

(Erase heading not required.)

Instructions regarding War Diaries and Intelligence Summaries are contained in F. S. Regs., Part II. and the Staff Manual respectively. Title pages will be prepared in manuscript.

Place	Date	Hour	Summary of Events and Information	Remarks and references to Appendices
SOUTHAMPTON	12.7.15	6 pm	Head Qtrs & No 1 Section 17th Signal Co Sailed for France	WRA
HAVRE	13.7.15	9 am	Arrived - Disembarked marched to Rest Camp No 5.	WRA
HAVRE	14.7.15	2.59 pm	Entrained	WRA
LUMBRES	15.7.15	9 am	Detrained & units billeted. No 2, 3, & 4 Sections came over with their respective Bdes - 50th, 51st, 52nd = Cable communication established with all Bdes & GHQ. Other units by D.R.	WRA
RENESCURE	18.7.15	2 pm	Marched new Signal Office opened at time indicated. Communication by Cable established with 50th Bde at ARQUES, 51st Bde at WALLOW CAPPEL and GHQ, other units by DR. Unit billeted	WRA
STEENVOORDE	19.7.15	9 pm	Marched here. Communication by cable with 5th Corps at ABEELE, 17th Divl ART. at CAESTRE, 51st Bde at EECKE, 52nd Bde at GODEWAERSVELDE. Other units by DR. Unit billeted	WRA
RENNINGHELST (ZEVECOTEN)	24.7.15	10 AM	MARCHED. Signal office opened at time stated - Cable communication established with 50th Bde at LA CLYTTE, 52nd near OUDERDOM and with 5th Corps. Telephonic Communication with 5 Corps, and G & Q branches 17 Divl Staff. Unit in huntments.	WRA

1577 Wt.W10791/1773 500,000 1/15 D. D. & L. A.D.S.S./Forms/C. 2118.

WAR DIARY
OF
INTELLIGENCE SUMMARY.

(Erase heading not required.)

Army Form C. 2118.

Place	Date	Hour	Summary of Events and Information	Remarks and references to Appendices
ZEVECOTEN	25/7	—	Lateral communication with 3rd, 46th and 28th Div established. The 17th Div are taking over this area from 3rd Div, when completed a diagram of the system of communications will be entered —	Appx. WW.1
"	31/7		Situation unchanged	

Army Form C. 2118.

WAR DIARY
of
INTELLIGENCE SUMMARY. of 17th Signal Co. R.E.
(Erase heading not required.)

Instructions regarding War Diaries and Intelligence Summaries are contained in F.S. Regs., Part II. and the Staff Manual respectively. Title pages will be prepared in manuscript.

Place	Date	Hour	Summary of Events and Information	Remarks and references to Appendices
SOUTHAMPTON	12.7.15	6 pm	Head Qtrs & No 1 Section 17th Signal Co. Sailed for France	WR24
HAVRE	13.7.15	9 am	Arrived - Disembarked marched to Rest Camp No 5.	WR34.
HAVRE	14.7.15	2.59 pm	Entrained	WR36
LUMBRES	15.7.15	9 am	Detrained & units billeted - No 2, 3, & 4 Sections came over with their respective Bdes - 50th, 51st & 52nd. Cable communication established with all Bdes of G.H.Q. Other units by D.R.	WR38
RENESCURE	18.7.15	2 pm	Marched here. Signal office opened at time indicated. Communication by Cable established with 50th Bde at ARQUES, 51st Bde at WALLOW CAPPEL and G.H.Q., other units by D.R. Unit billeted	WR4
STEENVOORDE	19.7.15	9 pm	Marched here. Communication by cable with 5th Corps at ABEELE, 51st Bde at EECKE, 52nd Bde at GODEWAERSVELDE. Divl ART. at CAESTRE. Unit billeted other units by D.R.	WR41
RENNINGHELST (ZEVECOTEN)	24.7.15	10 AM	MARCHED. Signal office opened at time stated - Cable communication established with 50th Bde at LA CLYTTE, 52nd near OUDERDOM and with 5th Corps. Telephone communication with 5 Corps, and Gr Q branches 17th DIVl Staff. Unit in huttments.	WR44

Army Form C. 2118.

WAR DIARY
or
INTELLIGENCE SUMMARY.
(Erase heading not required.)

Instructions regarding War Diaries and Intelligence Summaries are contained in F. S. Regs., Part II. and the Staff Manual respectively. Title pages will be prepared in manuscript.

Place	Date	Hour	Summary of Events and Information	Remarks and references to Appendices
ZEVECOTEN	25/7/-	–	Lateral communication with 3rd A.D. and 28th Div established. The 17th Div are taking over this area from 3rd Div, when completed a diagram of the System of communications will be entered –	msg. W24
"	31/7/-		Situation unchanged	

1577 Wt. W10791/1773 500,000 1/15 D. D. & L. A.D.S.S./Forms/C. 2118.

Army Form C. 21

WAR DIARY
or
INTELLIGENCE SUMMARY.
(Erase heading not required.)

Place	Date	Hour	Summary of Events and Information	Remarks and references to Appendices
RENNING-HELST	4.8.15		On 3rd August the 17th Div took over command of the area occupied by the 7th and 9th Brigades. Diagram was <s>Diagram of communication attached</s> sent	
"	"		On the night of the 3rd/4th August No 54154 Motor Cyclist Corporal MORGAN. A.P. was seriously injured by being run over by a motor ambulance. He was taken to the nearest Field Ambulance, & has been evacuated to the Base.	WD81
"	8.8.15		In accordance with W.O. letter A.G.2 B/5177 of 3.8.15 No 54215 Corporal Motor Cyclist BRADLEY E.T. was sent to England for the purpose of being appointed to a commission in the Naval air service.	WD81
"	12.8.15		The following reinforcement draft joined the company No 76572 Motor Cyclist Corporal CUTBUSH.F.S. " 64894 Lance Corp. WEBB. O.S. " 50442 Sapper MILES. A.E. " 51398 Sapper RAWLINSON. H.J. " 48216 Pioneer CORNISH. W	WD81

Army Form C. 2118

WAR DIARY
or
INTELLIGENCE SUMMARY.
(Erase heading not required.)

Instructions regarding War Diaries and Intelligence Summaries are contained in F. S. Regs., Part II. and the Staff Manual respectively. Title pages will be prepared in manuscript.

Place	Date	Hour	Summary of Events and Information	Remarks and references to Appendices
RENINGHELST	15.8.15		The following re-inforcement joined today No. 30393 Motor cyclist Corporal TAYLOR. N.C.	
	15.8.15		50th Inf. Brigade returned by the 51st Inf Brigade, came back from the front line to rest near RENINGHELST. No 3 Bde Signal Section relieve No 2 Section.	
	23.8.15		No 50180 Motor cyclist Corporal LOBB.G. who was admitted to hospital on the 13th instant was today sent down to the Base.	
	27.8.15		50 Inf. Bde relieved 51st Inf Bde, & consequently No 2 Signal Section relieved No 3.	
	31.8.15		During the month communications have been steadily improving. A diagram showing existing lines from the Divisional office is attached	

W.P. Ashton Major
Comdg 17th Signal Co RE

1577 Wt.W10791/1773 500,000 1/15 D.D. & L. A.D.S.S./Forms/C. 2118.

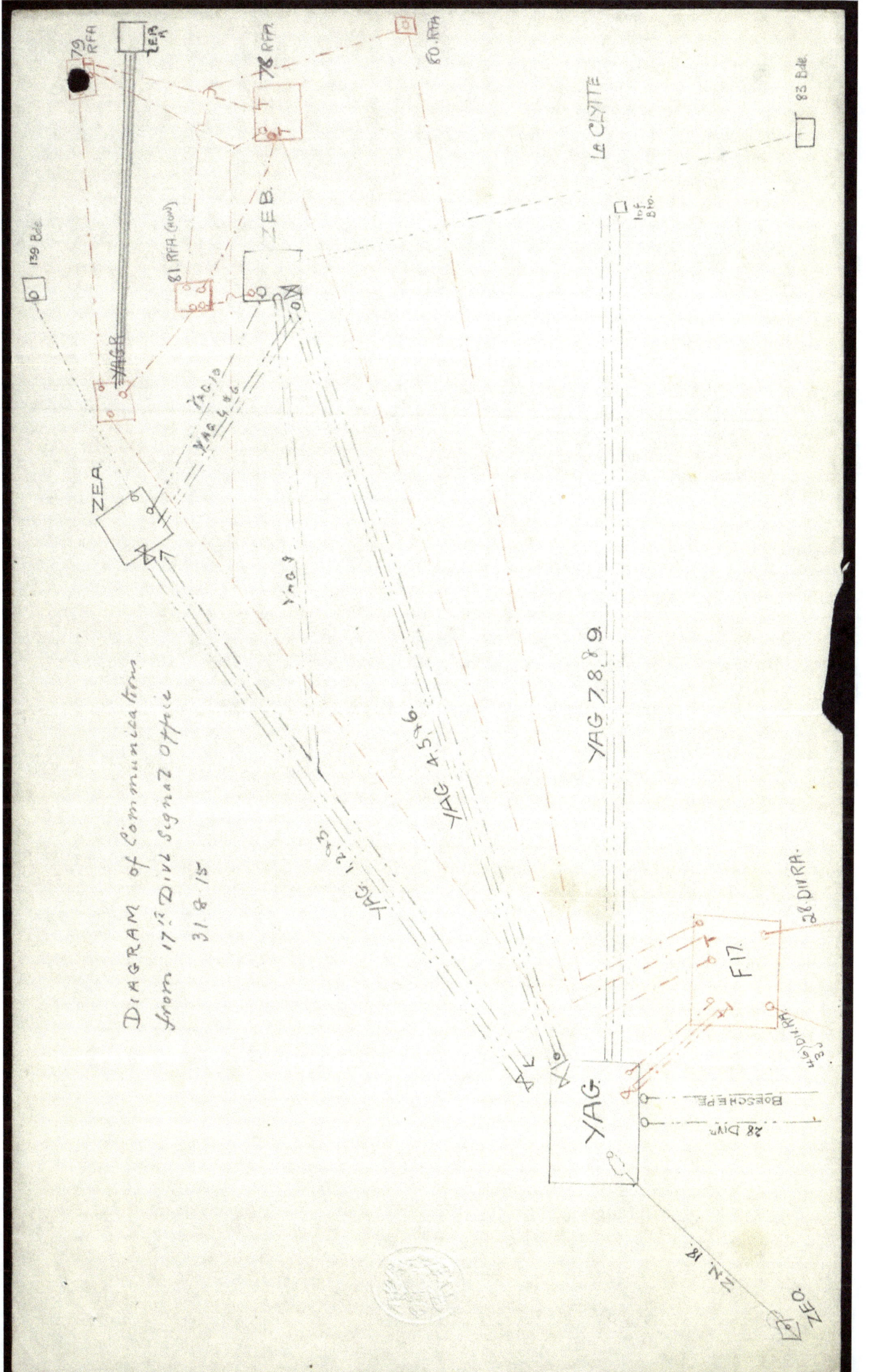

121/6907

17th Division

17th Signal Coy. RE.
Vol: II
From 4 - 31. 5. 15

WAR DIARY
or
INTELLIGENCE SUMMARY.

Army Form C. 2118.

Place	Date	Hour	Summary of Events and Information	Remarks and references to Appendices
RENNING- -HELST	4.8.15		On 3rd August the 17th Div took over command of the area occupied by the 7th and 9th Brigades. Diagram of Brigade Diagram of communication attached	
"	8.8.15		On the night of the 3rd/4th August No 54154 Motor Cyclist Corporal MORGAN A.P. was seriously injured by being run over by a motor ambulance. He was taken to the nearest Field Ambulance, & has been evacuated to the Base. In accordance with W.O letter A.G.2 B/5177 of 3.8.15 No 54215 Corporal Motor Cyclist BRADLEY E.T. was sent to England for the purpose of being appointed to a commission in the Naval air service.	WMS/ WMS/
"	12.8.15		The following reinforcement draft joined the Company No 76572 Motor Cyclist Corporal CUTBUSH F.J. " 64894 Lance Corp WEBB O.S. " 50442 Sapper MILES A.E " 51398 Sapper RAWLINSON H.J. " 48216 Pioneer CORNISH W	WMS/

Army Form C. 2118.

WAR DIARY
or
INTELLIGENCE SUMMARY.
(Erase heading not required.)

Instructions regarding War Diaries and Intelligence Summaries are contained in F. S. Regs., Part II. and the Staff Manual respectively. Title pages will be prepared in manuscript.

Place	Date	Hour	Summary of Events and Information	Remarks and references to Appendices
	13.6.15		The following re-inforcement joined today No. 30393 Motor cyclist Corporal TAYLOR N.C.	WAH
	15.8.15		50th Inf Brigade relieved by the 51st Inf Brigade, came back from the front line to rest near RENINGHELST No 3 Bde Signal Section relieves No 2 Section.	WAH
	23.8.15		No 50180 Motor cyclist Corporal LOBB.G who was admitted to hospital on the 13th instant was today sent down to the Base.	WAH
	27.8.15		50 Inf Bde relieved 51st Inf Bde, & consequently No 2 Signal Section relieved No 3.	WAH
	31.8.15		During the month communications have been steadily improved. A diagram showing existing lines from the Divl Signal Office is attached	WAH

W S Popham Major
Comdg 1st Signal Coy

RENINGHELST

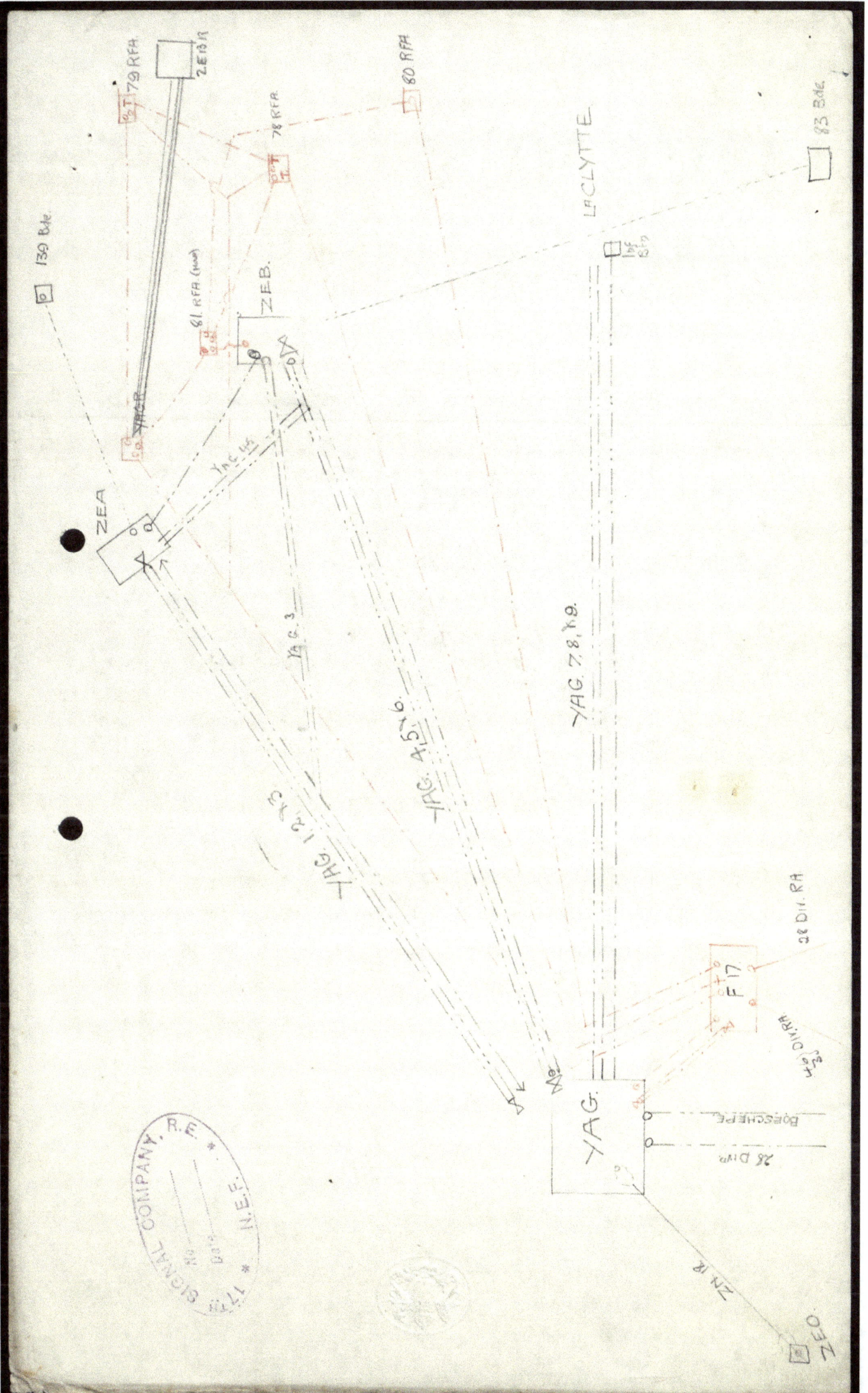

Secret

50th. Infantry Brigade.
51st.   "   "
52nd.   "   "
C. R. A.
C. R. E.
A.
Signals.
~~Pioneer Battalion~~
~~Motor Machine Gun Battery.~~

It is probable that the 17th. Division will be relieved from the trenches and moved into rest area early next week. The programme of relief will be, as far as is known at present, as below. Definite orders will be issued later, and this must be taken as a preliminary warning.

Night.
4th.-5th.
(1) Two left Battns. 51st. Bde. will be relieved by a Bde. of the 9th. Division.

(2) The 50th. Bde. in ST ELOI sector will be relieved by a Bde. of the 14th. Division. Trenches 27 and 28 will not be relieved till following night.

(3) 52nd. Inf. Bde. will be relieved by a Bde. of Canadian Corps.

Night
5th.-6th.
(4) Remaining Battalions of 51st. Bde. and trenches 27 - 28 will be relieved by a Bde. 7th. Division.

Artillery reliefs will take place on nights of 3rd./4th. and 5th./6th. under arrangements made by C.R.As.

Command of ~~mark~~ front of two left Battns. of 51st. Bde. will be taken by 9th. Division and of front taken over from 52nd. Bde. will be taken over by 2nd. Canadian Division from completion of relief on 4th./5th. Remainder of front held by 17th. Division including portion taken over by Brigade 14th. Division will be retained by G.O.C. 17th. Division till completion of reliefs on 5th./6th.

TRENCH STORES AND GRENADES. Detailed orders will be issued later, but probably the following will be handed over - Catapults, grenade throwers, bulged rifles for firing rifle grenades, rifle grenade stands, rifle batteries, pumps other than mining, all telephones and accessories over regimental establishment.

MAPS. Orders will be issued about maps but units should be prepared to hand over in good order all trench maps.

2

HEADQUARTERS. Headquarters of 51st. Bde. will remain at
WOODCOTE HOUSE till completion of relief on 5th./6th.

NEW BILLETS & HEADQUARTERS. Orders will be issued later, but
it is probable that two Brigades will move to an area west of
POPERINGHE.

DEFENCE SCHEMES. Brigadiers will endeavour to send in their
defence schemes for original areas to this office by Monday
morning.

OFFENSIVE MACHINE GUNS. Will be taken out of position before
sunrise on Tuesday and put into a thorough state of repair.
If arrangements can be made with relieving formations to replace them/before
Tuesday orders will be issued for their earlier removal.

OFFICERS N.C.Os. and MEN ABSENT ON INSTRUCTIONAL COURSES
Application has been made for their return to their respective
units, but as the list made up in this office may not be complete
Brigade and other formations will forward a list to this office
of all whom they wish recalled.

TRENCH WARDENS. Will be relieved at same time as Brigades.

2/10/15.

Lieut. Col.
G.S. 17th. Division.

	Monday night	Tuesday night 5	Wednesday night 6
Inf. 50 Inf. Bde.	Move to Reninghelst	Billets Steenvoorde area	Rest
51st Inf 7 Borders 10 Sherwoods 7 Lincolns 8 S. Staffs	Reninghelst	} Rest } Reninghelst	Billets at Eecke
52 Inf & 9 N.F.	La Clytte, Mille-Kruis & St Hubertshoek	billets GODEWAERSVELDE area	Rest.
R.A.		Remain present lines unless fresh orders.	
77. 7" Co. 78. 43.		March with 50" " 50"	March to billets at Eecke with 51
A S. York Dp	Remain at Boescheppe		
Cyclist Co.			WINNEZEELE (J.17)
12. M.M.G. 17 Div. Train	Remain at Godewaersvelde.		
34 San. Sec. Mob. Vet. Sec. Field Ambs		Billets in square R1 with their respective Brigade	Steenvoorde
Div H Q			To Steenvoorde

.... Major.
Commanding 17th. Signal Coy. R.E.

17th Div. Op. order no 19. (Extracts)

The 7th Lin. Regt, 8. S. Staffs & two coys E Yorks will be relieved by the 27th Inf. Bde & march to Reninghelst.

2. Moves from bivouacs to rest billets as below.

Unit	Bivouac	Destination	Route	Starting point	Time
50 Inf. Bde. less 2 coys 7 E Yorks 78 RE	Reninghelst	Steenvoorde	Ren. Poperinghe Abeele Steenvoorde	Rd June G.34 d 4.2	6 pm
53 F. Am.	Boeschepe	Steenvoorde	Godewaers-velde		5.30
52 I. Bde	La Clytte Mic Kemis St Huberts wood	Godewaers velde	La Clytte Reninghelst Westoutre Boeschepe &	Rd June G. 34 d 10.6	7.0
Mob Vet Sec	Present billets	Billets in R.1	Under arrangements of ADVS		4-0

Brigades to report to Div. HQ when clear of their starting pts.

O.C. My dist. Coy will arrange to block roads & provide guides etc.

_____ Major,
Commanding 17th. Signal Coy. R.E.

Copy. No. 12

17th. DIVISION OPERATION ORDER No. 20.   5/10/15.

1. The following moves will take place to-morrow :-

Unit	Bivouacs & Billets	Destination	Route	Starting Point.	Time.
Hd.Qrs.	RENINGHELST	STEENVOORDE	Under arrangements of Camp Commandant.	Under arrangements of Camp Commandant	a.m 11.0
34th.San. Sect.	do	do	do	do	
Cyclist Co	do	WINNEZEELE	By small parties during day under arrangements of O.C Cyclist Coy.		
12th.M.M.G Btty.	do	do	do under arrangements of O.C. M.M.G.Bty.		
Mob.Vet. Sect.	do	Billets in R.1	Under arrangements of A.D.V.S.		11.0
Bde.Am.Col.			Under arrangements of C.R.A	Clear of RENINGHELST	p.m 5.45
51st.I.Bde 51st.Fd.Amb. 77th.Fd.Co. R.E.	RENINGHELST	EECKE	RENINGHELST WEST OUTRE R.16c.4.8 BOESCHE E R.1d.3.4 GODEWAE SVELDE EECKE	Rd.Junc. B.34d.4.2 & 7.3	6.0
2.Cos.E. Yor's	RENINGHELST	STEENVOORDE	POPERINGHE ABEELE STEENVOORDE	RENINGHELST	5.30

2. O.C. Cyclists will make arrangements for blocking the roads and providing guides for the Inf. Bde., reporting to Brigadier 51st. Inf. Bde., arrangements made before noon.

3. R.A. will march under arrangements made by C. R. A.

Issued at 6 p.m.   (sgd) A. H. Marindin, Lieut. Col.
G.S. 17th. Division.

Copies to:-
50th.I.Bde.   Copy No.1
51st.I.Bde.   " 2
52nd.I.Bde.   " 3   A.D.V.S.   Copy No.8   C.R.A.   Copy No.13.
Cyclist Coy.   " 4   *5th.Corps   " 9   Office   " 14
Q.   " 5   *24th. Div.   " 10   "   " 15
C.R.E.   " 6   *2nd.Can.Div. " 11   " 16
A.D.M.S.   " 7   Sign.Co.   " 12   *For information.

17th Division Order No. 7

Ref. Map 1/40,000 Sheet 28.   RENINGHELST
                                                1.8.15.

1. 52nd Bde. and 93rd Fld. Co. R.E. will take over on the night of 1st/2nd Aug. the trenches now held by 9th Bde. The trench line runs approximately from the VIERSTRAAT - WYTSCHAETE road to 250 yds. south west of ST. ELOI. These troops are to be clear of the VLAMERTINGE - VOORMEZEELE road by 11 pm.

2. 50th Bde. and 78th Fld. Co. R.E. will move on the night of the 1st/2nd Aug. to H 23 c where they will halt, with a view to taking over the trenches of 7th Bde. on the night of the 2nd/3rd Aug. The trench line runs from the left of 52nd Bde. to the canal (excl.) These troops are to be clear of the cross roads between H 16 and H 22 by 1 a.m.

3. The above reliefs will be carried out under the orders of 3rd Div. All trench stores, including grenades on charge of Bdes. are being handed over to the relieving Bde.

4. The 51st Bde. and 77th Fld. Co. R.E. will move on the night of the 1st/2nd Aug. to the CHATEAU in H 23 b, where they will remain in Corps Reserve. These troops must not reach the cross roads between H. 16 and H 22 before 1 a.m.

5. The 17th Div. assumes command of the section to be occupied by 50th and 52nd Bdes. on completion of relief on night of 2nd/3rd Aug. when the artillery now in action under 3rd Div. covering the front of 9th & 7th Inf. Bdes. will come under the orders of 17th Division.

6. The 27th (2") and 32nd (4pr.) Trench Howitzer Btys. now with 3rd Division will be transferred to 17th Division on completion of relief on night 2/3rd August.

7. Progress and completion of reliefs to be reported to this office.

                                    E. Humphreys fed
                                    Jn. Lt. Col.
                                    G.S., 17th Division.

Issued at 12 noon to
50th Bde.   3rd Div.
51st Bde.   Train
52nd Bde. 3 copies   A.D.M.S.
C.R.A.
C.R.E.
A.A. & Q.M.G.
Signal Co.

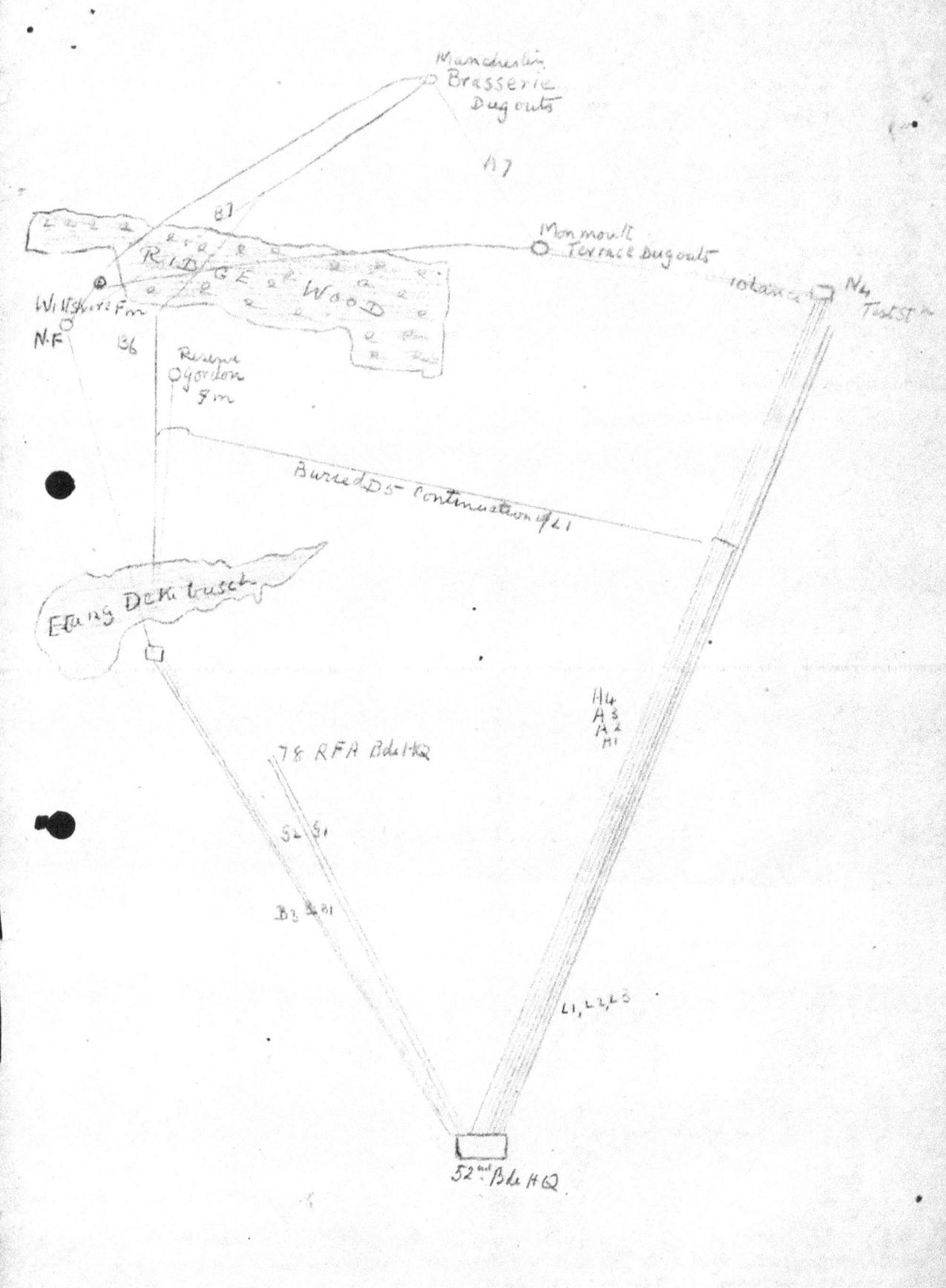

D/7050

17th Division

17th Signal Company R.E.
Vol: 3
Sept 15.

WAR DIARY
or
INTELLIGENCE SUMMARY.

(Erase heading not required.)

Army Form C. 2118.

Place: RENINGHELST

Date	Hour	Summary of Events and Information	Remarks and references to Appendices
3.9.15		51st Infantry Brigade relieved 50th Inf Bde	WSP
12.9.15		50th Inf Brigade relieved 51st Inf Bde	WSP
14.9.15		No 58082 Sapper PRESTON P.S. transferred from 17th Signal Co RE To Headquarters Signals 2nd Army	WSP
		No 34006 Sapper MacLENNAN, K. transferred from Signals 2nd Army to 19th Sig Co RE	WSP
26.9.15		51st Infantry Bde relieved 50th Infantry Bde.	WSP
		No 53105 Gunner CROWTHER, J. admitted to hospital	WSP
28.9.15		No 58360 Sapper LEWIS J transferred from 17th Signal Co. RE To Headquarters Signals 2nd Army.	WSP
		No 34008 Sapper ROSE M.M transferred from Signal 2nd Army to 17th Signal Co RE	WSP
		Corporal L0133 G.V. discharged from hospital	WSP
29.9.15		No 50180 Corporal L0133 G.V. discharged from hospital	WSP
		50 Inf Bde relieved K 51st Inf Bde	WSP

W.M.Shan

Army Form C. 2118.

WAR DIARY
or
INTELLIGENCE SUMMARY.

(Erase heading not required.)

Place: RENINGHELST

Date	Hour	Summary of Events and Information	Remarks and references to Appendices
3.9.15		51st Infantry Brigade relieved 50th Inf Bde	Appx
10.9.15		50th Inf Brigade relieved 51st Inf Bde	Appx
14.9.15		No 58082 Sapper PRESTON R.S. transferred from 17th Signal Co R.E. To Headquarters Signals 2nd Army.	Appx
		No 34006 Sapper MacLENNON, K. transferred from Signals 2nd Army K 14th Sig Co. R.E.	Appx Appx
20.9.15		51st Infantry Bde relieved 50th Infantry Bde.	Appx
"		No 53105 Driver CROWTHER, J. admitted to hospital	Appx
25.9.15		No 57360 Sapper LEWIS J. transferred from 17th Signal Co R.E. To Headquarters Signals 2nd Army.	Appx
		No 34008 Sapper ROSE M.M. transferred from Signals 2nd Army to 17th Signal Co R.E.	Appx
		No 50180 Corporal LOTT G.V. discharged from Hospital	Appx
29.9.15		50 Inf Bde relieved to 51st Inf Bde	Appx

W.M.Sloan Major,
Commanding 17th. Signal Coy. R.E.

WAR DIARY
or
INTELLIGENCE SUMMARY.
(Erase heading not required.)

Army Form C. 21

Place	Date	Hour	Summary of Events and Information	Remarks and references to Appendices
RENING-HELST	1.X.15		Dennis Motor Lorry (No 585T) transferred (with A.S.C Drivers Pte. LINDBERG G.P. No M2/098083 and TUGWELL A.E. No M2/035181) to Divisional Headquarters	used.
	1.X.15		No 54265 Corp. HARRISON P.A. accidentally burnt & admitted to hospital	used
	1.X.15		No 53090 Dr WHITTLE awarded days field punishment (No 2) for insubordinate conduct.	used.
	2.X.15		No 3 Brigade Signal Section 17th Div Completed taking over the Communications of the 137th & 139th Infantry Brigades also on the night of the 1st/2nd Oct	used.
	3.X.15		No 46031 Sap. ENGLAND } admitted to hospital	
	5.X.15		No 66865 Dr BARNES } discharged from hospital	used
			No 53105 " CROWTHER R J } rejoined unit.	
	5.X.15		On the night 4/5 Oct the following reliefs took place:- (1) Two left Batt ns 51st Bde relieved by a Bde 9th Div (2) 50th Inf. Bde in ST. ELOI Sector except trenches 27 & 28 were	used

Army Form C. 2118

WAR DIARY
or
INTELLIGENCE SUMMARY.
(Erase heading not required.)

Place	Date	Hour	Summary of Events and Information	Remarks and references to Appendices
		6.x.15	Relieved by a Bde 14th Division. (3) 52nd Inf Bde were relieved by a Bde of the 7th Division Remaining Bnt ys 51st Bde and finishes no/ 27 & 28 were relieved by a Bde. 7th Div. Artillery reliefs took place on the nights 3/4th Oct & 5/6th Oct under orders of C.R.A.s. All reliefs were carried out without interruption of communication -	appx.
	5.x.15		After relief on the 5 Oct. No 2 Bde Signal Sec. with 50th Inf Bde moved into rest area at STEENVOORDE. No 4 Bde Section with 52nd Inf moved into rest area at GODEWAERSVELDE No 3 Bde Sec with 51st Inf Bde moved into rest area at EECKE	appx.
STEEN-VOORDE	6.x.15		Head Qrs & No 1 Sec Tion 17th Signal Co moved into rest area at STEENVOORDE.	appx.

Army Form C. 21

WAR DIARY
or
INTELLIGENCE SUMMARY.
(Erase heading not required.)

Instructions regarding War Diaries and Intelligence Summaries are contained in F. S. Regs., Part II. and the Staff Manual respectively. Title pages will be prepared in manuscript.

Place	Date	Hour	Summary of Events and Information	Remarks and references to Appendices
STEEN-VOORDE	7.X.15		Communications in Div'l area as follows:— Telegph. direct line to 50th Inf Bde, continued to 51st Inf Bde at EECKE. To 52nd Inf at GODEWAERSVELDE, thro 3rd Corps Signal Office. Telephonic Direct line to 50th Inf Bde. To 51st & 52nd Inf Bdes thro' Signals 1st Army. Communication with other units by messenger or D.R.	
	3.X.15		No 48037 Sapper ENGLAND.P. admitted to hospital	
	5.X.15		Despatch rider Corporal HARRISON P.A. no. 54285 admitted to hospital	
	16.X.15		No 44697 Corporal CAMPBELL H. reinstated from Pioneer (Corporal) to Sapper (Corporal) with effect from 11.9.15	
	"		No 44115 Pioneer BATTY A.E. reinstated Sapper with effect from 8.9.15	
	"		No 52122 Pioneer LYE W.F. reinstated Sapper with effect from 9.9.15	
	"		No 60676 No HOWARD F. admitted to hospital	
	19.X.15		No 45234 Sapper GILLESPIE. F accidently injured & admitted to hospital	
	20.X.15		17th Division ordered to take over trenches held by 3rd Division	

WAR DIARY
or
INTELLIGENCE SUMMARY.

Army Form C. 2118.

Place	Date	Hour	Summary of Events and Information	Remarks and references to Appendices
STEEN-VOORDE	21.X.15		During the night of the 20/21 Oct. the 51st Infy Bde relieved the 8th Infantry Brigade & took over their communications.	west
	22.X.15		During the night of the 21/22nd the 50th Infy Bde relieved the 9th Infy Bde & took over their communications.	west
	23.X.15		During the night of the 22nd/23rd 52 Infy Bde moved into 3rd Divl area to rest billets. 3rd & 4th Divs moved to RENINGHELST area and took over the Divl communications from 3rd Div.	west
RENING-HELST	26.X/15		Sapr 58338 Sapper CUNNINGHAM J.M. wounded in the head by shell fire - admitted to hospital	west
	31.X.15			

WPB Wan Major.
Commanding 17th. Signal Coy. R.E.

121/7431

17th Kurwn

17 Topical Coy R.E.
Vol 4
Oct 15

WAR DIARY
or
INTELLIGENCE SUMMARY.
(Erase heading not required.)

Army Form C. 2118.

Place	Date	Hour	Summary of Events and Information	Remarks and references to Appendices
RENING- HELST	1 x 15		Dennis motor Lorry (No 585-) transferred (with A.S.C. Drivers Pte LINDBERG. G.P. No M2/098083 and TUGWELL A.E. No M2/035181) to Divisional Headquarters	appx.
	1 x 15		No 54265 Corp. HARRISON P.A. accidently burnt & admitted to hospital	appx.
	1 x 15		No 53090 Sr. WHITTLE awarded days Field Punishment (No 2) for insubordinate conduct	appx
	2 x 15		No 3 Brigade Signal Section 17th Div completed taking over the communications of the 137th & 139th Infantry Brigades on the night of 1/2 - 2/2 Oct	appx
	5 x 15		No 46031 Sapr. ENGLAND } admitted to hospital No 60865 Dr. BARNES } & discharged from hospital No 53105 " CROWTHER J.S. } & rejoined unit	appx
	5 x 15		On the night 4/5 Oct the following reliefs took place (1) Two left Batt of 51st Bde relieved by a Bde 9th Div (2) 50th Inf Bde in ST. ELOI Sector except trenches No 27 & 28 were	

Army Form C. 2118.

WAR DIARY
or
INTELLIGENCE SUMMARY.
(Erase heading not required.)

Place	Date	Hour	Summary of Events and Information	Remarks and references to Appendices
			Relieved by a Bde 14th Division (3) 52nd Inf Bde were relieved by a Bde of the 7th Division	
		6.15	Remaining Bns of 51st Bde and Lewises on 27 & 28 were relieved by a Bde 7th Div. Artillery reliefs took place on the nights 3/4 Oct and 5/6 Oct under orders of C.R.A's. All reliefs were carried out without interruption of communication.	
		5.15	After relief on the 5 Oct. No 2 Bde Sigl Sec with 50th Inf Bde moved into rest area at STEENVOORDE. No 4 Bde Section with 52nd Inf moved into rest area at GODEWAERSVELDE No 3 Bde Sec with 51st Inf Bde moved into rest area at ECKE	
STEEN- VOORDE		1.15	Head Qrs & No1 Section 17 Signal Co moved into rest area at STEENVOORDE.	

Army Form C. 2118.

WAR DIARY
or
INTELLIGENCE SUMMARY.
(Erase heading not required.)

Place	Date	Hour	Summary of Events and Information	Remarks and references to Appendices
STEEN-VOORDE		7.x.15	Communications in Div'l area as follows - Telegraph. Direct line to 50th Inf Bde, continued to 51st Inf Bde at ZECK. To 52nd Inf at GODEWAERSVELDE, also 5th Corps Signal Office. Telephonic. Direct line to 50th Inf Bde. To 51st & 52nd Inf Bdes HQrs. Signals 2nd Army. Communication with other units by messenger or D.R.	WH/SJ
		3.x.15	Sapper No 46031 ENGLAND J. P admitted to hospital	WH/SJ
		5.x.15	Despatch rider Corporal HARRISON P.A. no. 54285 admitted to hospital	WH/SJ
		16.x.15	No 44697 Corporal CAMPBELL H nominated from Pioneer (Corporal) to Sapper (Corporal) with effect from 1.9.15 No 44115 Pioneer BATTY A E nominated Sapper with effect from 8.9.15	WH/SJ
		"	No 52122 Pioneer LYE W F nominated Sapper with effect from 9.9.15	WH/SJ
		"	No 60676 Dvr HOWARD F admitted to hospital	WH/SJ
		19.x.15	Sapper No 45234 GILLESPIE accidentally injured & admitted to hospital	WH/SJ
		20.x.15	17th Division ordered to take over trenches held by 3rd Division	WH/SJ

WAR DIARY
of
INTELLIGENCE SUMMARY.

Army Form C. 2118.

Place	Date	Hour	Summary of Events and Information	Remarks and references to Appendices
STEEN-VOORDE		21.x.15	During the night of the 20/21 Oct. the 51st Infantry Bde relieved the 8th Infantry Brigade & took over their communications	W.R.H
		22.x.15	During the night of the 21st/22nd the 50th Inft Bde relieved the 9th Inft Bde & took over their communications	W.R.H
RENING-HELST		23.x.15	During the night of the 22nd/23rd 52 Inft 13de moved into 3rd Div. area to rest-billets. Brit HQ Divn moved to RENINGHELST	W.R.H
		26/x/15	Sn and took over the Divl communications from 3rd Div. No 58338 Sapper CUNNINGHAM J M wounded in the head by shell fire - admitted to hospital	W.R.H

31.X.15

W.R.H Wm.

SECRET.   COPY No. 13

OPERATION ORDER No. 21.

****

STEENVOORDE.

20/10/15.

1. The 17th Division will take over the trenches held by the 3rd Division. Reliefs will take place according to the attached table.

2. The front will be occupied as follows:-

   Right Section,   Trench A.4. inclusive,(I.30.B.1.5) to trench B.8. inclusive,(J.13.c.1.5).

   Left sector,   Trench C.1. inclusive,(J.13.c.1.5) to trench C.7. inclusive,(I.12.c.5.1).

   The right sector will be held by the 51st and 52nd Brigades alternately, four battalions in line.

   The left sector will be held by the 50th Brigade one and a half battalions in line, half a battalion at Half Way House, (I.17.c.4.8), one battalion in ramparts YPRES between SALLY PORT and LILLE GATE and one battalion in rest billets.

   The Pioneer Battalion will for the present be at ZILLEBEKE POND and will be under orders of the right Brigade for tactical purposes.

   Headquarters of the Brigades in the trenches are at ZILLEBEKE POND.

3. Further orders will be issued to the Pioneer Battalion and other troops not mentioned in the table.

4. Command of the front remains with the 3rd Division till completion of reliefs on night of   22nd/ 23rd after which G.O.C., 17th Division takes Command.

                                    (Sd)   A.H.MARINDIN. Lieut-Colonel.
Issued at:-   G.S., 17th Division.

Copies. No.1. 50th Inf.Bde.   No.10. Yorkshire Dragoons.
       " 2.   51st Inf.Bde.   " 11.   12th M.M.G.Bty.
       " 3.   52nd Inf.Bde.   " 12.   A.D.V.S.
       " 4.   C.R.A.   " 13.   Signal Company.
       " 5.   C.R.E.   " 14. *Fifth Corps.
       " 6.   A.A. & Q.M.G.   " 15. *3rd Division.
       " 7.   A.D.M.S.   " 16.   Office.
       " 8.   Pioneer Battalion.   " 17.   "
       " 9.   Cyclist Coy.

                        * For Information.

RELIEFS OF 3rd DIVISION BY 17th DIVISION.

Date	Moves	Remarks
Wednesday 20th Sept.	51st Inf. Bde. ⎫ 77th Field Co., R.E. ⎬ Move into 3rd Div. area 51st Field Amb. ⎭ G.11d.1.2 - G.17b.8.8 - G.18a.6.4 - G.11a.9.8 G.17a.8.7 - G.18a.2.5. Officers of 51st Inf. Bde. to trenches of 8th Inf. Bde. 76th Inf. Bde. moves out of above area to area west of Poperinghe.	Route - The road YPRES - POPERINGHE - ABEELE is allotted to 3rd Division. 51st Bde. can use any road south of the above. Hour of start any time after 2 p.m. Busses will be arranged for Officers going to trenches.
Thursday 21st Sept.	50th Inf. Bde. ⎫ 78th Field Co. R.E. ⎬ Move to same area as 53rd Field Amb. ⎭ above. Officers of 50th Inf. Bde. to trenches of 9th Inf. Bde. 76th Inf. Bde. moves into area vacated by 51st Inf. Bde. 51st Inf. Bde. relieves 8th Inf. Bde. in trenches. 8th Inf. Bde. moves to its own billeting area	Route - 50th Inf. Bde. moves by main ABEELE - POPERINGHE road. 76th Inf. Bde. uses roads to the south of the main road. Hour of start any time after 2 p.m. Busses will be arranged for Officers going to trenches. Route to be detailed later.
Friday 22nd Sept.	52nd Inf. Bde. ⎫ 93rd Field Co. R.E. ⎬ Move into 3rd Div. area 52nd Field Amb. ⎭ to rest billets. 8th Inf. Bde. move to STEENVOORDE 50th Inf. Bde. relieves 9th Inf. Bde. in trenches. 9th Inf. Bde. moves to bivouacs.	Route - 8th Inf. Bde. via main road through ABEELE 52nd Bde. by roads south of main road. Hour of start any time after 2 p.m. Route to be detailed later.
Saturday 23rd Sept.	Hd. Qrs. move into 3rd Division area * Artillery reliefs commence. 9th Inf. Bde. moves to GODEWAERSVELDE.	17th Division use main road. 9th Inf. Bde. use roads to the south of main road.
Sunday 24th Sept.	* Artillery reliefs completed	* Artillery reliefs to be carried out under arrangements to be made between C.R.A.s.

Reference 1/10,000   Copy No. 8

28 N.W. Sheet 4
28 N.E. Sheet 3

17th. DIVISION OPERATION ORDER NO. 23.   7/11/15.

1. The following changes on 17th. Division front will take place:-

    (a) The 52nd. Infantry Brigade will hand over the front it now occupies to the 27th. & 28th. Infantry Brigades.

    (b) The 51st. Infantry Brigade will take over the ~~area~~ line now held by the 6th. Division up to I.5.d.3.2

2. Reliefs will take place as shown on attached table. Details will be arranged between Brigades.

    Completion of each relief will be notified to Divisional Headquarters.

3. From completion of relief boundaries of areas will be as follows :-

    (a) Between 9th. and 17th. Divisions - From junction in front line J.13.c.2.3 to road junction I.24.b.2.5 to bend in road at I.24.a.1.7, westwards along south of road to I.16.d.6.1, thence to crossing of ZILLEBEKE SWITCH over road in I.18.d.2.5 (defence of road to 17th. Division), thence westwards south of farms to north corner of ZILLEBEKE POND, along west edge of pond to I.21.b.1.5, thence to present boundary I.21.a.5.5

    (b) Between 50th. and 52nd. Infantry Brigades - The present line between 17th. & 6th. Division.

    (c) Between 17th. Division and 6th. Corps - From I.5.d.3.2 to I.11.a.5.5 to I.10.a.5.5, to MENIN ROAD I.9.d.5.5, along road to MENIN GATE (defence of gate to 17th. Division), thence westwards by GRANDE PLACE and RUE D'ELVERDINGHE to level crossing in I.7.s. (streets and crossing to 17th. Division).

4. 177th. Tunnelling Coy. R.E. (less detachment with Canadian Corps) will be attached to 17th. Division.

5. Orders as to trench stores will be issued later.

6. Brigade Headquarters of 51st. Infantry Brigade will be established in YPRES. The O.C. Signals will arrange communications accordingly.

7. Please acknowledge.

                                               (sgd) A. H. Marindin, Lieut. Col.
                                                              G.S. 17th. Division.

Issued at   p.m.

50th. Inf. Bde.	Copy No. 1	A.D.M.S.	Copy No. 9
51st. " "	" " 2	Q.	" " 10
52nd. " "	" " 3	Office	" " 11
Cyclist Coy.	" " 4	"	" " 12
C. R. E.	" " 5	5th. Corps)	" " 13
C. R. A.	" " 6	6th. ") For	" " 14
Pioneer Battn.	" " 7	9th. Divn.) Information	" " 15
Signal Coy.	" " 8	6th. ")	" " 16

TABLE OF RELIEFS.

DATE.		REMARKS
	Brigades	
8th.	Officers 27th. and 28th. will be shewn trenches.	
8th./9th.	The 50th. Infantry Brigade will extend its right to right of B.8 (J.13.c.2.2)	
	28th. Infantry Brigade takes over trenches up as far as the road I.30.b.7.8 exclusive.	
	27th. Infantry Brigade takes over trenches from above road to /A.12 exclusive (I.24.d.8.9) trench	
9th.	Officers and Machine Guns 51st. Infantry Brigade go into trenches of 16th. Infantry Brigade.	
9th./10th.	27th. Infantry Brigade takes over trenches of 52nd. Infantry to right of B.8 (J.13.c.2.2) Bde.	On completion of relief 9th. Divn. takes over command of this front.
	One Battalion 51st. Infantry Brigade relieves Battalion of 16th. Infantry Brigade now in Ramparts YPRES and its detachments.	
10th./11th.	51st. Infantry Brigade completes relief of 16th. Infantry Brigade front	On completion of relief 17th. Divn. takes over command of this front.

Artillery reliefs will be arranged between C.R.As. of Divisions.

C.R.A. will arrange relief of Trench Howitzers.

WAR DIARY
or
INTELLIGENCE SUMMARY.

Army Form C. 2118.

Place	Date	Hour	Summary of Events and Information	Remarks and references to Appendices
RENING-HELST	1.xi.15		On night of 30/31 Oct 52nd Infantry Brigade relieved the 51st and 53rd Bdes Signal Section took over communications	Appx
	6.xi.15		Sapper No 45234 GILLESPIE T. Struck off strength on account of having been invalided home	Appx
	8/9.xi.15		50th Infantry Bde extended to-night to right of trench B.8. (J.13.c.2.2.)	Appx
	9/10.xi.15		27th Infy Bde took over trenches held by 52nd Inf Bde to right of B.8. (J.13.C.2.2) On the same night our Batt. 51st Inf Bde relieved a Battalion of the 16th Inf Bde in RAMPARTS YPRES and 15 detachments	Appx
	12th Nov		On night of 10/11 Nov 51st Inf Bde completed relief of 16 Infantry Brigade	
	15 Nov		52nd Inf Bde relieved 50th Inf Bde.	
	23rd Nov		Corporal No 54285 HARRISON P.A. struck off strength on	

WAR DIARY

of

INTELLIGENCE SUMMARY.

(Erase heading not required.)

Army Form C. 2118.

Place	Date	Hour	Summary of Events and Information	Remarks and references to Appendices
RENING HELST	24/11/15		Account of having been invalided to England. No 50644 2nd Cpl. CARESWELL J. sentenced by F.G.C.M. to be reduced to rank of Driver (sentence confirmed by G.O.C. 4th days F.P. No 1	
			No 58339 Sap. BRETHERICK T. wounded on duty 11.11.15	
			No 50166 Sap. WHITTON S. wounded on duty 11.11.15	
			No 45736 Cpl. BATES W. wounded on duty 15.11.15	
			No 64833 Sap. BACON A.G. and No 43326 Pioneer EDWARDS S.A. Accidentally burned and admitted to hospital	
			No 50690 Sergt ATTAWES F.C. Sentenced by F.G.C.M. to be reduced to rank of Corporal. with effect from 14/11/15.	
			No 44697 Corpl. CAMPBELL H. appointed paid acting Sergeant with effect from 15/11/15	
			No 80646 L. Cpl. THOMPSON S. appointed paid acting 2nd Corporal vice CARESWELL reduced.	

WAR DIARY
INTELLIGENCE SUMMARY

Army Form C. 2118.

3.

Place	Date	Hour	Summary of Events and Information	Remarks and references to Appendices
RENING-HELST			No 60867 Dr BATCHELOR A E appointed Lce Corpl with effect from 15.11.15	WRAP
			No 50644 Dr CARESWELL J admitted to hospital 17.11.15 -	WRAP
			Reinforcements received	
			No 28148 Motor Cyclist-Corporal TAYLOR A.D. 19.11.15 -	WRAP
			— 34033 Sapper LARDNER L 19.11.15 -	WRAP
			— 71437 " BAKER A G 19.11.15 -	WRAP
			— 75566 " LAWRIE J 19.11.15 -	WRAP
			— 62316 " ARTHUR R 19.11.15 -	WRAP
			No 49274 2nd Cpl. GIBBS. D appointed acting paid Corpl. 19.11.15 - vice Corpl BATES in whose in whose place	WRAP
			No 50632 Dr HOLT J appointed Lce Corpl. 19.11.15	WRAP
			No 60876 Dr HOWARD F. Struck off Strength 20.11.15 invalided	
	24/11/14		50" Inf Bde relieved 55nd Infantry Bde on night 24/25 Nov.	WRBT WRDY

WAR DIARY or INTELLIGENCE SUMMARY.

Army Form C. 2118.

Place	Date	Hour	Summary of Events and Information	Remarks and references to Appendices
RENING - HELST	25/11/15		No 58338 Sapper CUNNINGHAM J M rejoined after recovery from wound –	
			No 54212 M Corp HELLIER W transferred to 5 "Corps"	
			No 50161 M Corp BEAVLANDS H.E transferred from 5 Corps.	
			No 47076 Lce Corp LAST H.C. transferred to Home establishment as proving N.C.O instructor	
			No 56014 Sapper WAFE H.W. appointed Lance Corp with effect from 24/11/15	
	26.11.15		No 64833 Sap BACON H.G. No 43326 Pioneer EDWARDS S.A. and No 50144 S CARESWELL J. Struck off strength on account of Illness	
			No 58095 Sapper WILTSHIRE S. was transferred whilst on duty and admitted to hospital on 24/11/15 –	

WKS Blanchard
Lieut 17 Sig Co R.E.

131/7621

17th Kuwain

17th Signal Corps Rg.
Vol. 5

Nov. 15

Army Form C. 2118

WAR DIARY
or
INTELLIGENCE SUMMARY.
(Erase heading not required.)

Instructions regarding War Diaries and Intelligence Summaries are contained in F.S. Regs., Part II. and the Staff Manual respectively. Title pages will be prepared in manuscript.

Place	Date	Hour	Summary of Events and Information	Remarks and references to Appendices
RENING-HELST	1.XI.15		On night of 30/31 Oct 52nd Infantry Brigade relieved the 57th and Bde Signal Section took over communications	WD/APP
	6.XI.15		Sapper No 45234 GILLESPIE T. struck off strength on account of having been invalided home	WD/APP
	8/9.XI.15		50th Infantry Bde extended to-night to right of Trench B.8. (J.13 c.2.2.)	WD/APP
	9/10.XI.15		27th Inf. Bde took over trenches held by 52nd Inf. Bde to right of B.8. (J.13.c.2.2.) On the same night one Batt. 51st Inf. Bde relieved a Battalion of the 16th Inf. Bde in RAMPARTS YPRES and its detachments.	WD/APP
	12th Nov		On night of 10/11 Nov 57th Inf. Bde completed relief of 16th Infantry Brigade.	WD/APP
	15th Nov		52nd Inf. Bde relieved 50th Inf. Bde.	
	23rd Nov		Corporal No 54285 HARRISON P.A. struck off strength on	

Army Form C.2

WAR DIARY
or
INTELLIGENCE SUMMARY.
(Erase heading not required.)

Instructions regarding War Diaries and Intelligence Summaries are contained in F. S. Regs., Part II. and the Staff Manual respectively. Title pages will be prepared in manuscript.

Place	Date	Hour	Summary of Events and Information	Remarks and references to Appendices
RENING HELST	24/11/15		account of having been involved to England. No 50644 2/Corpl. CARESWELL. T. Sentence by F.G.C.M. to be reduced to rank of Driver (Sentence confirmed 6th) 14days F.P. No 1.	appx
			No 58339 Sap. BRETHERICK. T. wounded on duty 11.11.15	appx
			No 50166 Sap. WHITTON. S. wounded on duty 11.11.15	appx
			No 45738 Corp. BATES. W. wounded on duty 15.11.15	appx
			No 64833 Sap. BACON. A.G. and No 43326 Pioneer EDWARDS. S.H Accidentally burned and admitted to hospital	appx
			No 50690 Sergt ATHAWES F.C. Sentenced by F.G.C.M. to be reduced to rank of Corporal - with effect from	appx
	14/11/15		No 44697 Corp. CAMPBELL H. appointed paid acting Sergeant with effect from 16/11/15	appx
			No 57646 L. Cpl THOMPSON. S. appointed paid acting 2nd Corporal vice CARESWELL reduced.	appx

Army Form C. 2118.

WAR DIARY
or
INTELLIGENCE SUMMARY.

(Erase heading not required.)

No. 3.

Place	Date	Hour	Summary of Events and Information	Remarks and references to Appendices
RENING-HELST			No 60867 Lt BATCHELOR A.E. appointed Lce Corpl with effect from 15.11.15	West
			No 56644 Dr CARESWELL J. admitted to hospital 17.11.15	West
			Reinforcements received	
			No 28148 Motor cyclist-Corporal TAYLOR A.D. 19.11.15	West
			" 34033 Sapper LARDNER L. 19.11.15	West
			" 71437 " BAKER A.G. 19.11.15	West
			" 75568 " LAWRIE T. 19.11.15	West
			" 62316 " ARTHUR R. 19.11.15	West
			No 49274 2nd Cpl. GIBBS D. appointed acting 2nd Corp. 19.11.15 - vice Corp BATES invalided	West
			No 50632 Dr HOLT J. appointed Lce Corp. 19.11.15	West
			No 66876 Dr HOWARD F. struck off strength 20.11.15 invalided	West
	25/11/14		50th Inf Bde relieved 52nd Infantry Bde in night 24/25. Nil.	West

Army Form C. 2118.

WAR DIARY
or
INTELLIGENCE SUMMARY.

(Erase heading not required.)

4

Place	Date	Hour	Summary of Events and Information	Remarks and references to Appendices
RENING-HELST	25/11/15		No 58338 Sapper CUNNINGHAM. J.M. rejoined after recovery from wound.	
			No 54212 M.C. Corp. HELLIER W. transferred to 5 "Corps.	
			No 56161 M.C. Corp. BEANLANDS H.E. transferred from 5 Corps.	
			No 47076 Lce Corp. LAST H.C. transferred to Home establishment as junior N.C.O. instructor	
			No 56014 Sapper WHITE H.W. appointed Lance Corp with effect from 24/11/15	
	27/11/15		No 64833 Sap. BACON A.G. No 43326 Pioneer EDWARDS. SA and No 58144 Sap CARESWELL J. Struck off strength on account of illness	
			No 58090 Sapper WILTSHIRE. S, was wounded whilst on duty and admitted to hospital on 29/11/15	
	30/11/15			

WRS Colommayor
Army 17. Syd. RE.

WAR DIARY
or
INTELLIGENCE SUMMARY

Army Form C. 2118.

Place	Date	Hour	Summary of Events and Information	Remarks and references to Appendices
RENING	1.12.15		No 91336 Driver PARKIN C. and no 73086 Driver HAYHOE R. Transport to Coy from Signal Depot	WM&Y
HELST	2/12/15		52nd Bde relieved 50th Bde in front line	WM&Y
	6/12/15		M.C. Corp. LOBB G. transferred to 2nd Army Signals	WM&Y
	8/12/15		M.C. Corp. CAMPBELL T.J. Transferred to Company from Signal depot.	WM&Y
	10/12/15		50th Inf Bde relieved 52nd Inf Bde in front line	WM&Y
	11/12/15		No 44665 Serjt. HODGKINS C.A. selected for training Signal hands at Home, left for Base & struck off Strength	WM&Y
	13/12/15		Sapper WHITTEN S. (wounded) transferred to FENNY STRATFORD Signal Depot & struck off Strength	LOCAL
	14/12/15		No 50119 Corp MINNEAR C. transferred to 24th Sig'l RE	WM&Y
	"		No 43797 Pion BAKER W.C. transferred from 24th Sig'l G.R.E.	WM&Y
	15/12/15		No 75731 Sap. HAMPTON S.A. Transferred from 2nd Army Signals	WM&Y
	"		No 15712 Sap GREENALL J.B. " " " " "	WM&Y
	"		No 48216 Pion CORNISH W " " to " " "	WM&Y

WAR DIARY
or
INTELLIGENCE SUMMARY.

Army Form C. 2118.

Place	Date	Hour	Summary of Events and Information	Remarks and references to Appendices
RENING - HELST	17th		A.S.C.  (No. M2. 073525 Pte JONES. J.L.G. Struck off Strength (Sick) No 46036 2nd Corp BUDGE A. appointed paid acting Corp with effect from 11.12.15 vice Corp MINNEAR transferred No 64766 L/Corp HAYES H. appointed Paid acting 2nd Corp and vice 2nd Corp Budge promoted - No 44793 Sgt DENMAN H.W. appointed paid L/Corpnl vice HAYES promoted - 52nd Inf Bde relieved 50th Inf Bde No 50356 L/Corp PEATY H.W. wounded while repairing lines Struck off Strength	wdy wdy wdy wdy wdy wdy
	18th			wdy wdy
	19th			wdy wdy
	20th		No 50690 Cpl. ATHAWES F.C. appointed paid acting Sergeant No 7018 L/Corp LAST H.C. Struck off Strength having been transferred to B 1st Sqnd to R.E No 5738 Corp BATES W. Struck off Strength - No 56090 Sgt WILTSHIRE S. (wounded) Struck off Strength	wdy wdy wdy1

WAR DIARY
or
INTELLIGENCE SUMMARY.
(Erase heading not required.)

Army Form C. 2118.

Place	Date	Hour	Summary of Events and Information	Remarks and references to Appendices
RENING -HELST	25/12/15		No 23452 Sap. McCORMACK P. and No 27216 Sap. WILLIAMSON H. Transferred to Company from 2nd Army Signals. No 4566 Sap. DREW T.G. and Sap. EDWARDS T.H. transferred to 2nd Army Signals.	W.H.H.
	" 26/12/15		No 44683 Sap BRAZELL M. Transferred from 1st Sig. G R.E. 50th Inf. Bn. Albania. /Pl. 525 Sap Bn. in turn in No 71973 Pion ASPLEN C.	W.H.H. W.H.H W.H.H
	"		58543 " LETFORD H. 75992 Sap FORSYTH J. 75556 " WANT F.T. 71316 " WEBB P.W.	Reinforcement draft from Signal Company from Signal Depot R.E. Abbeville W.H.H
	27/12/15		58746 " BARRY B.R.S. and No 11023 Sap KNIGHTS A.J.L. transferred L Coy from Signal Depot. No 43797 Pion BAKER W.C. transferred to Signals 2nd Army	W.H.H W.H.H W.H.H
	28/12/15		M.C. Corp. TAYLOR A.D. (gassed) Struck off Strength	

Army Form C. 2118.

WAR DIARY
or
INTELLIGENCE SUMMARY.
(Erase heading not required.)

Place	Date	Hour	Summary of Events and Information	Remarks and references to Appendices
RENING	29/12/15		No 65001 Sap. PENNOCK H.L. dispatched to Signal Depôt, Bletchley with a view to being commissioned — 3 hrs dim'n "A" Strength	
HELST	31/12/15		No 54154 M.E. Corp. MORGAN A.P. reinforcement joined Coy — No 65013 Sap. ANDERSON A. appointed paid Lance Corporal vice L Corp. PEATY H.V. wounded + struck off Strength —	

W.S. Oldham Major
Comdg 17th Signal Co. R.E.

17th Lyrical Coy. 1812.
Vol: 6

121/7936

Army Form C. 2118

WAR DIARY
or
INTELLIGENCE SUMMARY.
(Erase heading not required.)

Place	Date	Hour	Summary of Events and Information	Remarks and references to Appendices
RENING	1.12.15		No 91336 Driver PARKIN. C. and No 73086 Driver HAYHOE R. transferred to Coy from Signal Depot	WRA/
HELST	2/12/15		52nd Bde relieved 50th Bde in front line	WRA/
	6/12/15		M.C. Corp. LOBB. G. transferred to 2nd Army Signals	WRA/
	8/12/15		M.C. Corp. CAMPBELL. T. G. transferred to Company from Signal depot.	WRA/
	10/12/15		50th Inf Bde relieved 52nd Inf Bde in front line	WRA/
	11/12/15		No 44665 Sergt. HODGKINS C.A. selected for training Signal lines "at home", left for Base at strength	WRA/
	13/12/15		Sapper WHITTEN. S. (wounded) transferred to FENNY STRATFORD Signal Depot + Struck off Strength	WRA/
	14/12/15		Corp. MINNEAR. T.C. transferred to 24" Signal R.E.	WRA/
	"		No 43797 Pion. BAKER. W.C. transferred from 24" Signal R.E.	WRA/
	15/12/15		No 75731 Spr. HAMPTON S.A. transferred from 2nd Army Signals	WRA/
	"		No 75712 Spr GREENALL J.B. " " " "	WRA/
	"		No 48216 Pion CORNISH. W. " " " "	WRA/

WAR DIARY
or
INTELLIGENCE SUMMARY.

Place	Date	Hour	Summary of Events and Information	Remarks and references to Appendices
RENING - HELST	17/12/15		A.S.C. N: M2. 073525 Pte JONES. J.L.G. Struck off Strength (sick)	MSS
			No 46036. 2nd Corp BUDGE A. appointed paid acting Corp with effect from 11.12.15 - Vice Corp MINNEAR transferred.	MSS
			No 64766. L Corp HAYES H.L. appointed paid acting 2nd Corporal vice 2nd Corp BUDGE promoted -	MSS
			No 44793 Sap DENMAN H.W. appointed paid Lce corporal vice HAYES promoted -	MSS
	18/12/15		52nd Inf Bde relieved 50th Inf Bde .	MSS
	19/12/15		No 50356 Le Corp PEATY. H.V. wounded while repairing lines, Struck off Strength	MSS
	20/12/15		No 50690 Corpl. ATHAWES F.C. appointed paid acting Sergeant No 47076. Le Corp LAST H.C. Struck off Strength having been transferred to 4th Signal Co R.E.	MSS
			No 45738 Corp BATES W. Struck off Strength -	MSS
			No 58090 Sap WILTSHIRE S. (wounded) struck off Strength	MSS

Army Form C. 2118

WAR DIARY
or
INTELLIGENCE SUMMARY.
(Erase heading not required.)

Army Form C. 2118

Place	Date	Hour	Summary of Events and Information	Remarks and references to Appendices
REMING -HELST	23/12/15		No 23452 Sap. McCORMACK. P. and No 27216 Sap. WILLIAMSON H. Transferred to Company from 2nd Army Signals	knelf
	"		No 42566 Sap. DREW.T.E. and Sap. EDWARDS.T.H. transferred to 2nd Army Signals	knelf knelf knelf
	26/12/15		No 44683 Sap. BRAZELL M. transferred from 1st Sig. Co R.E. 50th Inf. Bde whereas to 52nd Sig. Bde in turn him	knelf
	"		No 71973 Pion. ASPLEN C. ⎫ " 58543 " LETFORD H. ⎬ Reinforcement draft from " 75782 Sap. FORSYTH J. ⎬ Company from Signal " 75556 " WANT J.T. ⎬ Depot R.E. Abbeville " 71316 " WEBB P.W. ⎭	
	27/12/15		" 58746 " BARRY.B.R.S. and No 71023 Sap. KNIGHTS.A.J.L transferred E Coy. from Signal Depot-	knelf knelf
	"		No 43797 Pion BAKER.W.C transferred to Signals 3rd Army	knelf
	28/12/15		M.C Corp. TAYLOR. A.D (gassed) Struck off Strength	knelf

WAR DIARY
or
INTELLIGENCE SUMMARY.
(Erase heading not required.)

Army Form C. 2118

Place	Date	Hour	Summary of Events and Information	Remarks and references to Appendices
REMING	29/5/15		No 65001 Sap. PENNOCK H.L. dispatched to Signal Depot, BUCKLEY, with a view to being commissioned - Struck off Strength	LWM
HELST	31/5/15		No 54154 M.C. Cpl MORGAN A.P. reinforcement joined coy - No 65013 Sap. ANDERSON A. appointed paid Lance Corporal vice La Cpl. PEATY H.V. wounded + Struck off strength -	LWM LWM

W R Gilson Major
Comdg 17th Signal Co. R.E.

WAR DIARY
or
INTELLIGENCE SUMMARY.

Army Form C. 2118.

Place	Date	Hour	Summary of Events and Information	Remarks and references to Appendices
RENINGHELST	1916 Jan 1		Major D Haly (Queen's Westminster Rifles) (Reserve) transferred to Signals II Army. Work continued on laying cables on new report centre for left Div. V Corps at M.2.d.9.9. assistance received from small working party of Cable operators.	Strength: Officers 7 OR 202 209 Horses 107
	Jan 2		Work on buried lines in above continued – nothing new to report.	Casualties O.R.
	Jan 3		Capt. Naylor 2nd Div. came to arrange about relief when Division returned. Arrangements made to hand over to him the 2nd 39th Div. V Corps lines at YPRES. Scheme in Gold Fish Château M.M.67.D. & new V Cable damaged by enemy, patched & refused.	Casualties O.R.
	Jan 4		Work on above continued. O.C. V Corps Signals inspected the lines.	
	Jan 5		Advance parties of Divisions relieving us, viz. 2nd Div, 14 party & 17 Div.	

Army Form C. 2118.

WAR DIARY
or
INTELLIGENCE SUMMARY.
(Erase heading not required.)

Place	Date	Hour	Summary of Events and Information	Remarks and references to Appendices
RENINGHELST	Jan 6		Found up escorts for 10th Div. & C.R.A also Guard & all necessary conversations in and having completed. Orders movement lorries Coy cook & cooks in. & 52 I.B. in rest received by 17 I.B. "received" & cookers.	
	Jan 7		Coal train to Busseboom Damaged wagons - 51 & 50 I.B. returned 5.17 = 72.18. + promised Estaminet Willetz - 17 I.B. retained 273 I.B. the remount matters. We now is quartered at TIEQUET-17 Dm & Sigg. opposite 17 Dm class at noon 24 Div Hrs opens at RENINGHELST and 17 Dm class	
	Jan 8		at RENINGHELST and found moving Guard at TILQUES. "A" office came to meet. The company proceeded by route march (two practices & rests) quite into TILQUES) and bivouacked (billets) ARNEKE.	
	Jan 9		Own company arrived at rest billets in TILQUES. A Fatigue had had form motor car to connect C.R.A with D.H.Q. Cells cast cleared parent found to Sigllr. attached C.R.A. to help but hat from C.R.A th/ Sig artillery 1980 – Three further officers	
	Jan 10		from 20 Div. C.O B.n. in answer had home & hrs "A" B.(Oficers) and two H.R. to 5th Div. Fwd note write officers	

Army Form C. 2118.

WAR DIARY
or
INTELLIGENCE SUMMARY.
(Erase heading not required.)

Instructions regarding War Diaries and Intelligence Summaries are contained in F. S. Regs., Part II. and the Staff Manual respectively. Title pages will be prepared in manuscript.

Place	Date	Hour	Summary of Events and Information	Remarks and references to Appendices
TILQUES	June July		Divisional ammunition & Petroleum pk. wt. - TILQUES (D.H.Q.) to S.O.I.B. (NORD & PAS DE CALAIS) S.2.I.B. (FRANCE & PAS) They are here laid for 24 Brs. by G.H.Q. S.I.I.B. T.C. at an time 5. R.T.O. MATTER in TILQUES - Casualty O. C.R.A. continuation from S.O.F.S. (C/A) G. WOLPHUS (wd by 17 Dn C.R.A. K. Luttman Cath (Wd recvd D.S.) are wd 6 ZOUAFAUES, TOURNEHEM BONNINGUES, AUDRENEM, CLEAR PPS.) for parts of Infantry Br have were recvd now end - eturn 500 cases, 3000 gr. R. Wj, vite. Boulogne. Each furnished with 1 rule & g NORD & US & OES -	
	12			
	13		Tramp, theory, vig pony-waggon, humour + hermances. (ard) Dales to higher rate of J.E.P. Returns -	
	14		Tramp shut of ammunition stuffs. Lectun by Col A Wright R.E. on waters.	Casualty 1 Infantry wound
	15			end Mc
	16		1600 Schot of not hostile lost trak 6 watch or inspection - removed 4.30	ary end
	17		School Grand Carnival Tramp end pastoral Tramp cater -	amc any in

WAR DIARY
or
INTELLIGENCE SUMMARY.

Army Form C. 2118.

Place	Date	Hour	Summary of Events and Information	Remarks and references to Appendices
	Jan 19		General Training work	[illegible]
	Jan 20		General Training work	
	Jan 21		General Training work	
	Jan 22		General Training work	
	Jan 23		General Eng work	
	Jan 24		General Training work	
	Jan 25		General Training work	
	Jan 26		General Training work	
	Jan 27		General Training —	
	Jan 28		General work	
	Jan 29		General work	
	Jan 30		General work	
	Jan 31		General work	

17ᵗᵒ Agosto
fol: 7
Tan 16

Army Form C. 2118.

WAR DIARY
or
INTELLIGENCE SUMMARY.
(Erase heading not required.)

Instructions regarding War Diaries and Intelligence Summaries are contained in F. S. Regs., Part II. and the Staff Manual respectively. Title pages will be prepared in manuscript.

Place	Date	Hour	Summary of Events and Information	Remarks and references to Appendices
RENINGHELST	1916 Jan 1		(Queen's Westminster Rifles) Major O. Waley (Queens Westminsters) Took over command of 17 Signal Cy from Major H.R.B. Colvin 67 Pungahs transferred to Signals II Army — Work continued on loading cables in new spur centre to left Inn. V Corps at H.2.2a9.9. continue received from small working party V Corps sappers —	Strengthens Officers 7 OR 202 209 Horses 107
	Jan 2		Work on burying lines as above continued — Northern line to left higher end (Pauls) repaired —	Reports 1 first time OR casualty not Reinforcements 1 OR
	Jan 3		Capt. Naylor 24th Div came to arrange about relief when Division relieved. Arrangements made to have one 2 officers line to left B.G. wire. GOLDFISH CHATEAU H.11.a.7.0. & new V Corps lines into YPRES. Southern cable via K.V.016.7 & 9.8. Damaged by working parties & repaired. Work as above continued. O.C. V Corps signals inspected the lines.	Casualties 1 Feb O.R. wounded
	Jan 4			Reinf. Casualties lines
	5		Advance parties of teams exchange with 24th Div preparatory to going into at FLEURS for 17 Div ← RENINGHELST for 17 Div.	Casualty nil

Army Form C. 2118.

WAR DIARY
or
INTELLIGENCE SUMMARY.
(Erase heading not required.)

Instructions regarding War Diaries and Intelligence Summaries are contained in F. S. Regs., Part II. and the Staff Manual respectively. Title pages will be prepared in manuscript.

Place	Date	Hour	Summary of Events and Information	Remarks and references to Appendices
RENINGHELST	Jan 6		Found upon arrival from WR Div. & CRA obs. opened + all necessary connections in red lines completed — All unnecessary lines cut out & reeled in. 8 52 I.B. in use relieved by 17 I.B. Through to red cables.	[illegible]
	Jan 7		Laid line to BUSSEBOOM (engaged) refound — 51 & 50 I.B. relieved by 17 & 72 I.D. Through to red cables. 17 I.B. relieved 73 I.B. who came into billets at noon 24 Div. & cub. at TIEQUES [?] 17 Div. HQ opened at RENINGHELST and 17 Div. cable at RENINGHELST and temporary opened at TIEQUES.	
	Jan 8		The "A" office closed & Sunset. The Company proceeded by route march (two sections + motor cyclists went direct to TIEQUES) and bivouacked at WILLED ARNEKE.	
	Jan 9		Main Company arrived at that village in TIEQUES. A Forepart line laid from motor car to connect C.R.A. with D. H.Q. Cable cart & special party went to Sig Off. attached C.R.A. to lay line but from C.R.A. Hd [?] actually began there previous different from zee Div. 50 Bde in reserve had him to be H.Q. (B'Cula) [?] and new H.Q. & 51 Bde Hd. out & only HATTOU line [?]	
	Jan 10			

WAR DIARY or INTELLIGENCE SUMMARY

Army Form C. 2118.

Place	Date	Hour	Summary of Events and Information	Remarks and references to Appendices
TILQUES	Jan 11		Divisional communication established per wire – TILQUES (DHQ) to 50 I.B. (NORDAUSQUES) 52 I.B. (EPPERLEQUES) they on line laid for 24 Div by G.H.Q. 51 I.B. tied into line to R.T. o. WATTEN via 2 MERCKEGHEM – Casualty 0. C.R.A. continuation from 50 I.B. (cable) to MORPHUS (laid by 17 Div). nice 0. C.R.A. to batteries cable (D second D.S.) air laid to ZOUAFQUES, TOURNEHEM, BONNINGUES, AUDREHEM, CLERQUES. Line taps on batteries. De lines wire received + end – land lines to G.O.C., C.R.E., DADOS, G., Q., Q., V.J., + D.T. – BOISDINGHEM. Line forward with 1 mile of NORDAUSQUES. Trainy 0.	
	13		Training, theory, + ipany – wagon – drawn + instruments. Candidates for higher rate of P.E.P. tested.	
	14		Trainy school of instruction started + read out 36 from arty + infantry signal.	
	15		Lecture by Capt Wright R.E. on wireless.	
	16		160W school of instruction sent out to units as instructors – 2 new school of 72 assembled.	
	17		School opened. General Training cont.	
	18		General Training cont.	

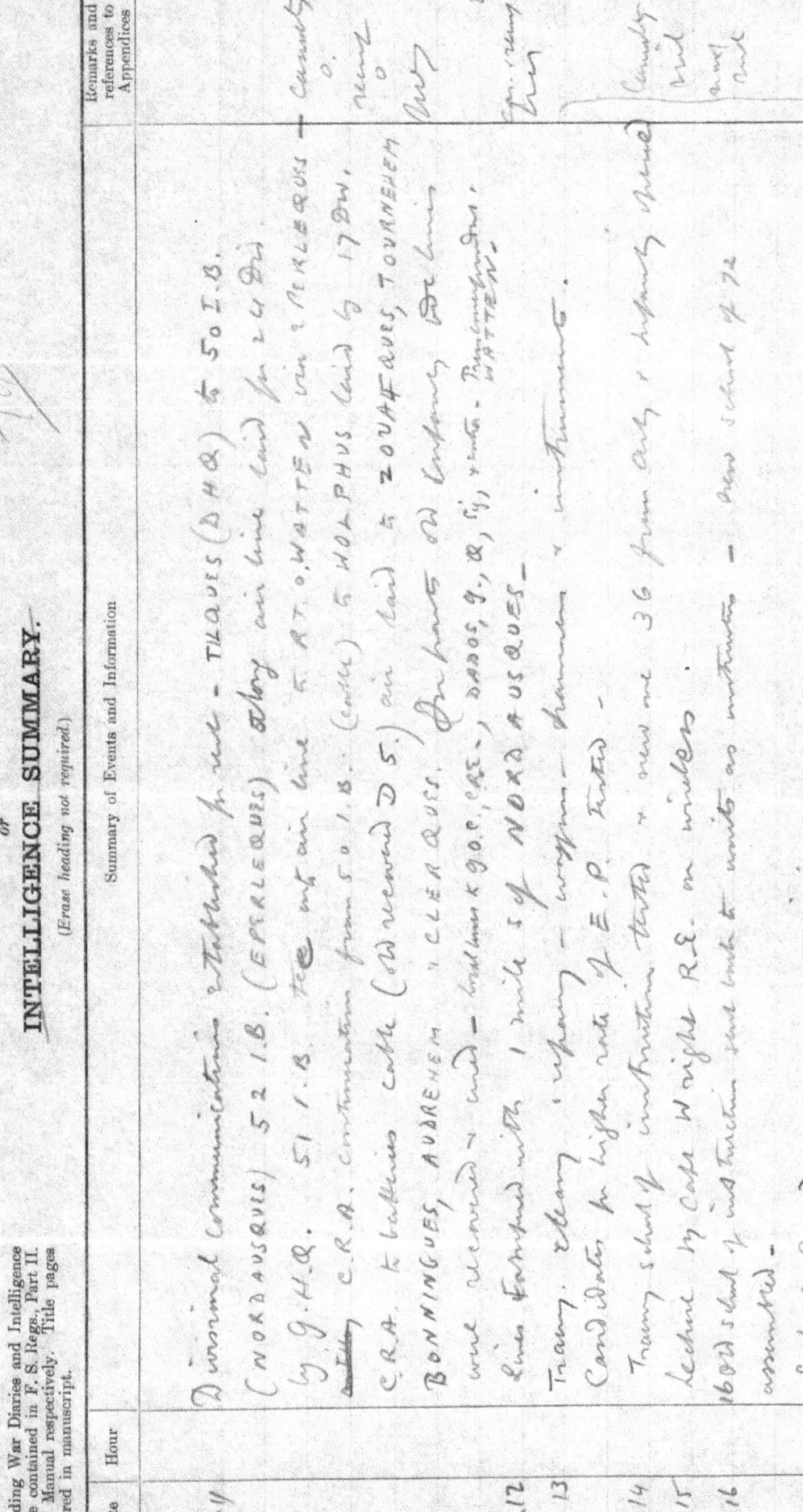

Army Form C. 2118.

WAR DIARY
or
INTELLIGENCE SUMMARY.
(Erase heading not required.)

Instructions regarding War Diaries and Intelligence Summaries are contained in F. S. Regs., Part II. and the Staff Manual respectively. Title pages will be prepared in manuscript.

Place	Date	Hour	Summary of Events and Information	Remarks and references to Appendices
	Jan 19		General Training work	
	Jan 20		General Train work	
	Jan 21		General Train work	
	Jan 22		General Train work	
	Jan 23		General Train work	
	Jan 24		General Training work	
	Jan 25		General Train work	
	Jan 26		General Train work	
	Jan 27		General Training	
	Jan 28		General	
	Jan 29		General Train	
	Jan 30		General Train	
	Jan 31		General	

WAR DIARY
or
INTELLIGENCE SUMMARY.
(Erase heading not required.)

Army Form C. 2118.

Place	Date	Hour	Summary of Events and Information	Remarks and references to Appendices
	Feb 1 1916		General Training	Strength 20 Officers 7 [illegible]
	Feb 2 1916		General Training	
	Feb 3 1916		Strength of NCOs & Men on the list was 5 3/2 Dec. and of the 1st completed 7"	R/R 8 OR
	Feb 4 1916		Officers went to view Demonstration trenches between our front & picket line	
	5 1916		Found burying came into TRNF1 view — Burying Party of company turned on later parties consisted of NCO & company. 52 I B came up road now to take up from 9 I B. line — Syer — Appli issued 5 each to each man —	R/R 10 IR
	6 1916		52 IB moved into our area — Took over 96 I D. lines.	
	7 1916		17 by Cab on our all communication from 3 by Sg. General issued a night.	
	8 1916		Communication working satisfactorily and of 2/Lt [illegible] 8 IB [illegible] returned — attempted with satisfactory.	
	9 1916		[illegible] Field — On leave was 13 [illegible]	
	10 1916		[illegible] — Hospital [illegible]	
	11 1916		[illegible]	

WAR DIARY
or
INTELLIGENCE SUMMARY.
(Erase heading not required.)

Army Form C. 2118.

Place	Date	Hour	Summary of Events and Information	Remarks and references to Appendices
	Feb 11		New stock issue (sought) of 9 P Irons issued to give Broken ground after Communication on VERMEZEEL F Rest Line —	
	Feb 12		Ten tons lead into Trenches — preparing to complete the new Drummed dugout Centre. Been patrols — Wirk any trestay had outfits in front Lines pushed —	
	Feb 13		General work continuing.	
	Feb 14 and 15		Enemy shelled the front line severely 10 aft + 11 started — Between trenches letter Communication through all through rifle remained through midgut — Staff were able to communicate with the Front. Brigade life through to Battalion + party with empty two improved Cut is regular during a sortie/party in Trench with R Bedson	
	Feb 15		Communication lifts lines frequently Cut + repaired. Not nearly complete lost part all types into Chous through air 6 begin to penetrate into Front upon officers so since one so communication reported by lines + telegraph to Brigade + Companies MET.	

Place	Date	Hour	Summary of Events and Information	Remarks and references to Appendices
	Feb 16		Heavy Artillery frequently opened fire - apparently between Spith check H29 a 68 and HOOGE 1075 HOUSE 1 - OC 5.12. Owing to destruction of observing bays - observers of 9 Div could not spot shots bursting in reserve. Communication poor. One Trench Mortar and several turned at night - response satisfactory. Plans in ——	
	Feb 17		Mortar bomb to HOOGLEDE HOUSE —— Own trenches - Returned - had opened with assy of V 10 for 10 minutes to our front from 17 C 38 K B.44 1 33 C 3.6 at night firing of 25 mm with 65 HISHMS between 1.05 on ammo from 450 rounds commencing of Toom Tam T 3 a c 79 K trench K . 33 h 5.6 trench K . 1 33 6 2 3 Boche K . 2 7 0 6 4. All trench patrolled and found. No other opening encountered.	

WAR DIARY
or
INTELLIGENCE SUMMARY.

(Erase heading not required.)

Army Form C. 2118.

Place	Date	Hour	Summary of Events and Information	Remarks and references to Appendices
	Feb 19		Communication through Company Head Quarters has improved. Telephony was improved by laying 1 34 (?) V. from 1339 to infantry HQ posts. No further wire wanted from 1277 & 64 to Woodcote Wood. Line 1371 64 R & 1611 51 neatly buried & station extended to road in side of road.	14h, 10h
	Feb 20		Road line VOORMEZEELE — Station 3, 1, Z3 a 5.5. Rammer line — (P. line road) begun. Station 1279 Q. Du Pepot centre no. 28 A Dt Ypres Nth F.W. extension ?? open more or less by 5 p.m. Line completed by 8 p.m.	Rh, 10h
	Feb 21		9 puntoons. Double Vormezeele & Sidney Drossroad to 1339 1.6. and to Hospice taken over silk O.C. 174 Coy. Installation made in new hut known as "Iberia" Junction communication station north of Coy.	

WAR DIARY
or
INTELLIGENCE SUMMARY.
(Erase heading not required.)

Army Form C. 2118.

Place	Date	Hour	Summary of Events and Information	Remarks and references to Appendices
Febr			76 I.B. occupied Armand line from 133 d 3.6 to 134 a 1 approx about I 34 a 0.0 Battalion to employ time repand reserves - in places wire around Front Trenches & communication trenches on whole Divisional area -	
Feb 23			Several work & upon - several continued - New work on wiring lines intertia & previsly lines intertained	
Feb 24			New line arranged from alternate route HOODCOTE HOUSE K 133 a 6.3 fr communication (shown attached plan at that point (BR Battery HR) with no interference to Battery position Chateau. Div. report wire completed & in working orders - spare BREALBUSH H 29 6.9t wire D5 laid for intelly from H 29 C 71 to Belgian Chateau.	

Army Form C. 2118.

WAR DIARY
or
INTELLIGENCE SUMMARY.
(Erase heading not required.)

Instructions regarding War Diaries and Intelligence Summaries are contained in F. S. Regs., Part II. and the Staff Manual respectively. Title pages will be prepared in manuscript.

Place	Date	Hour	Summary of Events and Information	Remarks and references to Appendices
Hom COTE HOUSE	Feb 26		Attended note. New line and PLAMERTINGHE front line on to LOMCOTE HOUSE via Amiers railway and KENNEL Beek. Our front upon with + Humphreys of calling in front Trenches N.E. I went to Athenian line (in) HOOD COTE HOUSE after with Humphrey then communications through Shannon & Bayuth.	R/r 20R
	Feb 27		Two front routes laid POILSAXX on ? Knowle at 133 a 63 to make latral to VANEELERE and Athenian front to Dr report Centre.	
	Feb 28		Brit Major Communication with I Corp GS Branch completing Fishery + Laundry of lines complete with + Humphreys Front line communications on ? by ? others in progress.	

WAR DIARY
or
INTELLIGENCE SUMMARY.

(Erase heading not required.)

Army Form C. 2118.

Place	Date	Hour	Summary of Events and Information	Remarks and references to Appendices
Feb 29			Further Feby - repairs - have between M & GC 9.1 & WOODCOTE House dwnwards say 20 hrs constantly cut. Afforded a supper of lines in at Feb 29 officers proves newly drowned, whilly term. Gunner Strength Feb 1 205 68 / 7 / 012 ← 4 1 / 7 / 203 6 / 9 / 202 wounded to hospital with scabies 4 / 202 / 6 Officer	

Walker Le Conely 2nd Lt
in command No Company

17th Signals
Vol: 8

Army Form C. 2118.

WAR DIARY
or
INTELLIGENCE SUMMARY.
(Erase heading not required.)

Instructions regarding War Diaries and Intelligence Summaries are contained in F. S. Regs., Part II. and the Staff Manual respectively. Title pages will be prepared in manuscript.

Place	Date	Hour	Summary of Events and Information	Remarks and references to Appendices
	Feb 1 1916		General Training	Sheet 203 W² 7/216
	Feb 2 1916		General Training	
	Feb 3 1916		Division ordered to take over the lines with 5 & 2nd Div. new Sta inspected 3,7 =	Att 1 O.R.
			Officers went to view communication lines.	
	Feb 4 1916		Advance wiremen party proceed to patrol lines —	
	5 1916		Fourth Army came into the 4 & 5 Div. area — Recon party & Company Ersatz on offensive jersey annual of D.A.R. company. 5 & 2 I.B. moved into new area & took over 9 I.D. lines. Sig Coy = tested & proved by road to new area —	R/L 1 O.R.
	6 1916		5 I.D. moved into new area & took over 9 6 I.D. lines.	
	7 1916		17 Sig Coy took over all communications from 3 Sig Coy — Command handed over night.	
	8 1916		Communications working satisfactorily — 2 line 5'' I B line & repaired — attention with interparty.	
	9 1916		Lines patrolled — no new work started.	
	10 1916		Lines patrolled — Hudson spoken at connected with telephone exchange —	
	11 1916		Lines arranged to improve communication for Premier Exchange —	

Army Form C. 2118.

WAR DIARY
or
INTELLIGENCE SUMMARY.
(Erase heading not required.)

Instructions regarding War Diaries and Intelligence Summaries are contained in F. S. Regs., Part II. and the Staff Manual respectively. Title pages will be prepared in manuscript.

Place	Date	Hour	Summary of Events and Information	Remarks and references to Appendices
	Feb 11		New Staff piece (Lergt) G.P. Thorn burned to give Brown forward spare Communication via VORMEZEELE first line —	
	Feb 12		Test lines laid into observations - preparing to complete the new Divisional report centre. Room prepared - Work no nearly lines installed in front. Lines installed — General work continuing.	
	Feb 13			
	Feb 14 and 15		Enemy shelled the front line especially 10 left + outskirts - Column reserves later. Communication through all through in the reserves through and fwd - Staff are able to communicate all the time. Brigade hope through to Battalions + forth well. Company lines suffered - all 8 separate lines by own circuits in touch with ambulances.	
	Feb 15		Communication fair. lines frequently cut + repaired but never complete break. Fair till 6 p.m. when 10 lines damaged in 6 mins to permanent until - Trenches upon affected in 2 sections and communication maintained by phone + telegraph - own company installed	enemy [illeg] command

1577 Wt.W10791/1773 500,000 1/15 D.D.&L. ADSS./Forms/C. 2118.

Army Form C. 2118.

WAR DIARY
or
INTELLIGENCE SUMMARY.
(Erase heading not required.)

Instructions regarding War Diaries and Intelligence Summaries are contained in F. S. Regs., Part II. and the Staff Manual respectively. Title pages will be prepared in manuscript.

Place	Date	Hour	Summary of Events and Information	Remarks and references to Appendices
	Feb 16		Heavy shelling throughout January hours — especially between Sp.14 where H 29 a 6.8 and WOODCOTE HOUSE 1 2 0 C 5.12. Owing to destruction of numerous dugouts — alternative quarters had to be found — new upper limits taken into service. Communication poor. One time when hyperia were seen been used at night. Response smaller [illegible] then one —	
	Feb 17		Drawn near to HOODCOTE HOUSE [illegible] Range extends anything now over description — Reinforcement had reported with help of large working parties.	
	Feb 18		At night party of 25 men worked at H/34000 and put up posts in [illegible] from 1 7 C 3 8 K 6 7 a d 1 3 3 d 3 6 another party of 500 wound as arranged of g.P. from from T 3 4 c 7 9 to U.12 c t. 1. 3 3 d 3.6 thence 5. 1. 33 a 2.3 thence 5.1. 2 7 c 6 4. all have patrolled and spread. Work on lines upon [illegible]	

Army Form C. 2118.

WAR DIARY
or
INTELLIGENCE SUMMARY.
(Erase heading not required.)

Instructions regarding War Diaries and Intelligence Summaries are contained in F. S. Regs., Part II. and the Staff Manual respectively. Title pages will be prepared in manuscript.

Place	Date	Hour	Summary of Events and Information	Remarks and references to Appendices
	Feb 19		Communication trench — Company & Battalion bones improved in the every jum/trench g had I 34 c 7.9 to I 3 3 9 3 6 completed and further bone laid westward from I 27 c 6.4 to W.8.8 c.0.7 8 via I 2 0 c 5.2	12A 10A
	Feb 20		New Line I 27 c 6.4 to I 30 c 5.5. I 30 c 5.5. (continued) to J 09 late House. New line VORNEZEELE to Scheme 8, I 32 a 5.5. Ammunition from — Scheme 8. I 32 a 5.5 Ammunition from — Scot. barn tramway. — Work on new y Sap Refped Centre at 28 d 0.2 begun. — Work of so continued. — Heavy supine wire on every trades which went out by 8 Batt. — Communication tramway tranches by Piscinsterm.	11A 12A
	Feb 21			
	Feb 22		Bonus laid VORNEZEELE F Schmy 8 (continued) to I 33 a 1.6 — and IN H 0 8 c 07 8 head been both completed & further tramway tranches on new line — tramway on railway at an been. — Communication tranches Pinestem.	

1577 Wt.W10791/1773 500,000 1/15 D.D.& L. A.D.S.S./Forms/C. 2118.

WAR DIARY
or
INTELLIGENCE SUMMARY.
(Erase heading not required.)

Army Form C. 2118.

Place	Date	Hour	Summary of Events and Information	Remarks and references to Appendices
Feb 22			76 I.B. commenced Armoured line from I 33 d 3.6 to I 34 a, right about I 34 a 0.0. Battalion to employ lines repaired renewed — in places with armoured lines [illegible] of various communication trenches in whole divisional area —	
Feb 23			General work of repair and renewal continued — New work — renewing lines installed & providing lines [illegible].	
Feb 24			New line armoured from alternative route WOODCOTE HOUSE K I 33 a 6 3 for communication between artillery Officer at that place (189 Brigade H.Q.) with his batteries at Belgian Chateau. Div. [illegible] centre completed & in working order — open at DICKEBUSCH H 29 c 9.4. New D5 [illegible] for artillery from H 29 c 9.1 to Belgian Chateau	

WAR DIARY or INTELLIGENCE SUMMARY

Army Form C. 2118.

Place	Date	Hour	Summary of Events and Information	Remarks and references to Appendices
	Feb 26		HONS COTE HOUSE joined unit 24 Other Ranks in an afternoon work. New line laid VLAMERTINGHE part Post km to WIPCOTE HOUSE via RAMLERS section and KENNEL BEEK. Re general upon work + tightening of cables in front trenches M & S of canal. Afternoon unit (W) WOOD COTE HOUSE to upper centre to strengthen communications when possible.	R/C 2 OR
	Feb 27		Two shore units laid SCOTT BANK on canal to 133 a 6.3 to make lateral to VANEZEELE and alternative trench to Div upper Centre. Draw Hunt communication with 2 Coy Ord Nance. Company testing + junction off line.	
	Feb 28		Company work to strengthen front line communications as ordered by Signr to majestec Division.	

WAR DIARY
or
INTELLIGENCE SUMMARY.

Army Form C. 2118.

Place	Date	Hour	Summary of Events and Information	Remarks and references to Appendices
Feb 24			Further testing of wiring - Wire between H 29 C 9 & 1 & WOODCOTE HOUSE deviated owing to being constantly cut. Arranged a program of wire as at Feb 27 & these have been freely deranged anything since. Summary Strength 203 OR Fit 1 / 7 Sick / 210 Casualties wounded 1 accidentally injured 1 Sick 4 To Company 1 7 / 203 Reinforcements 6 / 209 By 202 OR & 7 Officers.	

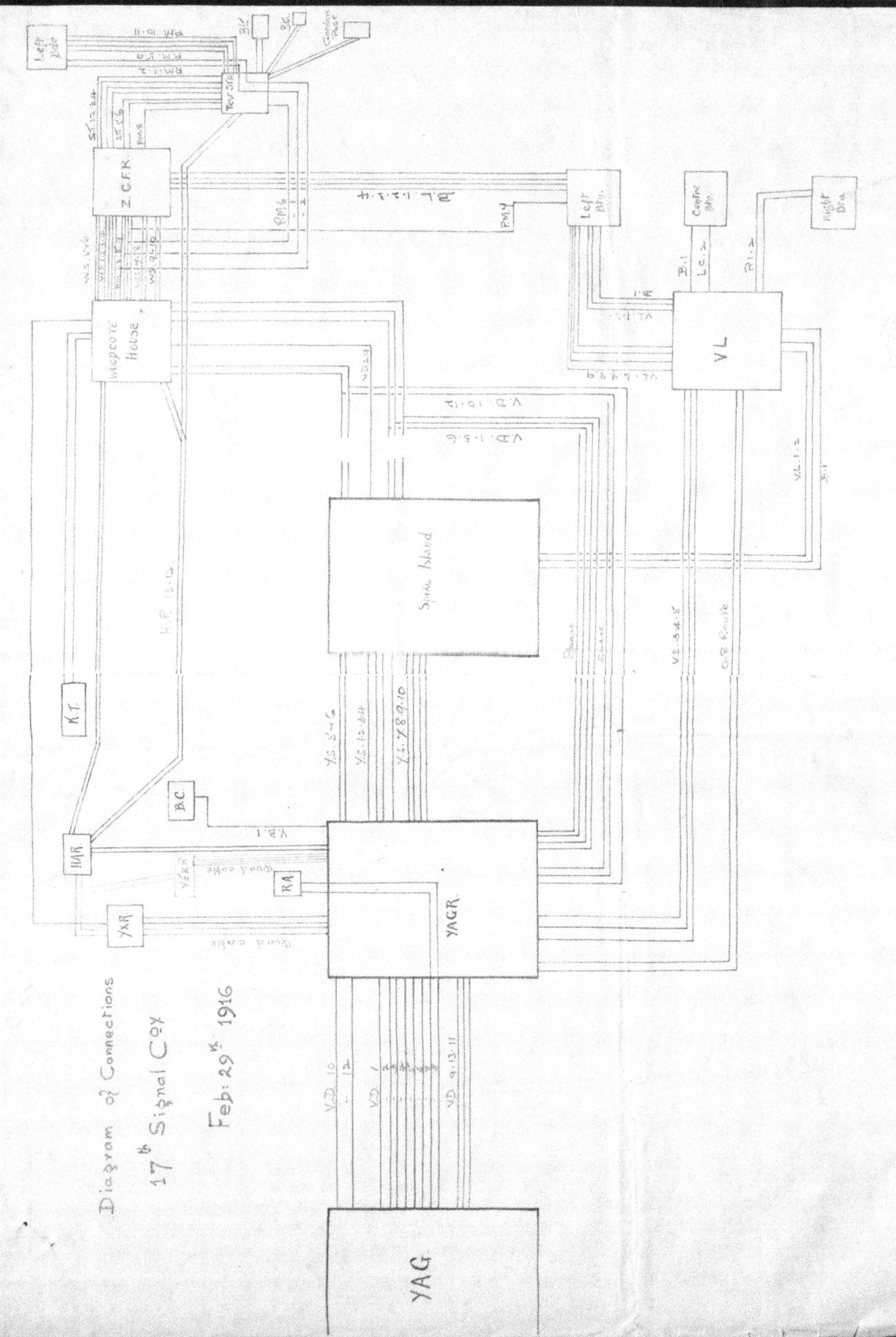

17th Divl Sig: Co.

Army Form C. 2118.

WAR DIARY
or
INTELLIGENCE SUMMARY.
(Erase heading not required.)

Place	Date	Hour	Summary of Events and Information	Remarks and references to Appendices
Chatham	1916		Cpl Lewis (Cable) with detachments of 3 from in preparations for magnetic signalling — Commanded private — 13 line Kennington to H 29 C 91.	Chap of 7 OR 202 /207
			H 29 C 91, from lines on two trenches and one road C.A.A. — H 24 C 91.5 WOODCOTE HOUSE.	
			Three 6 in line trenches and 1 cable, WOODCOTE HOUSE to 1.33 a 5.4 Bryant H8.	
			Attempts been in use 24 hrs. Communication to WOODCOTE from the Gaspers Chateau direct — Alternates from the Gaspers Chateau	
			WOODCOTE HOUSE to A 29, 14.9 & 6.5 ft. Found 1.33 a 5.4, removed and gave to bury E.D. in 1 sec. and a trench area was run to be again for twenty Tuesday — and a second aerial to from pole — as 11 pm communication from improved circuit Bush Hill.	enough with OR Most

WAR DIARY
or
INTELLIGENCE SUMMARY.

Army Form C. 2118.

Place	Date	Hour	Summary of Events and Information	Remarks and references to Appendices
[illegible] 2			Lines to BHQ 1:30am [illegible] - [illegible] communication from HQ to Division - Battalion commanders [illegible] in captured trenches N of Canal — we fell heavy morning shelling at 12:25 pm — Left Division [illegible] in front trench Charge 50 [illegible] — no news from D Coy in front until 10 [illegible] from Battle Stops (?R.O.) Then [illegible] 4 men were laid up right we fix — Communications of [illegible] Stationary [illegible] to Battalion 7:50 [illegible]	Casualty OR wounded OR duty
[illegible] 3			Brigade commentators [illegible] communications that [illegible] Division [illegible] at 7am at 7am [illegible] [illegible]	[illegible]

Army Form C. 2118.

WAR DIARY
or
INTELLIGENCE SUMMARY.
(Erase heading not required.)

Place	Date	Hour	Summary of Events and Information	Remarks and references to Appendices
Marchy			By means of buried cable communication to the forward headquarters in the Captured Trenches. Owing to the absence of any communication trenches & the impossibility of staying work parties till the new positions were consolidated, only alternative route by sugged cables were used. The wiring parties had carry the greatest were retained on the Tot Platform to help were maintained any heavy enemy bombardment.	
Annentieres			Evidence from 3rd Division arrived & appeared 17 Dvn men as in 6 room the new routes & repair centre Tent stations. Two Officer and photography to station the two Brigade HQ. in reporte Centre to Spike Island was in Charge but twee was able to the hard range in relief of 5 O I B by 5 2. I B All found were on by 3 w and any refuge	
March 6			6/7 and 17 Dir Invenience withdrawn.	

Army Form C. 2118.

WAR DIARY
or
INTELLIGENCE SUMMARY.

(Erase heading not required.)

Place	Date	Hour	Summary of Events and Information	Remarks and references to Appendices
	March 7		3rd Div. relieved 17 Div on up row — At relief all three infy. bdes. 17 Div manoeuvring ground STEEN VOORDE with all permanent offrs.	Cavalry Arty Inf
	March 8		Div HQ at STEEN VOORDE — Two Bgdes & arty BA with 3 Div — 57 I B with 2 Corps	Cavalry Arty Inf
	March 9		as March 8	
	March 10		17 Div relieved 2 & 5 Div at MERRIS in our and Corps into 2nd Corps area — many units not yet arrived	Cavalry Inf Arty
	March 11		On rest — have returned to Brigade HQ	
	March 12		On rest — have weekly inspections — Parades 10.30 & 2.15 —	
	March 13		In rest. Lectures to instruments — led 9 and returned to Bathe.	Cavalry Arty Inf

WAR DIARY or INTELLIGENCE SUMMARY.

Army Form C. 2118.

Place	Date	Hour	Summary of Events and Information	Remarks and references to Appendices
	March 14th		In rest - La Crèche Billets. Weather: dull but no [illegible]	
	March 15th		In rest - Improvements continued and no games played.	
	March 16th		G.S.O./1 informed this unit that Don Hulys at Armentières were going to be changed.	
	March 17th		New Hulys inspected and arrangements made for our to be taken	
	March 18th		Working party proceeded to Armentières with the object of laying turn between old Hulys at École to New Hulys. 5th Bn. Bell left Bailleul and took up their Hulys in Armentières. Working party employed in digging between École and New Hulys in the nature of communication	
	March 20th		52nd Bn. Bou moved from Outersteene to Bailleul, communication through 2nd Corps. Working party laying local line about New Hulys at Armentières.	
	March 21st		52nd Bell left Bailleul. In Armentières communication through 2nd Corps and 2nd Div. Working party in line in Armentières.	

WAR DIARY
or
INTELLIGENCE SUMMARY.

Army Form C. 2118.

(Erase heading not required.)

Place	Date	Hour	Summary of Events and Information	Remarks and references to Appendices
	March 22nd		5th Bttn marched from Stragele to Balleul Common cantonments through 2nd Corps	
	March 23rd		5th Bttn marches to Amentum about W.M 11.14. Bn took over area from 2nd Dvn. Signal office at —	
	March 24		1.30 p.m. Same Runner Change, men quite successful. Working Party hotly engaged in making a few discovery alterations to trenches.	
	March 25		Brother's birthday.	
	March 26		Moved an officer at 143 Rue Nationale — Supple in Thorough with unit in rest secretly	
	March 27		All been waiting until H. Bleuten aeroplane tracked with Mondo	
	March 28		Arrangements made for move of Bath to left Brigade ready to change of positions	

Army Form C. 2118.

WAR DIARY
or
INTELLIGENCE SUMMARY.
(Erase heading not required.)

Instructions regarding War Diaries and Intelligence Summaries are contained in F. S. Regs., Part II. and the Staff Manual respectively. Title pages will be prepared in manuscript.

Place	Date	Hour	Summary of Events and Information	Remarks and references to Appendices
	March 29		Lines working well —	Smothers end
	March 30		Lines working well — between two parties of strengthening of forward lines — many of which are (?) + broken —	
	March 31		Detail but between left + left centre between are given fair — Have been taken by plenty wirings. Sth very exposed.	

Strength 1.3.16 O.R. 7
O.R. 202
209

Casualties November 2 6
to commencers 2 203
sick 5
total 9 209

2nd Lieut Langton
W.38th Feb 1916

[signature] Major
Queen's Westminster Rifles,
Commanding 17th Signal Co., R.E.

1577 Wt. W10791/1773 500,000 1/15 D. D. & L. A.D.S.S./Forms/C. 2118.

17 Sig Coy
R?

Vol-9

Army Form C. 2118.

WAR DIARY
or
INTELLIGENCE SUMMARY.
(Erase heading not required.)

Place	Date	Hour	Summary of Events and Information	Remarks and references to Appendices
[Hooge?]	1916		Gas kills (?) all infantry on 3 from in Shrapnel 7 Trenches [Inspired Desertions] - (Communication trenches) 13 hrs Kennington to Cells - H2qc9.1, Bn lines in two Trenches and one kid H2qc91, H2qc91 to Woodcote House. Thos, 6 in Mam Trenches and 1 coch, Woodcote House to 1.33.a.5.4. Bryant H.Q. Alternate hrs in 2u Bn Kennington to Woodcote House direct - alternate from via Festrid Chateau Woodcote House to Kenninghurst. Forward of 1.33.a.5.4. on a trench arm via from to hvy OP. In 1.34 and in a trench arm via from to 8" bore to avoid Turkey - and a second around to form part - at 11 pm communication from - reports to all Batt. HQrs.	Shrap. Off 7 OR 202 20? — Casualty Pub. OR — M??

WAR DIARY
or
INTELLIGENCE SUMMARY.

Army Form C. 2118.

Place	Date	Hour	Summary of Events and Information	Remarks and references to Appendices
	March 2		Lines to Bde 1.30a held well + uninterrupted communication from Bde to Division — Battalion Communication rifts to 5 Battalions in Coy lines Trenches N. of Canal — and led till heavy enemy shelly at 12.25 p.m. — Reptd Bttln ready in tents Through 50 Dum — No lines forward of 10.5 in Coy tranches to Coy posts from Bttle HQ stood "to" then reported — 4 new lines laid out night we feel — Communication S. of Canal continuing through to Battalion 7.50 I.B.	Casualties OR wounded in duty. Ring 1 OR
	March 3		Brigade Communication renewed — Communication to buff restablished — all non two other lines returns.	Capt'ns [illegible]

Army Form C. 2118.

WAR DIARY
or
INTELLIGENCE SUMMARY.
(Erase heading not required.)

Place	Date	Hour	Summary of Events and Information	Remarks and references to Appendices
[illegible]			By means of ladders calls communications to the forward headquarters in the Captains trenches. Owing to the absence of any communication trenches & the impossibility of staying unduly parties till the new posts had consolidated, only alternative route by logged carr was used. The enemy front and rear the question was returned on the fort stations & help lines mentioned any they always bombardment.	[illegible]
[illegible]			Emerson from 3 Division arrived & supplements 17 Dn mtn as a team. He and another & upper centre Fest station. Two other ends corresponding to start Notes targets held in whose centre & Stokes stand we not charge. The line was alter 5th sect through orient & S D I B by 5 2 I B	[illegible]
[illegible]			all fixed than have now by 3 widows any by [illegible] 6/7 and 17 Div become integrated.	[illegible]

Army Form C. 2118.

WAR DIARY
or
INTELLIGENCE SUMMARY.
(Erase heading not required.)

Instructions regarding War Diaries and Intelligence Summaries are contained in F. S. Regs., Part II. and the Staff Manual respectively. Title pages will be prepared in manuscript.

Place	Date	Hour	Summary of Events and Information	Remarks and references to Appendices
	March 7		3rd Div. relieved 17 Div. at Ypres — at work all time with M.M. 17 Div transferring personnel & reinforcements but not permanent officers. Div. H.Q. at STEENVOORDE. Two Brigades ready with 3rd Div. 57 I.B. with 2nd Corps.	
	March 8.		as March 8	
	March 9			
	March 10		17 Div relieved 25th Div. at MERRIS in reserve to 2nd Corps area — many units not yet arrived	
	March 11		In rest — times opened to Brigade H.Q.	
	March 12		In rest. known heavy maintenance — Practice (2nd) call —	
	March 13		In rest. Return to instruments — half day granted to holders.	

Army Form C. 2118.

WAR DIARY
or
INTELLIGENCE SUMMARY.
(Erase heading not required.)

Place	Date	Hour	Summary of Events and Information	Remarks and references to Appendices
	March 14th		In rest. Lectured Coln. Woolead and Lieutenant Marshall	
	March 15th		In rest. Instruments rehearsed and wagon washed.	
	March 16th		G Staff informed this unit that Dvt Welfs at Armentieres were going to be changed	(Copy sent)
	March 17th		Lieut Hodges instructed and arrangements made for lorries to be collected	
	March 18th		Working party proceeded to Armentieres with the object of laying lines between Dvt Welfs at Pont de Nieppe	
	March 19th		51st Bttn left Bailleul and took up their Hdqrs in Armentieres. Working party employed in digging pole and line Hdqrs for the purpose of communication between	
	March 20th		52nd Bttn arrived from Bailleul. Communication through 2nd Corps. Working party laying field lines about New Hdqrs at Armentieres	
	March 21st		52nd Bttn left Bailleul for Armentieres. Communication through 2nd Corps and 2nd Div. Working party on lines in Armentieres	(Canady)

WAR DIARY
OR
INTELLIGENCE SUMMARY.

(Erase heading not required.)

Army Form C. 2118.

Place	Date	Hour	Summary of Events and Information	Remarks and references to Appendices
	March 22nd		51th Bttn marched from Strazeele to Bailleul. Ammunition carried through as ordered	
	March 23rd		8th Bttn marched to Caestre. Also W/O cyclist Desp to no area from S.I. Divn. Signal Office at 136 Rue Salle Carnot. Change over quite uneventful. Working hasty engageclerks making a few necessary alterations in lines.	
	March 25th		Nothing to report	
	March 26		Moved an office at 143 Rue Nationale in ruins. Tn the small units in that vicinity.	
	March 27		all lines working well. St-Bleien area officer evacuated into Meroles.	
	March 28th		Arrangements made for move of office to Eps. Avrycke moving to charge of Hazebrouck	

WAR DIARY
or
INTELLIGENCE SUMMARY.

Army Form C. 2118.

Place	Date	Hour	Summary of Events and Information	Remarks and references to Appendices
	March 29		Lines working well.	
	March 30		Lines working well. Schemes being prepared for strengthening of forward lines — many of which are O + Betsy.	
	March 31		Lateral line between left + left centre Battalion cut. Shell fire — Repair line broken by heavy wirechops. Both again repaired.	

Strength 1.3.16. Off 7
OR 202
209

Casualties: wound. 2
To Common 2
Sick 2 6
203

Reinf. underway 1
OR 5 6
209
7 Offrs
202 OR

[Signature] Major
Queens W. H. Officers R. Engrs. 1 Coy R.E.

WAR DIARY
INTELLIGENCE SUMMARY

Place	Date	Hour	Summary of Events and Information	Remarks and references to Appendices
	April 1		Heavy shelling of left sector - Directed on to right & right centre - [illegible]	
	April 2		Knees all good	
	April 3		Knees all good	
	April 4		[illegible]	
	April 5		[illegible]	
	April 6		[illegible]	
	April 7		[illegible]	

Army Form C. 2118.

WAR DIARY
or
INTELLIGENCE SUMMARY.
(Erase heading not required.)

Instructions regarding War Diaries and Intelligence Summaries are contained in F. S. Regs., Part II. and the Staff Manual respectively. Title pages will be prepared in manuscript.

Place	Date	Hour	Summary of Events and Information	Remarks and references to Appendices
	April 8		Louis Front - held Enemy Infantry testing activity -	
	April 9		Enemy have taken up right, left & centre sectors comments. 2.56.6 & 10.3 hyper water to left sector. Enemy Inspection posts removed.	Capt. Ramsey to hospital 13th to this date Ram 16 R
	April 10		Enemy on line H.Q.E. L.417412.6577E to 3222Y and B30 D 41 & C 19 Z oss. B.Th. have completed sector. Line complete to Newbury. arrangements for RTO to make II Cuba.	Gnr.K 10 R
	April 11		Ryth. Inspn. altimeters - line by 20th/0th veteran were still fair & efficient - Others leaving gas.	

1577 Wt.W10791/1773 500,000 1/15 D.D. & L. A.D.S.S./Forms/C. 2118.

WAR DIARY
or
INTELLIGENCE SUMMARY.

(Erase heading not required.)

Army Form C. 2118.

Place	Date	Hour	Summary of Events and Information	Remarks and references to Appendices
Westhof Farm			During the week ending April 12 the new constitution was carried on Company & Battn. orders of Company group by intensive recruits of company groups. Several front lines were visited to the variety & depth in loss of ground. There were casualties in serveral. Fire Central men were had along left of coast between left OC & get regts N & O's by night. New trails in rear laid severely with left company & right ?Brigade? Between in repair. A command ?post? in rear to between ?Bryan? ?Bryan? area was ?decided on?. By taking left O on from I, 2, 3, OC, ?&?, & ? ? light on the ? as to ? has his suggested to make a ? ? Extra ?seconds? ? ? ? to ? ?	

WAR DIARY
or
INTELLIGENCE SUMMARY.

(Erase heading not required.)

Army Form C. 2118.

Place	Date	Hour	Summary of Events and Information	Remarks and references to Appendices
	April 13		General duty	
	April 14		General duty — One [company?] have [been] out on [exercise?]	1 OR (William) sick
	April 15		[ditto]	
	April 16		[ditto]	
	April 17		General duty — Two horses [cast?] and [ ] [ ]	1 OR sick, 1 M sick, 1 OR Rejoin
	April 18		[ ] [ ] [ ] 1 OR [ ]	
			Marching to [ ]	

Army Form C. 2118.

WAR DIARY
or
INTELLIGENCE SUMMARY.
(Erase heading not required.)

Instructions regarding War Diaries and Intelligence Summaries are contained in F. S. Regs., Part II. and the Staff Manual respectively. Title pages will be prepared in manuscript.

Place	Date	Hour	Summary of Events and Information	Remarks and references to Appendices
	April 21		wet day. nothing to report	
	April 22		Quiet day do do	
	April 23		Quiet day do do	
	April 24		Quiet day do do	
	April 25		Rather an than the two previous. General Cameron returned	introduced
	April 26		Major Chin went on leave to Phila. took over command. Our to Capt Brigade out up trying to find enemy reported to soon in front. nothing to report.	
	April 27th			got order 1 on left
	April 28th		Gun battery have the during the morning	

WAR DIARY
or
INTELLIGENCE SUMMARY
(Erase heading not required.)

Army Form C. 2118.

Place	Date	Hour	Summary of Events and Information	Remarks and references to Appendices
	April 28		Opened quickly in the evening. Shrapnel fire three tried trench ever at happen where we were shelled. 21st thunder effects attached. Instructions type- for Fifth Corps.	
	April 29th		All lines in good working order. New station erected at J10 & 5.2 Cell C35 Station C30, C5, C4 and C2 instead of E. Gas started from many trench legs – all lines O.K.	Strength mess- Inv arrival Strength Off 9 OR 212
	April 30		Sgm Anthony to report	
	May 1st			
	May 2nd		Lee & Sgt Dr RE Cln pulled up quickly from lines to 5 D & 5.11 gr Am - trg were gone repaired along toying hasty on back line	
	May 3rd		D in on main line in front section but now repaired and in working order	delays

1577 Wt.W10791/1773 500,000 1/15 D.D.&L. A.D.S.S./Forms/C-2118.

WAR DIARY
or
INTELLIGENCE SUMMARY.

(Erase heading not required.)

Army Form C. 2118.

Place	Date	Hour	Summary of Events and Information	Remarks and references to Appendices
	April 28	cont	Japanese Advance in evening. Enemy tried Forward service ordered lines at Ruyth when wires were repaired by Thomas	
	April 29th		Offr attached for instruction L/1-1m 3rd Corps. All lines OK. New station opened at J.10.b.5.2 Calls g 38 Station C.30, C.5, C.21, C.22 handed over to Anzacs. Gas reported from many forces. All have OK.	
	April 30th		Strength 1-4-11 Off 4 OR 222 Off 9 OR 202 Casualties sick & funeral 2 6 Arrivals 6	Off 4 & OR 202 105 arrival

Queen's Westminster Rifles,
Commanding 17th. Signal Coy. R.E.

Major

17 Signals
Vol 10

Army Form C. 2118.

WAR DIARY
or
INTELLIGENCE SUMMARY
(Erase heading not required.)

Instructions regarding War Diaries and Intelligence Summaries are contained in F. S. Regs., Part II. and the Staff Manual respectively. Title pages will be prepared in manuscript.

Place	Date	Hour	Summary of Events and Information	Remarks and references to Appendices
	April 1		Heavy shelling of left section — Direct lines to right & right centre battalion out — but alternative via left centre & internal renewed good — lines repaired as soon as battery ceased —	Sky R. Direct Off 7 — OR 202 209 [illegible] Rayform 1/b R 1 on Rayform
	April 2		lines all good.	
	April 3		lines all good.	
	April 4		lines good — one line repaired.	
	April 5		lines good	
	April 6		looked between Inyati & [illegible] centres out & repaired — O'Kennie [illegible]	
	April 7		Lines good —	

Army Form C. 2118.

WAR DIARY
or
INTELLIGENCE SUMMARY.
(Erase heading not required.)

Instructions regarding War Diaries and Intelligence Summaries are contained in F. S. Regs., Part II. and the Staff Manual respectively. Title pages will be prepared in manuscript.

Place	Date	Hour	Summary of Events and Information	Remarks and references to Appendices
	April 8		Lines quiet —	
	April 9		New line taken rightfully [illeg] 1,9c,6,3,c,2,1,b,b type centre dates commenced — (mattr superior ne renewed)	Opt Quemen[?] then to [illeg] Pen 18 R
	April 10		New on line NLR L.17756.8 to [illeg] to BIZET land B30 D 4.3 to C.17 d 0.5. B.M lines compared [?] posters. Line completes to Newbury II Corps.	Crok 10 R
	April 11		Rifles [illeg] attacks — [illeg] by lot/view brown ine cattle fire + [illeg] — other river good).	

WAR DIARY
or
INTELLIGENCE SUMMARY.

(Erase heading not required.)

Army Form C. 2118.

Place	Date	Hour	Summary of Events and Information	Remarks and references to Appendices
Waterlot Farm			During the week ending April 12 the new communication was brought to Company's the battery up laterally by installing circuits of Company HQrs. Several front lines were found to be likely to come in bad repair. These were renewed in sections. A new wired pair was run and many joints had between W.85 right hyn & W.L. & W.R. hyn. New lines has been laid connecting with left company & left Bgdr. & Dovernn & right S.B. comm. Hill notes. Also a new report between Bryn upon contact by on M Contacty line - cut - from W.P. 2, 3, 0, & W.P. 1,2,3 Several wires being run out to supply R.E. reqts a suitable circuit. Total wires comm say to become between	

WAR DIARY
or
INTELLIGENCE SUMMARY.

Army Form C. 2118.

(Erase heading not required.)

Instructions regarding War Diaries and Intelligence Summaries are contained in F. S. Regs., Part II. and the Staff Manual respectively. Title pages will be prepared in manuscript.

Place	Date	Hour	Summary of Events and Information	Remarks and references to Appendices
[illegible]	April 14		General Day	
[illegible]	April 15		General Day — Division have now been reorganised	15 R[?] Hall 2 C[?]
[illegible]	April 16		Quiet Day	
[illegible]	April 17		Quiet Day	
[illegible]	April 18		Quiet Day — Trenches and road repaired	1 Or [?], 1 M. Ack, 1 Or [?]
[illegible]	April 19		Quiet Day — Enemy shelled [illegible] 9 Div [illegible]	
[illegible]	April 20		Nothing to report	

Army Form C. 2118.

WAR DIARY
or
INTELLIGENCE SUMMARY.
(Erase heading not required.)

Instructions regarding War Diaries and Intelligence Summaries are contained in F. S. Regs., Part II. and the Staff Manual respectively. Title pages will be prepared in manuscript.

Place	Date	Hour	Summary of Events and Information	Remarks and references to Appendices
	April 21		Quiet day. Nothing to report	
	April 22		Quiet day — do do	
	April 23		Quiet day do do	
	April 24		Quiet day do do	
	April 25		Enemy aeroplane twice attempted approach. Communications intercepted.	
	April 26		Major Chew went on leave to Phyllis took over command. Lieut. Longall cut up trying to find ordnance returned as soon as possible nothing to report.	10th arrival 1pm left
	April 27		Our battery have been on during the morning	

1577 Wt. W10791/1773 500,000 1/15 D. D. & L. A.D.S.S./Forms/C. 2118.

Army Form C. 2118.

WAR DIARY
or
INTELLIGENCE SUMMARY.
(Erase heading not required.)

Instructions regarding War Diaries and Intelligence Summaries are contained in F. S. Regs., Part II. and the Staff Manual respectively. Title pages will be prepared in manuscript.

Place	Date	Hour	Summary of Events and Information	Remarks and references to Appendices
	April 28 (?)		Opened quickly in the evening. Shrapnel from strike tended to spread wide or happen short. Were then opened – 6" Howitzer officers attached for instruction. Left for Fifth Corps	
	April 29th		All lines in good working order. New Station Munich at J.10.f.6.2. Call C.3.B. station C.30, C.5, C.21 and C.22 handed over to Fifth Corps	
	April 30		Gas reported from many trucks slight – bombardment in...? All lines O.K.	Strength off. 4 O.R. 212
	May 1st		Nothing to report	
	May 2nd		Line to 9th Div R.C. Chu. patched up quickly Ran lines in 50th & 51st Gpr Chu– from Howard also, working party on track ?	
	May 3rd		D is on main line in front section but now restored and ? in ?	delays

WAR DIARY
or
INTELLIGENCE SUMMARY.
(Erase heading not required.)

Army Form C. 2118.

Place	Date	Hour	Summary of Events and Information	Remarks and references to Appendices
April	28	Cont	Divine service ordered in evening. Shrapnel fire forced service ordered. Wire at supply where were soon repaired by Signallers. Officers attached for instruction apart for six weeks	
	April 29		All lines O.K. New stations C301, C5, C211, C22 Code G88 Station C301, opened out J10 $\frac{z}{6}$ 6.2 members	
	April 30		Dn. L. Anzacs Gas reported from many areas. All lines O.K.	15" divns

Strength 1-4-16 Off 4 OR 222 Off 4 OR 209
Sick & OR 2 ? 9
Casualties 2

6
Arrival 6.

[signatures]

Army Form C. 2118.

WAR DIARY
or
INTELLIGENCE SUMMARY.
(Erase heading not required.)

Instructions regarding War Diaries and Intelligence Summaries are contained in F. S. Regs., Part II. and the Staff Manual respectively. Title pages will be prepared in manuscript.

Place	Date	Hour	Summary of Events and Information	Remarks and references to Appendices
	May 1		Nothing to report —	Sheet # 7 202/209
	May 2		Line to gun Dir RC Chi - Mthn line in on & and 51st Bdes out - also Bat - all carried on. Delay Con'd were soon patched up	
	May 3rd		Dir & minor lines in front sections. They were soon repaired	and
	May 4		Quiet day all line all right.	
	May 5		Heavy Shelly from Trenches — several lines cut - we attention paid to trace up 8pes in front line was cut off — all were repaired by anyone	10R to [illegible]

Army Form C. 2118.

WAR DIARY
or
INTELLIGENCE SUMMARY.
(Erase heading not required.)

Instructions regarding War Diaries and Intelligence Summaries are contained in F. S. Regs., Part II. and the Staff Manual respectively. Title pages will be prepared in manuscript.

Place	Date	Hour	Summary of Events and Information	Remarks and references to Appendices
	May 6		Quiet generally —	Casualties nil
	May 7		Quiet generally —	nil (wounded)
	May 8		Iron huts taken by [lorry?] finished — at night —	recpt. 1 O.R. nil
	May 9		Keen huns opened & asphxnd calls us in to stick in nine.	recpt. 1 O.R.
	May 10		Quiet Day —	nil
	May 11		Quiet Day —	nil
	May 12		Quiet Day —	nil

WAR DIARY
or
INTELLIGENCE SUMMARY

Army Form C. 2118.

Place	Date	Hour	Summary of Events and Information	Remarks and references to Appendices
(May 13)			Londs ally crossed roughly 17/50. E 2 NZ Bgs relieved 51 NZ Bg when moved to ESTAIRES system. A.D.M.S. BG stationed moved at MORBECQUES inside the 2 Bg ref OR front of units of Bv en route to Trans area — SD Btn moved to MORBECQUES.	Casualty list
May 14			50 Bn moved to MORBECQUES — Commander via SCOUTS — right 13/4 out 51 = Bn. Lined by 1 N.Z. Bg & tooth over right sector 5.2 Bn. reported arrived have J. order landing on Road — 2.1 2.1 Bg relieved 1 = NZ Bg. — 2.51 Bn. moved to ESTAIRES — Communications to New Zealand Bg.	
May 15			Officer half 51 0.9 — to Estaires — Sent 1 off to NK scouts out half 52 Bg (left sector) relieved by 2 NZ Bg — and moved out the guard the TK Bvs Trans area	
May 16			right 7 15/16 Half 32 — 59 moved to MORBECQUES — 2 NZ Bg relieved 51 & 52 in the rear line OC — via Gorge to where May 16, 17 G.S. bucher & 7 NZ Spot by — of M. CON office on 7 IL ROLS	

Place	Date	Hour	Summary of Events and Information	Remarks and references to Appendices
	May 13/2		To prepare & sworn in the month the following supped arrangements were made:-
(1) ESTAIRES in ant 2 oc men are not available for units here though.
(2) in a set office was opened at DOULIEU towards suffering in the low Though.
(3) another was opened at MORBECQUE AREA was by units which billets & around there
(4) arrangements were for units to be (filled) from stores of units billets in HAZEBROUCK.	

WAR DIARY
or
INTELLIGENCE SUMMARY
(Erase heading not required.)

Army Form C. 2118

Instructions regarding War Diaries and Intelligence Summaries are contained in F. S. Regs., Part II. and the Staff Manual respectively. Title Pages will be prepared in manuscript.

Place	Date	Hour	Summary of Events and Information	Remarks and references to Appendices
	May 17		Communication established to NORTLEUVINGHEM from TILQUES — Cable by land from tn own north TILQUES-POLINCOVE road was tapped at EST MONT. Communication established to EPERLECQUES S17.B9. on permanent wire.	Convoy nil
	May 18		Subterranean Tramway	
	May 19		Ditto	
	May 20		Subterranean Tramway Easy Tramway	
	May 21		Subterranean Tramway	Convoy
	May 22		Subterranean Tramway	Convoy nil

Army Form C. 2118

Instructions regarding War Diaries and Intelligence Summaries are contained in F. S. Regs., Part II. and the Staff Manual respectively. Title Pages will be prepared in manuscript.

WAR DIARY
or
INTELLIGENCE SUMMARY
(Erase heading not required.)

Place	Date	Hour	Summary of Events and Information	Remarks and references to Appendices
May 24			Intensive Training	Casualty
May 25			Intensive training	
May 26			Intensive Training	nil
May 27			Intensive training.	
May 28			Rest	Casualties 18th May 10th
May 29			Intensive Training	
May 30			Intensive Training	
May 31			Intensive training.	

Summary strength Off 7 / OR 202 / 209

Battle casualties 2 / 3

To Command 13 / 206

Reinforcements 5 / 211

strength. Off 7 / OR 204

W Taylor [signature]

1875 Wt. W593/826 1,000,000 4/15 J.B.C. & A. A.D.S.S./Forms/C. 2118.

WAR DIARY
or
INTELLIGENCE SUMMARY.

Army Form C. 2118.

VOL II

Place	Date	Hour	Summary of Events and Information	Remarks and references to Appendices
	May 1		Nothing to report	Sheet #7 oct 20/9/19
	May 2		Line to g in Div R.C. Clr - Mtr. line in & & and 51st BCts Cut - also [?] all Cuned on delay and were soon patched up.	
	May 3rd		D in M [?] lines in front section. They were soon repaired	
	May 4		Quiet day - all wire all right	
	May 5		Heavy shelling of front trenches - several lines cut - no attention had to be no other in trace was cut off - all wires repaired by midnight	10A [?]

Army Form C. 2118.

WAR DIARY
or
INTELLIGENCE SUMMARY.
(Erase heading not required.)

Instructions regarding War Diaries and Intelligence Summaries are contained in F. S. Regs., Part II. and the Staff Manual respectively. Title pages will be prepared in manuscript.

Place	Date	Hour	Summary of Events and Information	Remarks and references to Appendices
	May 6		Quite friendly —	Cancelled
	May 7		Quite friendly —	on (November)
	May 8		Two men taken by Flurry Transho — at night —	supp. 10.8 nil
	May 9		Two men wounded & carried wells to be in to sun in sun	supp. 10.8
	May 10		Quiet day —	nil
	May 11		Quiet day —	nil
	May 12		Quiet Day —	nil

WAR DIARY
or
INTELLIGENCE SUMMARY.
(Erase heading not required.)

Army Form C. 2118.

Instructions regarding War Diaries and Intelligence Summaries are contained in F. S. Regs., Part II. and the Staff Manual respectively. Title pages will be prepared in manuscript.

Place	Date	Hour	Summary of Events and Information	Remarks and references to Appendices
	May 13		Lines all correct — night 12/13. 2ⁿᵈ N.Z. Bde (relieved) 50ᵗʰ Bde who moved to ESTAIRES — A. Bn. Sub-station moved to MORBECQUES between Bns 2ⁿᵈ Bde & rest of units of Bn. en route to Trany area — 50 Bde moved to MORBECQUES	Empty 10R
	May 14		50 Bde. moved to WARDRECQUES — Communication via 52ⁿᵈ Bde — night 13/14. 51ˢᵗ Bde. relieved by 1ˢᵗ N.Z. Bde. Lines good all handed over time — 2 N.Z. Bde received 1ˢᵗ N.Z. Bde — ½ 51 Bde moved to ESTAIRES — Communication by New Zealand Bde. night 14/15	no cas
	May 15		Second half 51 Bde — to Estaires — First half to WARDREQUES — Half 52 Bde (left party) relieved by 2ⁿᵈ N.Z. Bde — Advanced Signal Office opened at TICROSS taking over	nil
	May 16		night 15/16 Half 52ⁿᵈ Bde moved to WARDREQUES — ½ N.Z. Bde. relieved 52 I.D. in line from lines Oll [?] we hand over from May 16 17 by S.Bde. over to N.Z. Signal Coy. of the office at 7.16.2015 became permanent	nil

1577 Wt. W10791/1773 500,000 1/15 D.D.&L. A.D.S.S./Forms/C. 2118.

May 13/2/2

For purposes of ammunition on the march the following expend arrangements were made -
(1) ESTAIRES in ANZAC area was made available for units passing through.
(2) a salt office was opened at DOULIEU for units halting there on the way through.
(3) an office was opened at MORBECQUE ANZAC area for units which billeted & ammunition there
(4) arrangements made for units to be furnished from stores & units billets at HAZEBROUCK.

WAR DIARY or INTELLIGENCE SUMMARY.

Army Form C. 2118.

Place	Date	Hour	Summary of Events and Information	Remarks and references to Appendices
	May 17		Communication established to NORTLEULINGHEM from TILQUES — Cable by laid from the main route TILQUES POLINCOVE turn was looped at EST MONT. Communication established to EPERLECQUES SIT 8.91. on permanent lines	Country end
	May 18		Interior Survey	
	May 19		Ditto	
	May 20		Interior Survey	
	May 21		Easy Survey	reinforcement for
	May 22		Interior Survey	Country end
	May 23		Interior Survey	

WAR DIARY
or
INTELLIGENCE SUMMARY

Army Form C. 2118

(Erase heading not required.)

Instructions regarding War Diaries and Intelligence Summaries are contained in F.S. Regs., Part II. and the Staff Manual respectively. Title Pages will be prepared in manuscript.

Place	Date	Hour	Summary of Events and Information	Remarks and references to Appendices
	May 24		Intercom Training	Casualty
	May 25		Intercom Training	
	May 26		Intercom Training	and
	May 27		Intercom hour	
	May 28		rest	Owner 15m order
	May 29		Intercom Training	
	May 30		Intercom Training	
	May 31		Intercom hour	

Plan of CME with Artillery 52nd Brigade lines

	Trenches			
	Northumberland Fusiliers	Manchesters	W. Rid Regt	Lancashire Fus.
	P_6 P_4 P_3 P_2 P_1	O_4 O_3 O_2 O_1 N_6	N_5 N_4 N_3 N_2	N_1 M_3 M_2 M_1
Trenches covered by sight lines	D	B	A	C

D of W HQ

Manchesters HQ

Lancashire Fusiliers HQ

North'd Fus HQ

Howitzers C81

D   B   C   A

78th FAB

– – – – Trench to Battery
– · – · – Battalion to Battery
– ·· – ·· – Trench to Howitzer

Army Form C. 2118

WAR DIARY
or
INTELLIGENCE SUMMARY
(Erase heading not required.)

17th Div Signals
Vol 12

Place	Date	Hour	Summary of Events and Information	Remarks and references to Appendices
1915 June	1		Training	
	2		Training	
	3		Training	
	4		Training	
	5		Training. O.C. visited area to which Div. is moving	
	6		Training	
	7		Training	
	8		Advance party to new area at TREUX (Somme) & Div. H.Qtrs at HEILONVILLE near AMIENS.	
	9		Company training – advance office opened.	

Army Form C. 2118

WAR DIARY
or
INTELLIGENCE SUMMARY
(Erase heading not required.)

Instructions regarding War Diaries and Intelligence Summaries are contained in F.S. Regs., Part II. and the Staff Manual respectively. Title Pages will be prepared in manuscript.

Place	Date	Hour	Summary of Events and Information	Remarks, and references to Appendices
	June 10		50 I.B. with no 2 Sub. moved forward area — Eval lines to Bryour the land with all men through came — hyprio entrained for new area remaining	
	June 11		Offices at TILQV & Clarus & at MLO NURLUS in IV Army area opened the gun being heavy 15cwt —	
	June 12			
	June 13		Enemen funeral long was over	
	June 14		ditto —	
	June 15		MM. knee to codm via army 47 fouls.	

WAR DIARY
or
INTELLIGENCE SUMMARY

(Erase heading not required.)

Place	Date	Hour	Summary of Events and Information	Remarks and references to Appendices
	June 16		1st section wire up to H/Qrs Divisions in the line & to North and men & Officers trained in the areas where in may be called upon to work. Work in forward lines & employed & enats —	
	June 17.		Same	
	June 18		Same work. Preparation of So. I.B. [?] several communications opened for a special work allotted to them —	
	June 19.		Same work —	
	June 20			
	June 21		Two sections ready to 7 + 21 Divisions & Artillery So. I.B. & army at times & work for structures.	

Army Form C. 2118

WAR DIARY
or
INTELLIGENCE SUMMARY
(Erase heading not required.)

Instructions regarding War Diaries and Intelligence Summaries are contained in F. S. Regs., Part II. and the Staff Manual respectively. Title Pages will be prepared in manuscript.

Place	Date	Hour	Summary of Events and Information	Remarks and references to Appendices
	June 22		Bros. line from 7 Div HA at TREUX to 5.07.8 to Bde put in 2. Div area WILLOW AVENUE (incl) to forward stations.	
	June 23		General work - namely 7 & 2 Div.	
	June 24		do.	
	June 25		do	
	June 26		do	
	June 27		New lateral lines laid by forward sections from 9' BSM HQ, F.17.b May 62.C.63 & A1.30 F.B.Co. (see 62.C.6 sh.) to 54.09.40.	

1875 Wt. W593/826 1,000,000 4/15 J.B.C. & A. A.D.S.S./Forms/C. 2118.

WAR DIARY
or
INTELLIGENCE SUMMARY

Army Form C. 2118

Place	Date	Hour	Summary of Events and Information	Remarks and references to Appendices
	June 28		Group moved to HERICOURT + opened office — at the same time the 17 Fy Cy. provided operators for the lines from 7 Div. H.Q. at TREUX to that 7 Div Comd occupy its report centre. Line found up to Trigny. Unanswered to 21 + 7 Divs. Same wire.	
	June 29			
	June 30		Div. H.Q. moved to TRSVX + Futh men 20 1892 wages 21. Div. Comd. 7 Div. H.Q. the 51 1892 to NORCNCOURT into F $ 2 $ 21. The 5 2 to BOIS des THULES. Strength off 7 OR 20 4 June 1. 21 7 20 8 1 8 A.D.S.T. Form 2118. Return Two lieuts proceeded with — 7 proceeded in pursuit of — 7 Transfer on increase of establishment authorised W/o DTD 103	

Michael Gerales Major.
Queen's Westminster Rifles,
Commanding 17th Signal Coy., R.E.

Confidential.

WAR DIARY

of

17th DIVISIONAL SIGNAL COY.

July 1st – 31st 1916.

VOLUME 13.

WAR DIARY
or
INTELLIGENCE SUMMARY

(Erase heading not required.)

Army Form C. 2118

Place	Date	Hour	Summary of Events and Information	Remarks and references to Appendices
	July 1st		The forward lines as far as our front trenches laid by the 50th Brigade in the 21st Division area in connection with the attack on FRICOURT held extremely well and reflected the greatest credit on the Signal Officer of the 50th Brigade Signal Section who planned and carried out the work. The 50th Brigade were working under the 21st Division and their communications were satisfactory. The 10th West Yorks laid rapid lines to the German front lines behind the first assault which would have been available for communication had the assault succeeded. The 51st Brigade relieved the 50th Brigade.	
Night of July 1/2.				
	July 2nd		The attack on FRICOURT WOOD was successful and lines were laid & maintained right up to the Battalions Headquarters some Company lines beyond. The communications both by runner and wire worked	

WAR DIARY
or
INTELLIGENCE SUMMARY

Army Form C. 2118

Place	Date	Hour	Summary of Events and Information	Remarks and references to Appendices
	July 2nd (contd)		Lines were sufficient and it was unnecessary to use pigeons on July 1/2 though they were provided on both occasions. Wireless could not be put out because the Division was still working through the 21st Divisional Signal system and sharing the 21st Division Report Centre and the only set in position was a 1·50 wave length from which the 21st Division could not receive.	
	July 3rd		In order to strengthen lateral communications which were found to be unsatisfactory a line was laid from the left Brigade of the 15th Division (late position of the 21st Division) to the right Brigade of the 34th Division. This communication and later proved invaluable during the whole day and was laid under considerable shelling during the night	

Place	Date	Hour	Summary of Events and Information	Remarks and references to Appendices
July 3rd (Contd)			The 51st & 52nd Brigades laid the temporary laid line which was made forward through a captured trench by D5 pinned mostly in communication trenches. This formed a basis of communication during the next few days.	
	July 4th		The 17th Division Headquarters relieved the 21st Division at E.28.A.3.4 and took over. The Infantry of the 17th Division during the night having taken over the whole of the position of the 21st Division. A good many lines were cut during the day and a good many were repaired and communications were well maintained during the day. In order to further strengthen the lateral communications which were becoming important a pair was laid from the 51st Brigade to the 52nd Brigade Headquarters. This pair became at night	

WAR DIARY
or
INTELLIGENCE SUMMARY

Army Form C. 2118

Place	Date	Hour	Summary of Events and Information	Remarks and references to Appendices
July 4th (contd)			A most essential link in the communications became the whole line of the 17th Division during the night of 4/5th placed under command of the 52nd Brigade who remained in. And therefore by means of this lateral in addition to existing lines were able to make full use of the communications which have been laid by the 51st Brigade when they controlled the greater part of the 17th Division front. A heavy wireless set was set up at Divisional Headquarters and an attempt was made during the night to send to forward position a trench set but owing to a heavy "barrage" it was impossible to get it going. The likes held sufficiently will to make wireless unnecessary and as the fighting was at night the use of pigeons was not practicable.	

Place	Date	Hour	Summary of Events and Information	Remarks and references to Appendices
	July 5		With a view to providing safe lines from the present Artillery exchange to new forward Observation Posts on a system that could be afterwards drawn in to general utility when Divisional Headquarters went forward an armoured quad and two D5 lines were laid from X26D8.0 to X12&A2.4 in CRUCIFIX TRENCH. Owing to the heavy work of keeping the normal lines going which necessitated a good deal of maintenance a working party consisted of a party of 1 Yorks & Lancasters, 6 halfpast and 6 drivers. Great credit is due to Lieutenant Robertson Royal Engineers of this Company for the admirable way in which the work was carried out and to the working party for the admirable way in which they worked considering that half the distance of 2½ miles - was carried out under intermittent shell fire during the time the work was done.	

WAR DIARY
or
INTELLIGENCE SUMMARY

Army Form C. 2118

Place	Date	Hour	Summary of Events and Information	Remarks and references to Appendices
	July 6th		Lines to Brigade held well but the very heavy shelling East of Fricourt constantly cut the lines in advance. A heavy wireless set was working from FRICOURT FARM and a trench set from the DINGLE. Very heavy rain caused an enormous amount of induction on the lines and the maintenance was very heavy. The lines forward to Battalion Headquarters were constantly cut. A certain number of pigeon messages were sent and came in fairly well.	

Place	Date	Hour	Summary of Events and Information	Remarks and references to Appendices
	July 7th		Induction was still very bad in the open trenches. An alternative route was laid from F.8.A to FRICOURT CHATEAU so as to try and keep the telegraph system independent of the telephone. As Artillery Brigades were moving, new connections were made so as to keep the C.R.A in constant touch with all Brigades of Artillery.	
	July 8th		The 119th and 121st Brigades of Artillery came into the sector and communication was provided to them. The 119th Brigade by a short line from F.F.A and 121st by a junction with 79th Brigade at F.9 central. The trend of the Division being to sidestep to the East some of the Artillery lines East of SEQOURDEZ FRICOURT route were diverted either direct to E.2.F.A.3.4 Divisional Headquarters or the the exchange from the original exchange at Queens Redoubt.	

Army Form C. 2118

WAR DIARY
or
INTELLIGENCE SUMMARY

(Erase heading not required.)

Instructions regarding War Diaries and Intelligence Summaries are contained in F.S. Regs., Part II. and the Staff Manual respectively. Title Pages will be prepared in manuscript.

Place	Date	Hour	Summary of Events and Information	Remarks and references to Appendices
	July 9th		Work here practically this work was continued and in order to cope with in addition a certain number of low poles were made to lift telephone lines out of the cable trenches. On the night of July 9th a total many Artillery Brigades moved forward and a lot of cable had to be issued so that the lines from Brigades to Batteries might be extended and also from Batteries to forward F.O.O's. Some of the lines originally laid from our front trenches to CRUCIFIX TRENCH in anticipation of these Artillery moves were now brought into service. Some of these lines were also used by 23rd Division to subsidy to the great covering a considerable amount of the original 17/21st area.	
July 10th			Operators & linemen of the 21st Signal Company came to learn the lines as it was intended to relieve the 17th Division by 21st Division.	
July 11th			The 17th Division was relieved by the 21st Division	

1875 Wt. W593/826 1,000,000 4/15 J.B.C. & A. A.D.S.S./Forms/C. 2118.

WAR DIARY
or
INTELLIGENCE SUMMARY
(Erase heading not required.)

Army Form C. 2118

Place	Date	Hour	Summary of Events and Information	Remarks and references to Appendices
	July 11th		at 10. a.m - two officers & 14 Linesmen R.E. 17th Division being left behind to ensure that the 21st Division could follow out the system of communication as developed during the time of the 17th Division were in the line. During the time the 17th Division were in the line there was no moment when Divisional H.Q. were unable to communicate by telephone or telegraph with Brigades except for a few hours on July 5th when Battalions were cut off from Brigade Headquarters. Divisional Headquarters opened at CAVILLON and found lines which were pushed up by some of the Brigades and passed under 2nd Corps administration.	
	July 12th		The rest of the 17th Division came out on the night of July 12th. By 21st Division being satisfied the light left behind were withdrawn to rest.	

Army Form C. 2118

WAR DIARY
or
INTELLIGENCE SUMMARY

(Erase heading not required.)

Instructions regarding War Diaries and Intelligence Summaries are contained in F. S. Regs., Part II. and the Staff Manual respectively. Title Pages will be prepared in manuscript.

Place	Date	Hour	Summary of Events and Information	Remarks and references to Appendices
July	13th		Rest at CAVILLON. By request of the 21st Division an extra officer was sent them to help supervise the maintenance of signalling.	
July	14th		Rest at CAVILLON.	
July	15th		Division moved from CAVILLON to PONT REMY.	
July	16th		At PONT REMY.	
July	17th		Also at PONT REMY.	
July	18th		also at PONT REMY.	
July	19th		At PONT REMY.	
"	20th		Resting at PONT REMY.	
	21st		-do- -do-	

Army Form C. 2118

WAR DIARY
or
INTELLIGENCE SUMMARY
(Erase heading not required.)

Instructions regarding War Diaries and Intelligence Summaries are contained in F. S. Regs., Part II. and the Staff Manual respectively. Title Pages will be prepared in manuscript.

Place	Date	Hour	Summary of Events and Information	Remarks and references to Appendices
July	22		Company moved by route march	
	23		PONT REMY to DERNECOURT.	
	24		Signal offr spend at RIBEMONT. remainder to Brigadr's D.R.	
	"			
	25		recon + repair work XV Corps area	
	26		Remainder attached to 51 and 5 Divisions	
	27		front. rest of company engaged as before.	
	28		Ditto.	
	29		Ditto.	

1875 Wt. W593/826 1,000,000 4/15 J.B.C. & A. A.D.S.S./Forms/C. 2118.

WAR DIARY
or
INTELLIGENCE SUMMARY

(Erase heading not required.)

Army Form C. 2118

Place	Date	Hour	Summary of Events and Information	Remarks and references to Appendices
	July 30		BELLEVUE FARM, AZ 35 a 7 [?] engaged as a [?] HQ to wind up.	
	July 31		Two lines connected from south down to the corridor for 5 Divn. Strength July 31 Officers 7 Other Ranks [?] O.R. 218 / 226 / 11	

Casualties for month
Killed — 1
Wounded — 1 / 8
Sick — 5
Troops — 1 / 12
Horses — 4

[signature] Major
Queen's Westminster Rifles,
Commanding 17th. Signal Coy, R.E.

17th Divisional Engineers

17th DIVISIONAL SIGNAL COMPANY R. E.

AUGUST 1 9 1 6::::

WAR DIARY
or
INTELLIGENCE SUMMARY
(Erase heading not required.)

Army Form C. 2118

17th Signal Co:

Place	Date	Hour	Summary of Events and Information	Remarks and references to Appendices
	August 1st		The 17th Division absorbed the 5th Division going into new Headquarters at Bethune. Your station, System of communication - Test station, Signal Office & Exchange at FRICOURT, also at POMMIERS REDOUBT.	
	August 2nd		A derelict armoured cable in MONTAUBAN TRENCH between POMMIERS REDOUBT and Brigade H.Q. was brought into use and adapted and applied to and continued to POMMIERS REDOUBT so as to improve communication to the Brigade in the line.	
	August 3rd		Arrangements made for communication with Divisions taking over Right Brigade of 13th Corps Lines laid from their test truckle in front of MONTAUBAN by two miles thank to POMMIERS REDOUBT. One of these miles an armoured cable, not enf use was found for	

Place	Date	Hour	Summary of Events and Information	Remarks and references to Appendices
	August 4th		Quarter of way and was completed. Forward test Stations S.2.C of the Right Brigade and 2nd Division completed until medical circuit lines laid from S.16 to two Battalions in the front line at S. and junction with Left battalion of Right Brigade at S. when taking over. There was no Right communication further forward than S.2.B.C.	
	August 5th		The 51st Brigade relieved 99th Brigade, 2nd Division and sidedly completed. The two fighting Brigade Headquarters allotted in POMMIERS REDOUBT MONTAUBAN ALLEY having been rendered untenable.	
	August 6th		Two armoured cables laid along new communication trench from POMMIERS REDOUBT	

WAR DIARY
or
INTELLIGENCE SUMMARY
(Erase heading not required.)

Army Form C. 2118

Place	Date	Hour	Summary of Events and Information	Remarks and references to Appendices
Aug.	7th		No S.I.B.C. lines maintained though frequently cut.	
"	8th		Two armoured cables as far as S.I.B. carried on to two battalions in front Inf: one as additional communication for Brigade, the other as controlling O.P. line.	
"	9th		Maintenance and repair of lines.	
"	10th		An armoured cable laid from S.22.C up new communication trench to S.6.D.5. laid as far as new trench to DELVILLE WOOD.	
"	11th		D.S. came to DELVILLE Wood completed thus establishing communication on the Right Brigade area LONGUEVAL VALLEY.	
"	12th		Repair & maintenance of lines. All communication Right Division placed by lines at Divison owing to heavy shelling in MONTAUBAN ALLEY the line from PORTMIERS Division killed.	

WAR DIARY
or
INTELLIGENCE SUMMARY

Army Form C. 2118

Place	Date	Hour	Summary of Events and Information	Remarks and references to Appendices
	August 13		REDOUBT to S16D were very badly damaged. Large party sent out with rope to retour damage. Wire threaded over and nothing in thoroughly good order. One officer & 30 O.R. left behind to maintain this to 17th Divisional Artillery who remained in trenches 14th Division. W) ireless stations were established at 16 D and MONTAUBAN which kept communication with The Corps stationed FRICOURT. Pigeons were kept continually in the front line were invaluable especially from Companies who had no lines back to Brigade. On the night of 5/7 during some minor operations in DELVILLE WOOD the O.C. 7th Borders Regt	

Army Form C. 2118

WAR DIARY
or
INTELLIGENCE SUMMARY
(Erase heading not required.)

Instructions regarding War Diaries and Intelligence Summaries are contained in F.S. Regs., Part II. and the Staff Manual respectively. Title Pages will be prepared in manuscript.

Place	Date	Hour	Summary of Events and Information	Remarks and references to Appendices
	August 14		suffered to find a billeting pit. He had this brought into his Headquarters and by means of D3 telephones with earths in front line was able to send up support and stores as required to his Companies who there carrying out operations. Office maintained at BUIRE Company on the move.	
	" 15		Closed at BUIRE and opened at BERNAVILLE.	
	" 16		Closed at BERNAVILLE and opened at DOULLENS.	
	" 17		Visited lines in new Divisional area to be taken over. Six linesmen plus telephone operators went up to learn lines.	
	" 18		Learning lines in new area.	

Army Form C. 2118

WAR DIARY
or
INTELLIGENCE SUMMARY
(Erase heading not required.)

Place	Date	Hour	Summary of Events and Information	Remarks and references to Appendices
	August 19		Officers visited their new sections.	
	" 20		No 2, 3 & 4 Sections attached to 50th, 51st & 52nd Brigades took over lines from Brigade Headquarters at SAILLY. BIENVILLERS & CHATEAU LA HAIE.	
	" 21		The 17th Division relieved 56th Division. Laid all satisfactory. 10 a.m. system established. Headquarters H.E.N/s, Divisional Exchange and test station SOUASTRE. Thence traced lines to Three Brigade Headquarters.	
	" 22		Lines surveyed for 7th Corps. Put "S" tumbling Cap on telephone lines tested alright.	
	" 23		Lines built for 7th Bn. Loading Coy near SOUASTRE. Office to the 181 Loading Coy near SOUASTRE. Office from SOUASTRE temporarily at-hand grieved. Cause not known.	

WAR DIARY
or
INTELLIGENCE SUMMARY

Army Form C. 2118

Place	Date	Hour	Summary of Events and Information	Remarks and references to Appendices
	August 24		One of the jankers from SUSSITREM & SAILLY was destroyed by still fire. Other two had well hits in front of them. The Centre group Artillery limited into SUSSITRE and a part from SUSSITREM to NW thrown span having been constantly changed by war horse skins. Still held except one. All for outside left Battalion night Brigade cuf all lines between Brigade & Battalion Headquarters which and in communication to 10 minutes. Wireless stations established at HEBUTERNE and FONQUEVILLERS. Positions of 1 Battalion Headquarters of flashlamp chosen by 1 Battalion Brigadier.	
	August 25		Communication established with Corps wireless at ST AMAND.	

WAR DIARY
or
INTELLIGENCE SUMMARY

(Erase heading not required.)

Army Form C. 2118

Place	Date	Hour	Summary of Events and Information	Remarks and references to Appendices
August	27th		Lines patrolled and worked satisfactorily.	
"	28th		Quiet day. Corps permanent route into Divisional Headquarters finished but arrangements made to transfer their 12 line cover to this allotted to Corps route.	
"	29th		Transfer completed and working satisfactorily. Shelling at CHATEAU LA HAIE broke lateral communication to Artillery Group. Communication maintained via Division until lines could be repaired.	
"	30		52 B.Sr. H.Q. shelled & if CHATEAU LA HAIE J 6.81.9 ? mm had to evacuate — by means 1 Divisional Test return system this transfer was arranged without any real line [signature]	

Army Form C. 2118

WAR DIARY
or
INTELLIGENCE SUMMARY
(Erase heading not required.)

Instructions regarding War Diaries and Intelligence Summaries are contained in F. S. Regs., Part II. and the Staff Manual respectively. Title Pages will be prepared in manuscript.

Place	Date	Hour	Summary of Events and Information	Remarks and references to Appendices
Aug 31			Close range artillery round yards to DOOSTAR, showing [illegible] held to ELADAR (end) observers however opened. [illegible] of men f/dy [illegible] 4PA. Co [illegible] good billets in [illegible]. Two lines cal [illegible] General arrangements made for commence when around with [illegible] to forth communications.	

Strength Augt. 1916 Officers 7
                                    nurses 8
                          OR 218
                              246

Commanded OR 31
Sickness OR   5

Reports OR   5
              223

Infantry   3

Vol 14

Confidential
War Diary
of
17 Signal. Coy. R.E.
Aug 1 — 31 1916

Volume 14

Army Form C. 2118.

WAR DIARY
or
INTELLIGENCE SUMMARY.

(Erase heading not required.)

Instructions regarding War Diaries and Intelligence Summaries are contained in F. S. Regs., Part II. and the Staff Manual respectively. Title pages will be prepared in manuscript.

Place	Date	Hour	Summary of Events and Information	Remarks and references to Appendices
	August 1st		The 17th Division relieved the 5th Division going into new Headquarters at Bellevue Farm. System of communication:- Test station, Signal Office & Exchange at FRICOURT, also at POMMIERS Redoubt.	
	August 2nd		A derelict armoured cable in MONTAUBAN TRENCH ( ) between POMMIERS REDOUBT and Brigade H.Q. was brought into use and adapted and applied to and continued to POMMIERS REDOUBT so to improve communication to the Brigade in the line.	
	August 3rd		Arrangements made for communication in connection with Division taking over Right Brigade of 13th Corps. Lines laid from their test points in front of MONTAUBAN by two routes track to POMMIERS REDOUBT. One of these routes, an armoured cable not in use, was found for	

WAR DIARY or INTELLIGENCE SUMMARY

(Erase heading not required.)

Army Form C. 2118

Place	Date	Hour	Summary of Events and Information	Remarks and references to Appendices
	August 4th		Quarter of May and was completed. Forward Stations S.22.C of the Right Brigade and 2nd Division exchanged connected metal metallic circuit. Lines laid from S16D to two Battalions in the front line at S. and forecoming junction with left battalion of Right Brigade at S. Right Brigade at S. taking over when there was no telegraph communication further forward than S.22.C.	
	August 5th		The 51st Brigade relieved 99th Brigade, 2nd Division and violently completed. The 100 Fighting Brigade Headquarters allocated in POMMIERS REDOUBT, MONTAUBAN ALLEY having been rendered untenable.	
	August 6th		Two armoured cables laid along new Communication trench from POMMIERS REDOUBT	

WAR DIARY
or
INTELLIGENCE SUMMARY

(Erase heading not required.)

Army Form C. 2118

Instructions regarding War Diaries and Intelligence Summaries are contained in F.S. Regs., Part II. and the Staff Manual respectively. Title Pages will be prepared in manuscript.

Place	Date	Hour	Summary of Events and Information	Remarks and references to Appendices
Aug:	7th		To S.I.6.C. Lines maintained though frequently cut. Two Armoured cables as far as S.I.6. carried on to two battalions in front line; one as additional communication for Brigade, the other as controlling O.P. line.	
"	8th		Maintenance and repair of lines.	
"	9th		An armoured cable laid from S.22.C. up new communication trench to S.6.D.5. laid as far as new trench to DELVILLE WOOD.	
"	10th		D.S. laid to DELVILLE WOOD completed thus establishing communication in the Right Brigade across LONGUEVAL VALLEY.	
"	11th		Repair & maintenance of lines. All communication holding.	
"	12th		Division relieved by 14th Division. owing to heavy shelling in MONT AUBAN ALLEY the lines from POZIERES	

Army Form C. 2118

WAR DIARY
or
INTELLIGENCE SUMMARY
(Erase heading not required.)

Place	Date	Hour	Summary of Events and Information	Remarks and references to Appendices
	August 13		REDOUBT to S.16.D were very badly damaged. Large party sent out with cable to repair damage. Lines patched over and working in thoroughly good order. One officer & S.O.R. left behind to maintain lines to 17th Divisional Artillery who remained in under 14th Division.

Wireless stations were established at 16D and MONTAUBAN which kept communication with the Corps station at FRICOURT.

Pigeons were kept continually in the front line & were invaluable especially from Companies who had no line back to Brigade.

On the night of 6/7 during some minor operations in DELVILLE WOOD the O.C. ynk/Borderers | |

WAR DIARY
or
INTELLIGENCE SUMMARY
(Erase heading not required.)

Army Form C. 2118

Place	Date	Hour	Summary of Events and Information	Remarks and references to Appendices
	August 14		happened to find a listening post. He had this brought into his Headquarters and by means of D.3 telephones with earths in front line was able to send up supports and stores as required to his Companies who were carrying out operations. Office maintained at BUIRE. Company on the move.	
	" 15		Closed at BUIRE and opened at BERNAVILLE.	
	" 16		Closed at BERNAVILLE and opened at DOULLENS.	
	" 17		Visited lines in new Divisional area to be taken over. Six linemen plus telephone operators went up to learn lines.	
	" 18		Learning lines in new area	

WAR DIARY
or
INTELLIGENCE SUMMARY

Army Form C. 2118

Place	Date	Hour	Summary of Events and Information	Remarks and references to Appendices
August	19		Officers visited their new locations.	
"	20		No 2, 3 & 4 Sections attached to 50th, 51st & 52nd Brigades took over lines from Brigade Headquarters at SAILLY, BIENVILLERS & CHATEAU LA HAIE.	
"	21		The 17th Division relieved 56th Division. Lines all satisfactory 10 a.m. System established. Headquarters HENU, Divisional exchange and test station SOUASTRE. Thence buried lines to three Brigade Headquarters.	
"	22		Lines surveyed for 7th Corps. But 18" tunnelling Coy on telephone. Lines held alright.	
"	23		Lines built for 7th Corps from SOUASTRE Signal Office to the 181st Tunnelling Coy near SOUASTRE. Wire from SOUASTRE toSAILLY cut and repaired. Cause not known.	

WAR DIARY
or
INTELLIGENCE SUMMARY

Army Form C. 2118

Place	Date	Hour	Summary of Events and Information	Remarks and references to Appendices
	August 24		One of the tanks from SOUASTRE to SAILLY destroyed by shell fire. Other lines held well. The line from Hénu to Centre group Artillery diverted into SOUASTRE and a part from SOUASTRE to HÉNU thrown spare having been constantly damaged by new horse lines.	
	August 25		Lines held except one. Shell fire outside left Battalion right Brigade cut all lines between Brigade & Battalion Headquarters which lead in. Communication absent for 10 minutes. Wireless stations established at HEBUTERNE and FONQUEVILLERS Positions chosen by Battalion Headquarters of flanking Brigades. Communication established with Corps wireless at ST AMAND.	
	August 26			

Army Form C. 2118

WAR DIARY
or
INTELLIGENCE SUMMARY
(Erase heading not required.)

Place	Date	Hour	Summary of Events and Information	Remarks and references to Appendices
August	27th		Lines patrolled and worked satisfactorily.	
"	28th		Quiet day. Corps permanent route into Divisional Headquarters finished and arrangements made to transfer their 12 line comic to this allotted to Corps route.	
"	29th		Transfer completed and working satisfactorily. Shelling at CHATEAU LA HAIE broke lateral communication to Artillery group. Communication maintained via Division until lines could be repaired.	J6 B17
	30.		S.Z.D. Hqrs. H.Q. shells) one of CHATEAU LA HAIE. and moved back to SOUASTRE. By means of Divisional Trunk start in system this transfer was arranged without any new lines being opened.	

1875 Wt. W593/826 1,000,000 4/15 J.B.C. & A.   A.D.S.S./Forms/C. 2118.

WAR DIARY
or
INTELLIGENCE SUMMARY

Army Form C. 2118

Place	Date	Hour	Summary of Events and Information	Remarks and references to Appendices
	Aug 31		Central Group Artillery moved back to OSTART28. Lines from Nieuport to 5 & 22 HQ laid. Otherwise no wire repaired. A company of men (O Coy) spent 8.30 — a new line repaired to their billet in D.21b. Two lines were replaced. Special arrangements made to communicate when wires go to pieces. Communication.	

Strength Aug 1, 19b. Officers 7
attached 1
— 8
OR. 218
226

Casualties wounded. OR 2
Sick. OR 5 2 ✗ 1 transferred
+ other causes to base week 18.
Nieuport. OR 5 5
223

3 men have been transferred there.

[Signed] Major
Queen's Westminster Rifles, R.E.
Commanding 17th Signal Coy.

War Diary
17 Signal Coy
Aug 1 — 31
1916

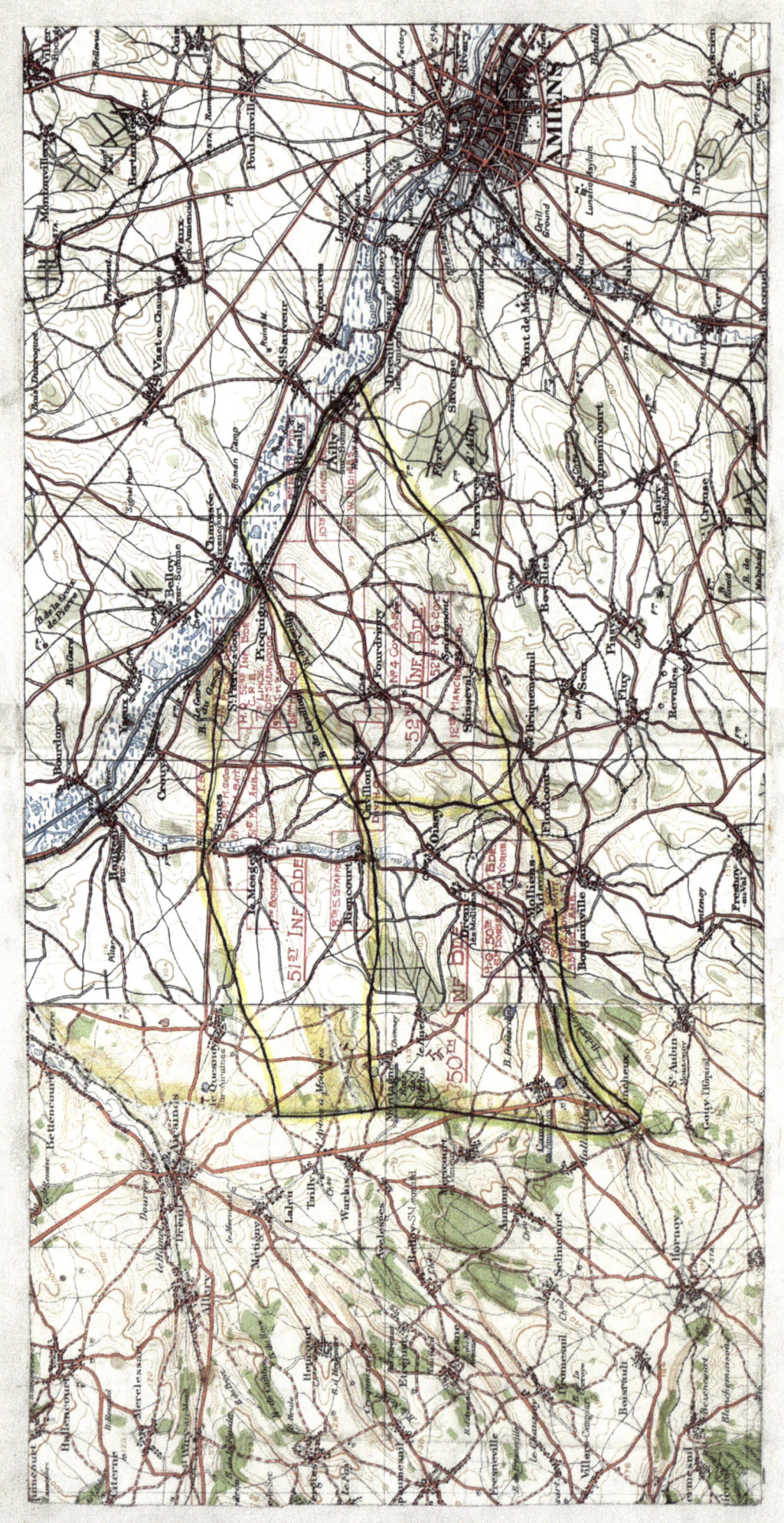

CONFIDENTIAL

Vol 15

Confidential.

War Diary

of

17th Divisional Signal Company, R.E.

September 1 - 30th 1916.

Volume 15.

Army Form C. 2118

WAR DIARY
or
INTELLIGENCE SUMMARY
(Erase heading not required.)

Instructions regarding War Diaries and Intelligence Summaries are contained in F.S. Regs., Part II. and the Staff Manual respectively. Title Pages will be prepared in manuscript.

Place	Date	Hour	Summary of Events and Information	Remarks and references to Appendices
April 1/4/15			Lines held satisfactorily	Strys. of 8 OR 2/3 2/3
	2nd		Quiet. Lines held well. Work commenced on an O.P. exchange system for the Artillery, the Northern end being taken in hand first.	
	3rd		Work continued. Material obtained for making 3 - 20 line metallic buzzer exchanges.	
	4th		One exchange made. Line traced & where necessary new lines laid	
	5th		O.P. system in Northern end in working order. Men diverted to old French from Brigade Headquarters to Battalion and batteries cut. Alterna tive route available so that no damage done. All work satisfactorily carried out.	
	6.		O.P. system working. Our lines through DAILY	

1875. Wt. W593/826. 1,000,000. 4/15. J.B.C. & A. A.D.S.S./Forms/C.2118.

WAR DIARY
or
INTELLIGENCE SUMMARY
(Erase heading not required.)

Army Form C. 2118

Place	Date	Hour	Summary of Events and Information	Remarks and references to Appendices
In the field	6th Aug		replaced by prepared line.	
	7th		Repaired lines. Two 20 line exchanges installed.	
	8th		Work commenced for possible offensive operations.	
	9th		Work for offensive operations continued. New twisted cable laid in bottom of communication trench to form communication in the event of "No Man's land" being crossed.	
	10th		Work continued as above. Lines holding well.	
	11th		Left sector relieved by 33rd Division Brigade. Went into rest at 16.00.	
	12th		Northern sector relieved by 33rd Divn. Lines altered so that 33rd Divn could work through Lt AMAND chipset & alternatively through	

WAR DIARY
or
INTELLIGENCE SUMMARY

(Erase heading not required.)

Army Form C. 2118

Place	Date	Hour	Summary of Events and Information	Remarks and references to Appendices
	12th		17 Divn advanced Signal Office at SOUASTRE	
	13th		Work in HEBUTERNE Sector continued. Arrangements commenced in view of 2 more groups of Artillery coming into this Sector.	
	14th		Preparations for possible offensive continued, cable being gradually carried up new trenches at present in advanced line.	
	15th		Work continued forward. 4 new working parties were placed at the disposal of Signals for starting & improving communication and arranging Headquarters and lines for battery & O.P. for one Hyphozal new Artillery group finished of the 2nd one got on with	
	17th		travel group arrangements completed.	

WAR DIARY
or
INTELLIGENCE SUMMARY

(Erase heading not required.)

Army Form C. 2118

Place	Date	Hour	Summary of Events and Information	Remarks and references to Appendices
	18th		New airline from Bayencourt to SAILLY built to provide communication to proposed Headquarters in new Artillery group.	
	19th		Arrangements made for handing new right sector to 33rd Divn. and replacing a junction so that the whole line could be controlled from HENU.	
	20th		Work in right sector completed and taken up to a point suitable for handling over.	
	21st.		Line held well. Division relieved by 33rd Divn. Command having at 10 a.m.	
FROHEN-LE-GRAND	22nd		Signal Company relieved by 33rd Divnl. Signals at 10 a.m. & travelled by road staying for the night at FROHEN-LE-GRAND	

Army Form C. 2118

WAR DIARY
or
INTELLIGENCE SUMMARY
(Erase heading not required.)

Place	Date	Hour	Summary of Events and Information	Remarks and references to Appendices
	2ʳᵈ			
	3ʰ		Arrived at STRIQUIER.	
	24ᵗʰ		Resting. Limbers & cable carts looked over & repaired as necessary. 10 visual established to 50th Brigade at DRUAT.	
	25ᵗʰ		Do.	
	26ᵗʰ		Do.	
	27ᵗʰ		Do.	
	28ᵗʰ		Do.	
	29ᵗʰ		Do.	
	30		Strength Sept. 1st — Officers 7+8 Strength Wireless men	
			O.R. 215 / 223 transferred to 3rd Army Signals	
				226
			Wulen as	
			Reinforcements O.R. 4	6
			Sick 1	220
			226	

Watts

WAR DIARY
or
INTELLIGENCE SUMMARY

Army Form C. 2118

Place	Date	Hour	Summary of Events and Information	Remarks and references to Appendices
Sailly	1/4/18		(hors had) interrupted Entry.	Strength 8 OR 275 / 223
"	2nd		Quiet. Line held well. Work commenced on an O.P. exchange system for the Artillery, the Northern end being taken in hand first.	
	3rd		Work continued. Material obtained for making 3-20 line metallic buzzer exchange.	
	4th		An exchange made. Line traced & where necessary new line laid.	
	5th		O.P. system in Northern end in working order. Main heads for alert French from Brigade headquarters to Battalions and Battery's out. Alternative routes available so that no damage done all work satisfactorily carried out.	
	6.		O.P. system working. Our line through SAILLY	

Army Form C. 2118

WAR DIARY
or
INTELLIGENCE SUMMARY
(Erase heading not required.)

Place	Date	Hour	Summary of Events and Information	Remarks and references to Appendices
In the Field	6th Aug		replaced by prepared line.	
	7th		Repaired lines. Two 20 lines exchanges installed.	
	8th		Work commenced for possible offensive operations.	
	9th		Work for offensive operations continued. New buried cable laid the bottom of communication trench to form communication in the event of "No Man's Land" being crossed.	
	10th		Work continued as above. Lines holding well.	
	11th		Left sector relieved by 33rd Division Brigade. Went into rest at Bakroy.	
	12th		Northern sector relieved by 33rd Div. Lines X'bred so that 33rd M'D ob. 'ed & worked through Br A M W D obs'ed & alternately through	

WAR DIARY
or
INTELLIGENCE SUMMARY

(Erase heading not required.)

Army Form C. 2118

Place	Date	Hour	Summary of Events and Information	Remarks and references to Appendices
	12th		17 Div advanced Signal Office at SOUASTRE.	
	13th		Work in HEBUTERNE Sector continued. Arrangements commenced in view of 2 more groups of Artillery coming into the Sector.	
	14th		Preparations for possible offensive operations continued. Cable being gradually carried up and trenches at present in advance in.	
	15th		Work continued forward. 4 new working parties were placed at the disposal of Signals for starting & improving communications and arranging Headquarters and lines for battery & O.P.'s one Offizers new Artillery group found in rear of the 2nd Div one got on with	
	16th			
	17th		travel group arrangements completed.	

Army Form C. 2118

WAR DIARY
or
INTELLIGENCE SUMMARY
(Erase heading not required.)

Instructions regarding War Diaries and Intelligence Summaries are contained in F.S. Regs., Part II. and the Staff Manual respectively. Title Pages will be prepared in manuscript.

Place	Date	Hour	Summary of Events and Information	Remarks and references to Appendices
	18th		New cable from Regiment to French communication to proposed Headquarters in new Artillery group.	
	19th		Arrangement made for handing over right sector to 33rd Divn. and replacing a junction so that the whole line could be controlled from HFW.	
	20th		Work in right sector completed and carried out to a point suitable for handing over.	
	21st		Line held until Division relieved by 33rd Divn. Command passing at 10 a.m.	
	22nd		10. a.m. 1 Knolled. Coy relieved by 33rd Div. by about 10. a.m. 1 Knolled by road staying for the night at FROHEN-LE-G(R)AND.	

WAR DIARY
or
INTELLIGENCE SUMMARY
(Erase heading not required.)

Place	Date	Hour	Summary of Events and Information	Remarks and references to Appendices
	2 3rd		Arrived at ST RIQUIER	
	24d		Resting - Limbers + cable carts looked over + repaired	
	25d		as necessary. Visual established to 50th Brigade at DRUCAT.	
	26d			
	27d			
	28d			
	29d			
	30			

Go.
B.S.M.
D.Q.

Strength Left D.O. Ar 7 officers 108 Strength
orderlies O.R 215 recalled now
O.R 215 transferred to
223 3rd Army troops
1 Reinforcement O.R 4 Wireless
Sick 1
226 226 220

[signature]

Army Form C. 2118

WAR DIARY
or
INTELLIGENCE SUMMARY
(Erase heading not required.)

Instructions regarding War Diaries and Intelligence Summaries are contained in F. S. Regs., Part II. and the Staff Manual respectively. Title Pages will be prepared in manuscript.

Place	Date	Hour	Summary of Events and Information	Remarks and references to Appendices
In the Field	October 1st		Resting at ST RIQUIER.	
	2		do	
	3		do	
	4		Working party sent up to SAILLY to carry out work already started.	
	5		Rest of Company resting at ST RIQUIER. Advance party went up to PAS to open office.	
	6		Company moved to FROHEN-LE-GRAND & billeted there for the night. Immediate preparing laying lines for future operations	
	7		Company arrived at PAS. Line taken over by 17 Division. Work continued.	
	8		Advance party sent on. Divisional Report Centre taken over at SUASTRE. All local deliveries for Corps understanding.	
	9		Lines strengthened from SOUASTRE forward.	

Army Form C. 2118

WAR DIARY
or
INTELLIGENCE SUMMARY
(Erase heading not required.)

Instructions regarding War Diaries and Intelligence Summaries are contained in F.S. Regs, Part II. and the Staff Manual respectively. Title Pages will be prepared in manuscript.

Place	Date	Hour	Summary of Events and Information	Remarks and references to Appendices
Oct.	10		Working party still continuing with lines right up to front trenches and up to Tunnels forward of area mined.	
	11		do	
	12		do	
	13		do	
	14		dis	
	15		All work in HEBUTERNE area completed for prospective operations. Two new Brigade advancing Report Centres wired up and all local lines including Prisoners Cage etc. Conducted as required by telephone.	
	16.		Working party testing all lines.	
	17		Working party brought in as Division warned to move.	
	18.		Handed over to 48th Division.	

1875 Wt. W593/826 1,000,000 4/15 J.B.C. & A. A.D.S.S./Forms/C. 2118.

Place	Date	Hour	Summary of Events and Information	Remarks and references to Appendices
	Oct. 19		Working party withdrawn to PAS. Owing to move of Brigade temporary office formed at DOULLENC. for Brigade's to Brigade in area of faced to move. Divisional H.Q. PAS. Report Centre still at DOULLENS	
	20		Company moved to BAIZEUX now on way to new area.	
	21		Company at BAIZEUX. New area having been changed. DOULLENS office handed over to 4 & 8. Division. Div Headquarters at PAS.	
	22		Divisional Headquarters closed at PAS & opened at TREUX & 4 in Army area. Company moved from BAISEUX to TREUX. Communications to Brigades on the march through nearest	

WAR DIARY
or
INTELLIGENCE SUMMARY

Army Form C. 2118

Place	Date	Hour	Summary of Events and Information	Remarks and references to Appendices
October	23	"	Signal Officers to their billets.	
	24	"	Divisional Headquarters remained at TREVA. Communications to Brigades either direct or through 14th Corps.	
	25	"	Division remained at TREVA.	
	26	"	do.	
	27	"	do.	
	28	"	Division moved from TREVA to the CITADEL.	
	29	"	Division remained at the CITADEL.	
	30	"	do.	
	31	"	do.	
		"	Division relieved 8th Division, Command passing	

WAR DIARY
or
INTELLIGENCE SUMMARY

Army Form C. 2118

Place	Date	Hour	Summary of Events and Information	Remarks and references to Appendices

October	31		at 10 a.m. Headquarters opened at MINDEN POST and Divisional Report Centre at BERNAFAY WOOD at 10 a.m. Lines to Brigades very erratic, mostly "dis" as taken over. Strength :- Officers 7
			 " attached 1
			  ————
			  8
			 O.R. 212
			  2 20
			 Sick 3
			 Reinforcements 1
			 ————
			 216	

Vol 16

Confidential
War ~~Diary~~
17th Signal Company, R.E.

Volume No 16.

WAR DIARY
or
INTELLIGENCE SUMMARY

(Erase heading not required.)

Army Form C. 2118

Place	Date	Hour	Summary of Events and Information	Remarks and references to Appendices
In the Field	October 1st		Resting at ST RIQUIER.	
	2		do	
	3		do	
	4		Working party sent up to SAILLY to carry out work already started.	
	5		Rest of Company resting at ST RIQUIER. Advance party went up to PAS to fix offices	
	6		Company moved to FROHEN-LE-GRAND & billeted there for the night. Lineman preparing laying line for future operations	
	7		Company arrived at PAS. Line taken over by 17 Division & Co. returned.	
	8		Advanced party sent on. Divisional Report Centre taken over at SOMASTRE. All local delivering for Corps	
	9		Kept taken over from SOUASTRE forward.	

Army Form C. 2118

WAR DIARY
or
INTELLIGENCE SUMMARY
(Erase heading not required.)

Place	Date	Hour	Summary of Events and Information	Remarks and references to Appendices
Oct	10		Wiring party still continuing with lines right up to front trenches and up to 1 tunnels forward of area wired.	
	11		do	
	12		do	
	13		do	
	14		do	
	15		All work in HEBUTERNE are completed for prospective operations. Two new Brigade advanced Report Centres wired up and all local lines including Prisoner Cage etc. connected as required by telephone.	
	16		Working party testing all lines.	
	17		Working party brought in as Division warned to move.	
	18		Handed over to 48 Div. Division	

WAR DIARY
or
INTELLIGENCE SUMMARY

(Erase heading not required.)

Army Form C. 2118

Place	Date	Hour	Summary of Events and Information	Remarks and references to Appendices
	Oct 19		D. o. hvy party withdrawn to PAS. Owing to move of Brigades temporary office formed at DOULLENS for Brigades in area preparing to move.	
	20		Divisional H.Q. PAS. Report came still at DOULLENS. Company moved to BAIZEUX now on way to new area.	
	21		Company at BAIZEUX. New area having been changed. DOULLENS office handed over to 48th Division. Divl Headquarters at PAS.	
	22		Divisional Headquarters closed at PAS & opened at REUTH, 4th Army area. Company moved from BAISEUX to TIREUX. Communication to Brigades on the march through nearest	

Army Form C. 2118

WAR DIARY
or
INTELLIGENCE SUMMARY
(Erase heading not required.)

Instructions regarding War Diaries and Intelligence Summaries are contained in F. S. Regs., Part II. and the Staff Manual respectively. Title Pages will be prepared in manuscript.

Place	Date	Hour	Summary of Events and Information	Remarks and references to Appendices
	October 23		Signal Officers to their billets.	
	24		Divisional Headquarters remained at TREUX. Communications to Brigades either direct or through 14 it Corps.	
	25		Division remained at TREUX.	
	26		do.	
	27		do.	
	28		Division moved from TREUX to the CITADEL	
	29		Division remained at the CITADEL.	
	30		do	
	31		do	
			Division relieved by it Division, Command passing	

WAR DIARY
or
INTELLIGENCE SUMMARY

Army Form C. 2118

Place	Date	Hour	Summary of Events and Information	Remarks and references to Appendices
October	31	10 a.m.	Headquarters opened at MINDEN POST and Divisional Report Centre at BERNAFAY WOOD at 10. a.m. Lines to Brigades very establishments "dis" as taken over. Strength:- Officers 7 Attached 1 ——— 8 O.R. 212 220 Sick 3 Reinforcements 1 ——— 216	

Major
Commanding Queen's Own Oxfordshire Yeomanry Signal Coy. R.E.

Army Form C. 2118

WAR DIARY
or
INTELLIGENCE SUMMARY
(Erase heading not required.)

Place	Date	Hour	Summary of Events and Information	Remarks and references to Appendices
Hethwl	1st Nov.		During the course of the day lines on the burried route provided by Corps for all Divisions in the area had to be gradually repaired. Linesmen were continually out repairing breaks on lines. During the course of the day communication was spasmodically established to all Battalions. One of Brigade Headquarters very lavishly shelled. Casualties 1 killed & 1 wounded.	
	2nd		Two Brigade Headquarters moved back from T.8 to WATERLOW FARM. Four pairs laid from GUILLEMONT test station to the new Brigade Headquarters, two for working from Headquarters to Division, one an alternative route to to left Brigade and one for two Brigades working forward to a joint station in T.8. Junction also made to a line around DELVILLE WOOD and T.8 to have two routes to forward line, one through DELVILLE WOOD very faulty faulty	

Place	Date	Hour	Summary of Events and Information	Remarks and references to Appendices
November 2			Enemy shelling fifty through Griffin lines through to both Nostalgia & Siffy Brigade. Telephone working to T. Bastakatory fully.	
	3rd		Brigade Headquarters again moved. Necessary alterations made to provide communication to ground. Lines partly & various shell cuts repairing. Front lines now in better condition, only fair but enthusiastic. Bold Diffsotn Headquarters cut whole of day back to Division. No lines telegraphically.	
	Night 4/5		Brigades have been through to Battalion on an average of 14 hours a day. Various small faults repaired on the whole the lines have been that worried by	
November 5				

WAR DIARY
or
INTELLIGENCE SUMMARY

Army Form C. 2118

Place	Date	Hour	Summary of Events and Information	Remarks and references to Appendices
November	5th		1st Div. since Divison came in. Was turned O.K.	
	6th		30th Regt. carried till working well. 2nd Regt. cut & filled in a C.T. Dis' [?] to 1st man behind and but through all the front lines except in one day. They improved the forward communication laterally by a which through night to constructions in our line.	
	7th		Very wet day. Everything old [?] was [?] rear Jets [?] full in holes. Lines may much damaged. 51st & 52nd Divs. left working with 61st Pile. Divs working well. Working party have	
	8th		been at work filling lines and relaying road frames.	

WAR DIARY
or
INTELLIGENCE SUMMARY
(Erase heading not required.)

Army Form C. 2118

Place	Date	Hour	Summary of Events and Information	Remarks and references to Appendices
	night 8th/9th		Air bomb fell quite near Divisional Headquarters and cut main lines forward at about 8.15 p.m. Lines repaired after half an hour.	
	9th		Shelling of back areas beyond Divisional Headquarters cut all lines to Corps & MINDEN Post Office and shelling of Railway cut lines forward. These lines have been repaired this morning. Various spare routes have been joined together to make alternative route to Bde. Flight to Centre Brigades from Divisional Headquarters working very satisfactory today. Preparing hard for new office. New office completed and taken into work between 12.1 a.m. and 2 a.m. morning	
	10th			

Place	Date	Hour	Summary of Events and Information	Remarks and references to Appendices
	10th		instant. This transfer was completed without a dislocation of any traffic. Enemy cut rail again damaged two permanent lines which were repaired, otherwise lines working fairly well.	
	11th		A quieter day. Lines through DELVILLE WOOD considerably damaged, otherwise no trouble.	
	12th		Lines on ground lifted & poled. Corps air line from Delville Wood to Waterlot Farm Commons. Good deal of trouble in centre section. Various Interruptions owing to shelling of back areas. Officers and men of Corps Signal Company relieving our lines.	

Army Form C. 2118

WAR DIARY
OF
INTELLIGENCE SUMMARY
(Erase heading not required.)

Instructions regarding War Diaries and Intelligence Summaries are contained in F. S. Regs., Part II. and the Staff Manual respectively. Title Pages will be prepared in manuscript.

Place	Date	Hour	Summary of Events and Information	Remarks and references to Appendices
		8th	Linemen of Signal Company went out on various lines to learn extent of damage preparatory to relief. Headquarters advised that no damage done to lines.	
		14	Division relieved at 10 a.m. by Guards Div. All lines accepted as working satisfactorily.	
		15	Company moved to TITEUR. Communication to Brigades via nearest telegraph office. Divisional H.Q. at CAVILLON. Communication opened with various Brigades as they came into the area.	
		16	All Brigades complete in the area. Communication established to three Brigade Headquarters.	

WAR DIARY
or
INTELLIGENCE SUMMARY

(Erase heading not required.)

Army Form C. 2118

Place	Date	Hour	Summary of Events and Information	Remarks and references to Appendices
	16		Transport portion of Company arrived in rest area	
	17		Rest area & training.	
	18		do.	
	19		do	
	20		do	
	21		do	
	22		do. Line laid to RIENCOURT from 51st BDE	
	23		do. cast down.	
	24		do	
	25		do	
	26		do	
	27		do	
	28		do	
	29		Party with 17st Divisional Artillery gradually	

WAR DIARY
or
INTELLIGENCE SUMMARY
(Erase heading not required.)

Army Form C. 2118

Place	Date	Hour	Summary of Events and Information	Remarks and references to Appendices
Albert	Nov. 29			
	30		Rest area & training	
		1st		

Strength of Company November 1st:

Officers 7
" attached 1

O.R. 212
220
Less
Reinforcements 1
216

Strength November 30th:

Officers 7 206
Reinforcements 13
219 Strength.

O.R. 212 Reinforcements 7
219 6/7
Killed   4
Wounded Sick 206

Confidential

Vol 17

WAR DIARY
17th Divl Signal Coy
November 1916

WAR DIARY
or
INTELLIGENCE SUMMARY

(Erase heading not required.)

Army Form C. 2118

Place	Date	Hour	Summary of Events and Information	Remarks and references to Appendices
In the Field	1st Nov.		During the course of the day lines on the Divisional route provided by Corps for all Divisions in the area had to were gradually repaired. Enemy were continually cutting breaks on lines. During the course of the day communication was spasmodically established to all Battalions. One of Brigade Headquarters very heavily shelled. Casualties 1 killed & 6 wounded.	
	2nd		Two Brigade Headquarters moved back from T.8 to WATERLOW FARM. Four pairs laid from GUILLEMONT test station to the new Brigade Headquarters, two for working from Headquarters to Division, one an alternative route to left Brigade and one for two Brigades working forward to a joint station in T.8. Junction also made to a line around DELVILLE WOOD and T.8 to have two routes to forward line. Lines through DELVILLE WOOD very faulty, partly	

WAR DIARY
or
INTELLIGENCE SUMMARY

Army Form C. 2118

Place	Date	Hour	Summary of Events and Information	Remarks and references to Appendices
	November 2nd		Through shell fire; partly through Infantry. Lines put through to both Battalions of 5th Iny. Brigade. Fullerphones working to T.B. Battalion only.	
	3rd		Brigade Headquarters again moved. Necessary alterations made to provide communication required. Lines faulty & various shell cuts repaired. Front lines now in better condition only four interruptions occurred to cut Headquarters to whole of lines back to Division but were repaired after half an hour's delay. The lines held erratically.	
	night 4/5		Brigades have been through to Battalion on an average of 14 hours a day. Various small faults repaired. On the whole the lines have been led worried by	
	November 5th			

WAR DIARY
or
INTELLIGENCE SUMMARY

(Erase heading not required.)

Army Form C. 2118

Place	Date	Hour	Summary of Events and Information	Remarks and references to Appendices
	November 3rd		Shell fire since Division came in. All lines all working well.	
	6th		50th Brigade forward O.P.	
	night 5/6		All lines cut by shell fire on a tree. "Dis" for 1½ hours by direct route but through all the time by indirect route. During day lines improved. Brigade communication intermittent. On a whole Brough right to battalions in front line.	
	7th		Very wet day. Strengthening all lines continued. New flits put in where lines very much damaged. 51st & 53rd lines all working well. Also 50th Bde.	
	8th		Lines working well. Working party laying been at work laying lines and ordering rear places.	

Army Form C. 2118

WAR DIARY or INTELLIGENCE SUMMARY

(Erase heading not required.)

Place	Date	Hour	Summary of Events and Information	Remarks and references to Appendices
	night 7/8th		Air bomb fell quite near Divisional Headquarters and cut main lines forward at about 8.15 pm. Lines repaired after half an hour.	
	8th		Shelling of back areas beyond Divisional Headquarters cut all lines to Corps & MINDEN Post again and shelling of railway cut lines forward. These lines have been repaired this morning. Various have routes have been joined together to make alternative route to 97th, 98th & Centre Brigades. Divisional Headquarters working hard supplying today preparing down for new office. New office completed and to be in use	
	9th		Work between 12.10 am and 2 am morning	

WAR DIARY
or
INTELLIGENCE SUMMARY

(Erase heading not required.)

Army Form C. 2118

Place	Date	Hour	Summary of Events and Information	Remarks and references to Appendices
			B. of 10th instant the enemy was considerably quieter, but at dusk a disturbance of enemy traffic. Enemy cut raid again damaged two permanent lines which were repaired, otherwise lines working fairly well.	
		11th	A quieter day. Lines through DELVILLE WOOD considerably damaged, otherwise no trouble.	
		12th	Lines on ground lifted & poled. Corps air line from Delville Wood to Waterlot Farm commenced. Good deal of trouble in Corps section owing to interruptions owing to shelling of back areas, officers and men of Corps Signal Company attending wire cuts.	

WAR DIARY
or
INTELLIGENCE SUMMARY

(Erase heading not required.)

Army Form C. 2118

Instructions regarding War Diaries and Intelligence Summaries are contained in F. S. Regs., Part II. and the Staff Manual respectively. Title Pages will be prepared in manuscript.

Place	Date	Hour	Summary of Events and Information	Remarks and references to Appendices
	13th		Linesmen of Guards Signal Company went out on various lines to Clamecy and Infantry to relief. Headquarters shelled but no damage done to lines.	
	14.		Division relieved at 10 a.m. by Guards Div. All lines accepted as working satisfactorily. Company moved to TREUX. Communication to Brigades via nearest telegraph office.	
	15.		Divisional H.Q. at GAVRELON. Communication opened with various Brigades as they came into the area.	
	16.		All Brigades complete in the area. Communication established to three Brigades by Brigade telegraph.	

1875 Wt. W593/826 1,000,000 4/15 J.B.C. & A. A.D.S.S./Forms/C. 2118.

WAR DIARY
or
INTELLIGENCE SUMMARY

Army Form C. 2118

(Erase heading not required.)

Place	Date	Hour	Summary of Events and Information	Remarks and references to Appendices
	16		Transport portion of Company arrived in rest area.	
	17		Rest area & training.	
	18		do	
	19		do do	
	20		do do	
	21		do do	
	22		do do	
	23		do do Line laid to RIENCOURT from C.17.36	
	24		do do and return.	
	25		do do	
	26		do do	
	27		do do	
	28		do do	
	29		Party with 17th Divisional Artillery gradually	

WAR DIARY
or
INTELLIGENCE SUMMARY

Army Form C. 2118

Place	Date	Hour	Summary of Events and Information	Remarks and references to Appendices
	November 29		Relieved.	
	30		Rest area & training	
	1		"	

Strength of Company November 1st

Officers 7
" attached 1

O.R. 212
     220
Sick 3
    216
Reinforcements 1
       206

Strength November 30th

Officers 7
O.R. 212 Reinforcements 1
     219 Strength
Killed 7
Wounded 4
Sick 2
     206

L Phipps Capt. Major.
Queen's Westminster Rifles,
Commanding 17th, Signal Coy, R.E.

Army Form C. 2118

WAR DIARY
or
INTELLIGENCE SUMMARY
(Erase heading not required.)

Instructions regarding War Diaries and Intelligence Summaries are contained in F.S. Regs., Part II. and the Staff Manual respectively. Title Pages will be prepared in manuscript.

Place	Date	Hour	Summary of Events and Information	Remarks and references to Appendices
in the Field	Dec 1916	1	Rest Area, easy morning	
		2	do	
		3	do	
		4	do	
		5	do	
		6	do	
		7	do	
		8	do	
		9	do	
		10	do	
		11	do	
		12	Arrival of new drafts from troops to France do	
		13	Capt B. moved from Camden to Bris and returned so to his Rest at ...	
		14		

WAR DIARY
or
INTELLIGENCE SUMMARY

(Erase heading not required.)

Army Form C. 2118

Instructions regarding War Diaries and Intelligence Summaries are contained in F.S. Regs., Part II and the Staff Manual respectively. Title Pages will be prepared in manuscript.

Place	Date	Hour	Summary of Events and Information	Remarks and references to Appendices
Lille to Lens	Dec 15th		Resting at Corbehem	
	16th		do	
	17th		do	
	18th		do	
	19th		do	
	20th		do	
	21st		2nd in Cmd. Rode over to reconnoitre position & HQ office closed at 10 am at results of the day. Car & horses moved out and gate. 8 am heavy firing about 1.30 pm. Advance troops of Division went up to relieve us to return home here.	
	23rd		Company moved off from CORBIE at 6 a.m. and marched before 14 Bty. arrived at 1.30 p.m. and bivouaced for night.	
	24th		Company relieved 20 KK Divisional Signal Company at 8 pm. Orders issued to it then kept Xmas till after flies.	

1875 Wt. W 593/826 1,000,000 4/15 J.B.C. & A. A.D.S.S./Forms/C. 2118.

Army Form C. 2118

WAR DIARY
or
INTELLIGENCE SUMMARY
(Erase heading not required.)

Instructions regarding War Diaries and Intelligence Summaries are contained in F. S. Regs., Part II. and the Staff Manual respectively. Title Pages will be prepared in manuscript.

Place	Date	Hour	Summary of Events and Information	Remarks and references to Appendices
Etaples	Oct 25		17th Div. Division relieved 20th Division taking over Command of front at 10 a.m. HQ at Inc 3 Inf	
	26th		HR No 2 of 4. Lines O.K.	
	27		All lines of Right & Left Bdes also working well except lines to D.S.g. dressing pet. & wound station at GINCHY put on telephone to 50 th Bde. orderlies in tests at ----	
	28		Lines working well.	

WAR DIARY
or
INTELLIGENCE SUMMARY

(Erase heading not required.)

Army Form C. 2118

Place	Date	Hour	Summary of Events and Information	Remarks and references to Appendices
			[illegible handwritten entries]	

Strength of Company
December 1st —

Strength of Company
December 31st —
O.R. 211
Sick 15
Reinforcements ___
Strength 214

Officers 8
O.R. 211
219

Officers 8

Army Form C. 2118

WAR DIARY
or
INTELLIGENCE SUMMARY
(Erase heading not required.)

19th Batt Signalling Vol 18

Place	Date	Hour	Summary of Events and Information	Remarks and references to Appendices
Etaples	Dec	1	Rest Area, and training	
		2	do	
		3	do	
		4	do	
		5	do	
		6	do	
		7	do	
		8	do	
		9	do	
		10	do	
		11	do	
		12	Signal office moved to Spain Farm Mongres do Daours do	
		13	17th Divl HQ moved from Corbie to Catin and relieved 20th Div	
		14	Resting at Corbie	

Army Form C. 2118

WAR DIARY
or
INTELLIGENCE SUMMARY
(Erase heading not required.)

Place	Date	Hour	Summary of Events and Information	Remarks and references to Appendices
H.Q. 2nd	Dec 15th		Resting at Mailly	
	16th		do	
	17th		do	
	18th		do	
	19th		do	
	20th		do	
	21st		52nd Sig Co office closed at 10 am at Mailly (Mare) 10 am. BRIQUETERIE	
	22nd		No 1 Cy. Column moved to Sandpits from Sandpits. There 1.30 pm. Advance party of linesmen sent up to relieve outstations at trenches.	
	23rd		Company moved off from CORBIE at 6 a.m. for Meaulte where they arrived at 1.30 p.m. and bivouaced for night.	
	24th		Company relieved 20th Divisional Signal Company at 6 a.m. to at them have Trunks out of line	

WAR DIARY
or
INTELLIGENCE SUMMARY

(Erase heading not required.)

Army Form C. 2118

Place	Date	Hour	Summary of Events and Information	Remarks and references to Appendices
In the Field	Oct 25		17th Division relieved 20th Division taking over Command of front at 10 a.m. H.Q. at M.C. 5.3 approx. H.Q. at 20.95	
"	26th		Lines O.K.	
"	27th		All lines of Right & Left Brigades working well except line to DS.G. Trench cut. Dugout Station at GINCHY put on telephone to 50th Brigadiers new HQrs at new HA	
"	28th		Lines working well. Four huns a good deal are about but not used	
"	29th		Telephones & Talkies) as far as Battalion HQrs - On both Brigade fronts & working satisfactorily	
"	30		Considerable difficulty owing to the effort to remove huns on Corps tramway T 8 to T 9. Wires have been repeatedly interfered	

Place	Date	Hour	Summary of Events and Information	Remarks and references to Appendices
Dec 31			with. General communications maintained satisfactorily. The enemy's friendly artillery some jerky. Work in progress satisfactorily - sundries further to Dec 30th. Strength of Company 1st December Officers 8 W.O.T. 211 / 219 Strength of Company 31st December Officers 8 O/T.R. 211 / Sick 10 / Reinforcements 5 / Strength 214 Walty Major Queen's Westminster Rifles, Commanding 17th Signal Coy, R.E.	

Vol 19

Confidential

War Diary

17th Divisional Signal Company, R.E.

January, 1917

Volume 19

Enclosures

Diagram of Lines.

Place	Date	Hour	Summary of Events and Information	Remarks and references to Appendices
In the field	1/1/17		Strength of Company :- Officers 8 O.R. 206 / 214 Lines working fairly well. Fullerphone working.	
	2nd		Lines working well.	
	3rd		All lines of 51st Bde working well except Heavy group artillery. Bde lines all through 52nd Bde lines working well. Fullerphone working 52nd Bde lines working well.	
	4th		Power buzzer installed in 51st Bde area. Results fairly satisfactory. All lines working well.	
	5		Power Buzzer moved from left battalion H.Q to Right Battalion H.Q. Jammed by D. Involution.	

Army Form C. 2118

WAR DIARY
or
INTELLIGENCE SUMMARY
(Erase heading not required.)

Instructions regarding War Diaries and Intelligence Summaries are contained in F. S. Regs., Part II. and the Staff Manual respectively. Title Pages will be prepared in manuscript.

Place	Date	Hour	Summary of Events and Information	Remarks and references to Appendices
In field	6		Power Buzzer from Right & Left Battalion Company H.Q. satisfactory but signals very very faint. Probable cause long range. Right Battalion H.Q. 5200 Power Buzzer at Right Battalion H.Q. working well. Both lines working well.	
	7		do	
	8		do	
	9		do	
	10		do	
	11		do	
	12		do	
	13		do	
	14		do	

1875 Wt. W593/826 1,000,000 4/15 J.B.C. & A. A.D.S.S./Forms/C.2118.

WAR DIARY or INTELLIGENCE SUMMARY

Army Form C. 2118

Place	Date	Hour	Summary of Events and Information	Remarks and references to Appendices
	15		Interview of 2g/h Divns sent out to outstations to relieve trainmen of 17th Divn.	
	16		Advance party of 17th Divn sent to Corbie to take over Corbie office	
	17		17th Divisien relieved by 2g/h Divn. 10 am	
			17th Divnl HQrs opened at Corbie at 10 am.	
			Rest area & training	
	18		do	
	19		do	
	20		do	
	21		do	
	22		do	
	23		do	
	24		do	
	25			

WAR DIARY
or
INTELLIGENCE SUMMARY

(Erase heading not required.)

Army Form C. 2118

Instructions regarding War Diaries and Intelligence Summaries are contained in F.S. Regs., Part II. and the Staff Manual respectively. Title Pages will be prepared in manuscript.

Place	Date	Hour	Summary of Events and Information	Remarks and references to Appendices
Jany	26		Advance party of Mr. Souvenir sent to Roms. Reno Cafe to return home etc. of 20th Div.	
	27*		Company moved at 6.30 a.m. relieving 20th Divisional Signal Company. Company H.Q. at CORBIE.	
	28th		17th Division relieved 20th Division. Command of line passing at 10 a.m. 40th Divisional Signal Company relieved party of 17th Signal Company at CORBIE being over filled at 10 a.m.	
	29th		Lines working well.	
	30th		Working party out getting well.	
	31st		Lines into the Party laying line to BRONFAY FARM.	

1875 Wt. W593/826 1,000,000 4/15 J.B.C. & A. A.D.S.S./Forms/C. 2118.

WAR DIARY
or
INTELLIGENCE SUMMARY

Place	Date	Hour	Summary of Events and Information	Remarks and references to Appendices
	January 31st		Strength of Company on January 1st 1927 Officers 8 O.R. 206 Total 214 Strength on 31st Officers 7 O.R. 206 213 Sick 1 212 Reinforcements 7 219	

Major J Waley Cohen p.s.o.
attached A.D. Signals
18 it Corps.

M Stiff-Cope
Major.
Commanding 17th Signal Coy. R.E.

Instructions regarding War Diaries and Intelligence Summaries are contained in F. S. Regs., Part II. and the Staff Manual respectively. Title Pages will be prepared in manuscript.

WAR DIARY
or
INTELLIGENCE SUMMARY
(Erase heading not required.)

Army Form C. 2118

Place	Date	Hour	Summary of Events and Information	Remarks and references to Appendices
January	31st		Strength of Company on January 1st 1917 Officers ~~7~~ 8 O.R. 206 Total 21~~3~~ Strength on 31st Officers 7 * O.R. 206 213 Sick 1 212 Reinforcements 7 219	Major J. Waley Cohen D.S.O. appointed A.D. Signals 8th Corps. J J Shippy[?] Capt RE

1875 Wt. W593/826 1,000,000 4/15 J.B.C. & A. A.D.S.S./Forms/C. 2118.

17th Division Communications.

Scale 1/20000 MAP 57c SW

All lines are metallic pairs unless marked otherwise.
Test points — ☐ HQ of units — ☐

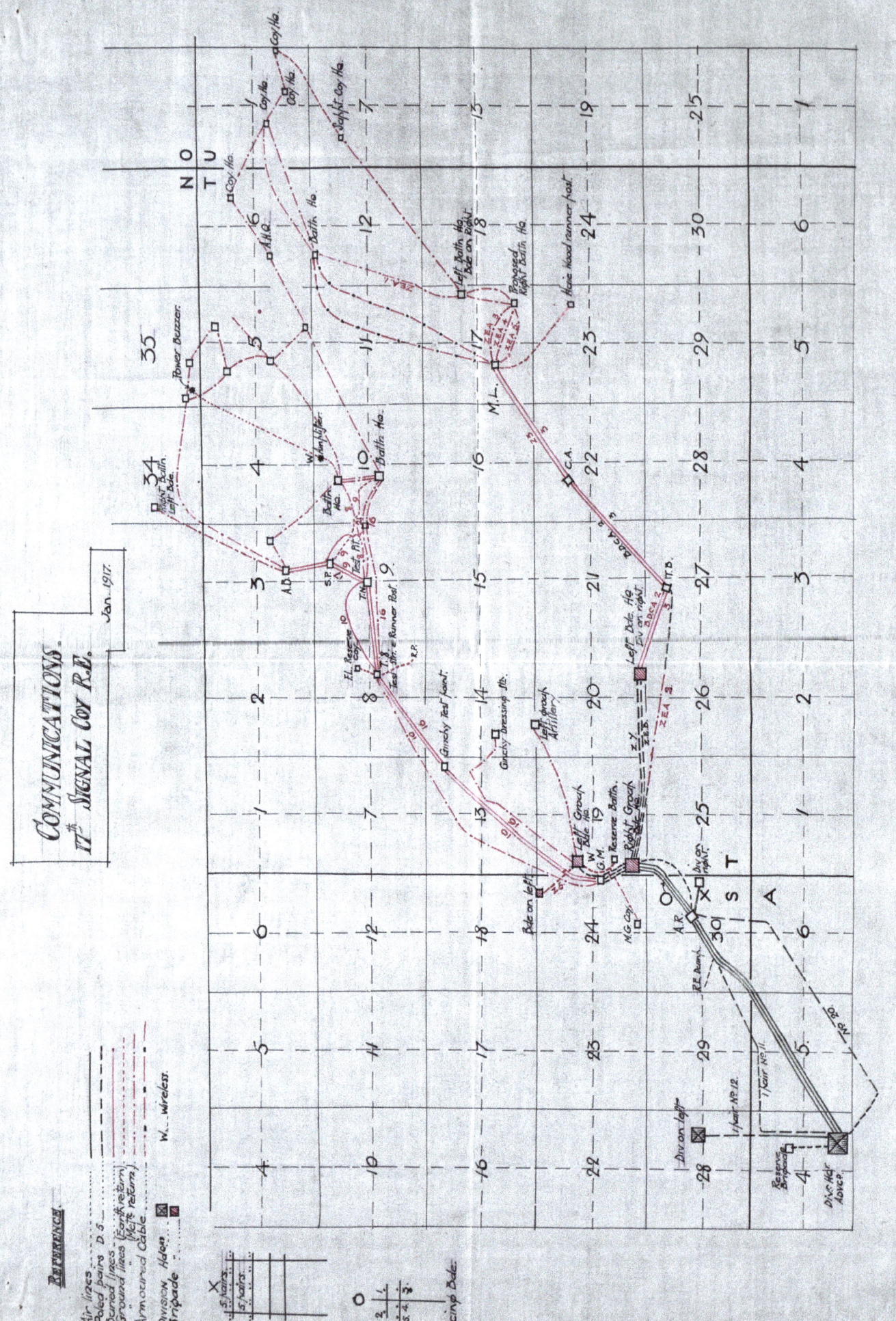

WAR DIARY
or
INTELLIGENCE SUMMARY

Army Form C. 2118

Place	Date	Hour	Summary of Events and Information	Remarks and references to Appendices
In the Field	1/1/17		Strength of Company Officers 8 O.R. 206 / 214	
	2nd		Lines working fairly well. Telephone working.	
	3rd		Lines everything well. All lines of 51st Bde working well except left group artillery. Polo lines all through. 52nd Bde lines working well. Fullerphone working to C.Lt battalion.	
	4th		Power buzzer installed in 51st Bde week. Results fairly satisfactory.	
	5		All lines working well. Power Buzzer relief for left battalion. H.Q to Right Battalion H.S. Jammed by D. Buchanan.	

WAR DIARY
or
INTELLIGENCE SUMMARY

Army Form C. 2118

Place	Date	Hour	Summary of Events and Information	Remarks and references to Appendices
H.Hill	6		Power Buzzer from Right & Left Battalion Company HQ satisfactory but signals very very faint. Relaid cause long range.	
	7		Power Buzzer at Right splitted H.Q. 52nd Bde working well.	
	8		58 Bdl lines working well.	
	9		Lines working well.	
	10		do do	
	11		do do	
	12		do do	
	13		do do	
	14		do do	

Army Form C. 2118

WAR DIARY
or
INTELLIGENCE SUMMARY
(Erase heading not required.)

Instructions regarding War Diaries and Intelligence Summaries are contained in F. S. Regs., Part II. and the Staff Manual respectively. Title Pages will be prepared in manuscript.

Place	Date	Hour	Summary of Events and Information	Remarks and references to Appendices
	15		In charge of Sgt. Brown sent out to outstations to relieve bearers of 37th Division	
	16		Advance party of 3 bearers sent to Corbie to be our Corpse office	
	17		19th Divisional returned by 39th Div. 10 am 17th Div. H.Q. opened at Corbie at 10 am	
	18		Rest and return	
	19		do	
	20		do	
	21		do	
	22		do	
	23		do	
	24		do	
	25		do	

1875 Wt. W593/826 1,000,000 4/15 J.B.C. & A. A.D.S.S./Forms/C. 2118.

WAR DIARY or INTELLIGENCE SUMMARY

Army Form C. 2118

(Erase heading not required.)

Place	Date	Hour	Summary of Events and Information	Remarks and references to Appendices
	28		Advance party of 0 Sgn [?] proceeded to have fresh lines of communication before leaving, lines etc. to 0 Bn	
	29		Company moved at 6.30 a.m. Subward Signal Company Commando opened at CORBIE.	
	2nd		17th Division relieved 26th Division at 10 a.m. 4 O.R. 17th Divisional Signal Company Commando party of 17th Signal Company relieved war [?] office at 19 a.m. every officer	
	"		Fine. Working well.	
	9		Working party out carrying line to BRONFAY FARM.	
	6th			
	7th		Line working fairly well.	

WAR DIARY
or
INTELLIGENCE SUMMARY

Army Form C. 2118

1st Bn Green Howards

Place	Date	Hour	Summary of Events and Information	Remarks and references to Appendices
Bn H.Qrs	1/2/17		Strength of Company Officers 7 O.R. 212/9	
	1st		Lines of 51st Brigade working well, time from Right Battalion to Right Company dis. All lines working well.	
	2nd		do	
	3rd		do	
	4th		Brigade report lines working well.	
	5th		do	
	6th		Working party engaged on new bury. Work postponed owing to ground being too hard.	
	7th		Lines working well.	
	8th		Division attached and captured SULLIVAN TRENCH and GREEN HOWARD TRENCH. 52nd Brigade reports &c.	

WAR DIARY or INTELLIGENCE SUMMARY

Army Form C. 2118

(Erase heading not required.)

Place	Date	Hour	Summary of Events and Information	Remarks and references to Appendices
Feb.	8th		All lines through to Contigious Battalions. Forward of left Battalion all lines cut.	A
	9th		Line to T.P. and M.C. through. Battalion by buzzer and fullerphone, through to right Battalion by buzzer 10.30 a.m. through to left still dis. Lateral between battalions	A
	10th		Lines working well	A
	11th		do do do	A
	12th		do do do	A
	13th		All lines through	A
	14th		Lines fairly satisfactory	A
	15th		All lines working well. Capt. F. Henry RE reported from 2716 Signal Co. C Common'd	A
	16th		do do	A
			Blowing up of ammunition dump at PLATEAU carried on by BRONFAY FARM. Left brigade to 91st div. 5th Brigade report all lines working satisfactorily.	A

WAR DIARY or INTELLIGENCE SUMMARY

Army Form C. 2118

Place	Date	Hour	Summary of Events and Information	Remarks and references to Appendices
Acroy Head Copse	19th		Chewing out at trenches but continuing of work	
	16th			
	19th			
	20th			
HEILLY	21st		on Tower to TOUASE road L.C.W. prepon at # SOS posopour	
	22nd		Bt. on enemy of CANAL MARUE & HEILLY hot mor Main at 10 am. (29th Div arding no 14 Brig)	
	23rd		Officer from at Mos Mohn at Spotting and medication of targets, our bomby of enterning slots	
	24th		Re supplying forces Company Parts Parade. Re supply of ammun of Training	
	25th			
	26th			
	27th			
	2nd			

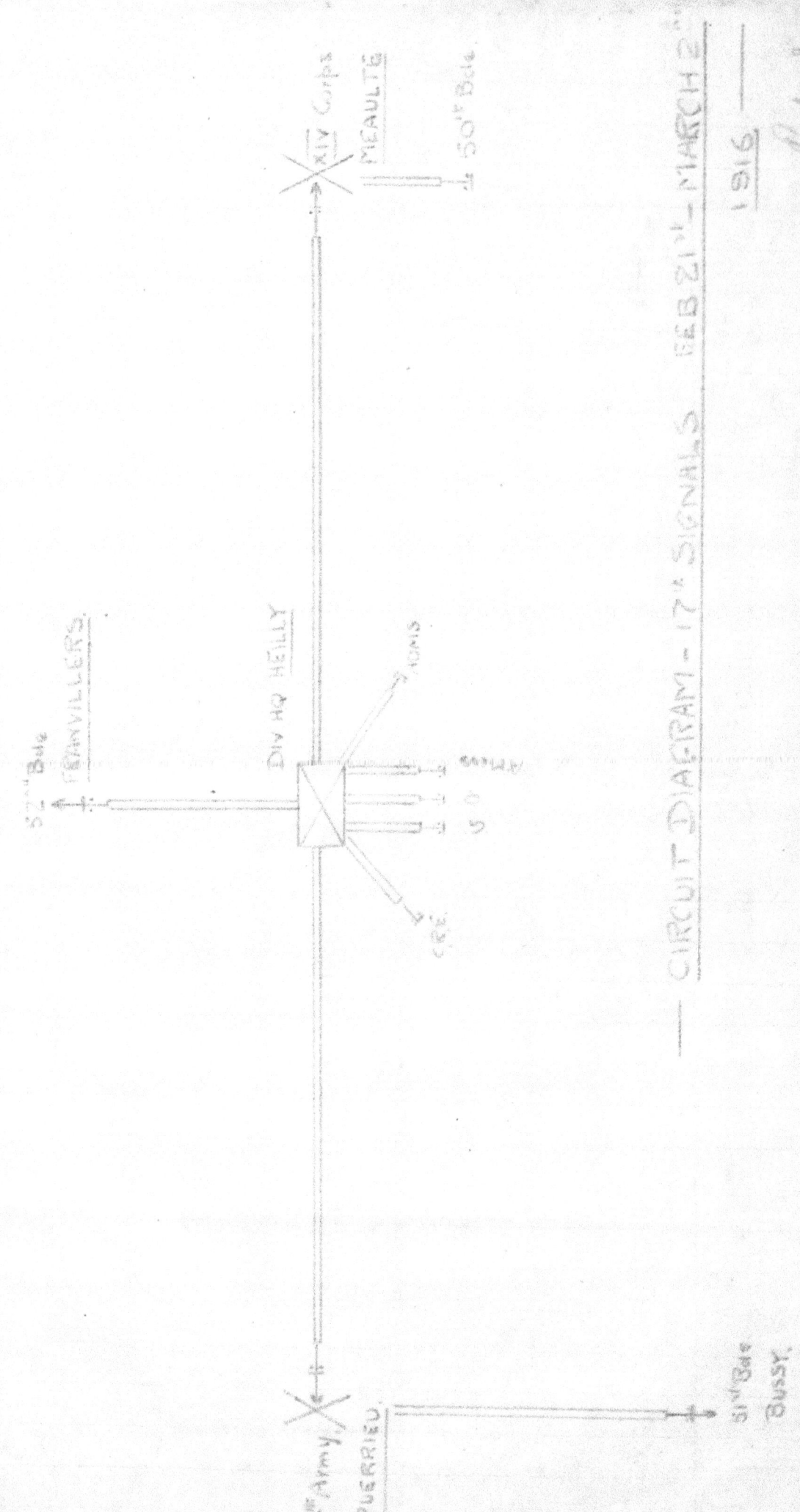

Vol 20

SECRET & CONFIDENTIAL

War Diary

-of-

17th SIGNAL COMPANY R.E.

Vol 20 - FEBRUARY 1917

Army Form C. 2118

WAR DIARY
or
~~INTELLIGENCE SUMMARY~~
(Erase heading not required.)

SECRET and CONFIDENTIAL

WAR DIARY

OF

17th SIGNAL COMPANY R.E.

VOL. 20. — FEBRUARY 1917.

Army Form C. 2118

WAR DIARY
or
INTELLIGENCE SUMMARY
(Erase heading not required.)

Instructions regarding War Diaries and Intelligence Summaries are contained in F. S. Regs., Part II. and the Staff Manual respectively. Title Pages will be prepared in manuscript.

Place	Date	Hour	Summary of Events and Information	Remarks and references to Appendices
In the Field	1/2/17		Strength of Company Officers 7 O.R. 212 / 219	A.
	1st		Lines of 51st Brigade working well. Line from Right Battalion to Right Company dis.	A.
	2		All lines working well.	A.
	3rd		do	A.
	4th		do	A.
	5th		Brigades report lines working well.	A.
	6th		Working party engaged on new bury. Work suspended owing to ground being too hard.	A.
	7th		Lines working well.	A.
	8th		Division attacked and captured SULLIVAN TRENCH and GREEN HOWARD TRENCH. 52nd Brigade report.	A.

1875 Wt. W593/826 1,000,000 4/15 J.B.C. & A. A.D.S.S./Forms/C. 2118.

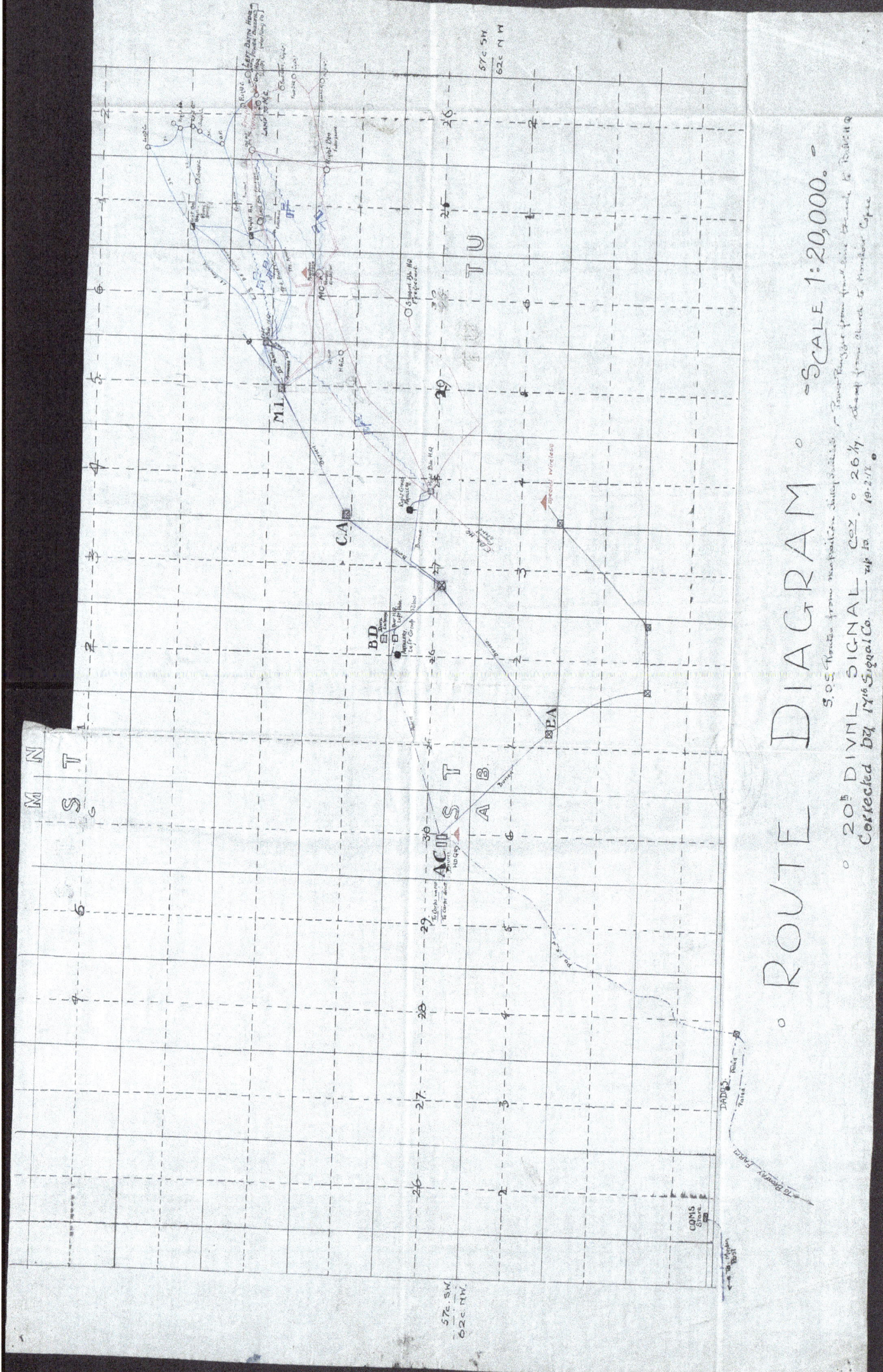

WAR DIARY
or
INTELLIGENCE SUMMARY

Army Form C. 2118

Place	Date	Hour	Summary of Events and Information	Remarks and references to Appendices
J.W.	8th		All lines through to Companies Battalions. Forward of Left Battalion all lines cut.	A.
	9th		Lines to T.P. and M.C. through. Through to right Battalion by buzzer and fullerphone. Through to left Battalion by buzzer 10.30 a.m. Lateral between Battalions still "dis".	B.
	10th		Lines working well.	C.
	11th		do do do	D.
	12th		All lines through.	E.
	13th		Lines fairly satisfactory.	F.
	14th		All lines working well. Capt: K.F. Rumpff reports from 23rd Divn in Command.	G.
	15th		do do do	H.
	16th		Blowing up of ammunition dump at PLATEAU caused Cy. lines to BRONFAY FARM Left Brigade to go "dis". 50th Brigade report all lines working satisfactorily.	I.

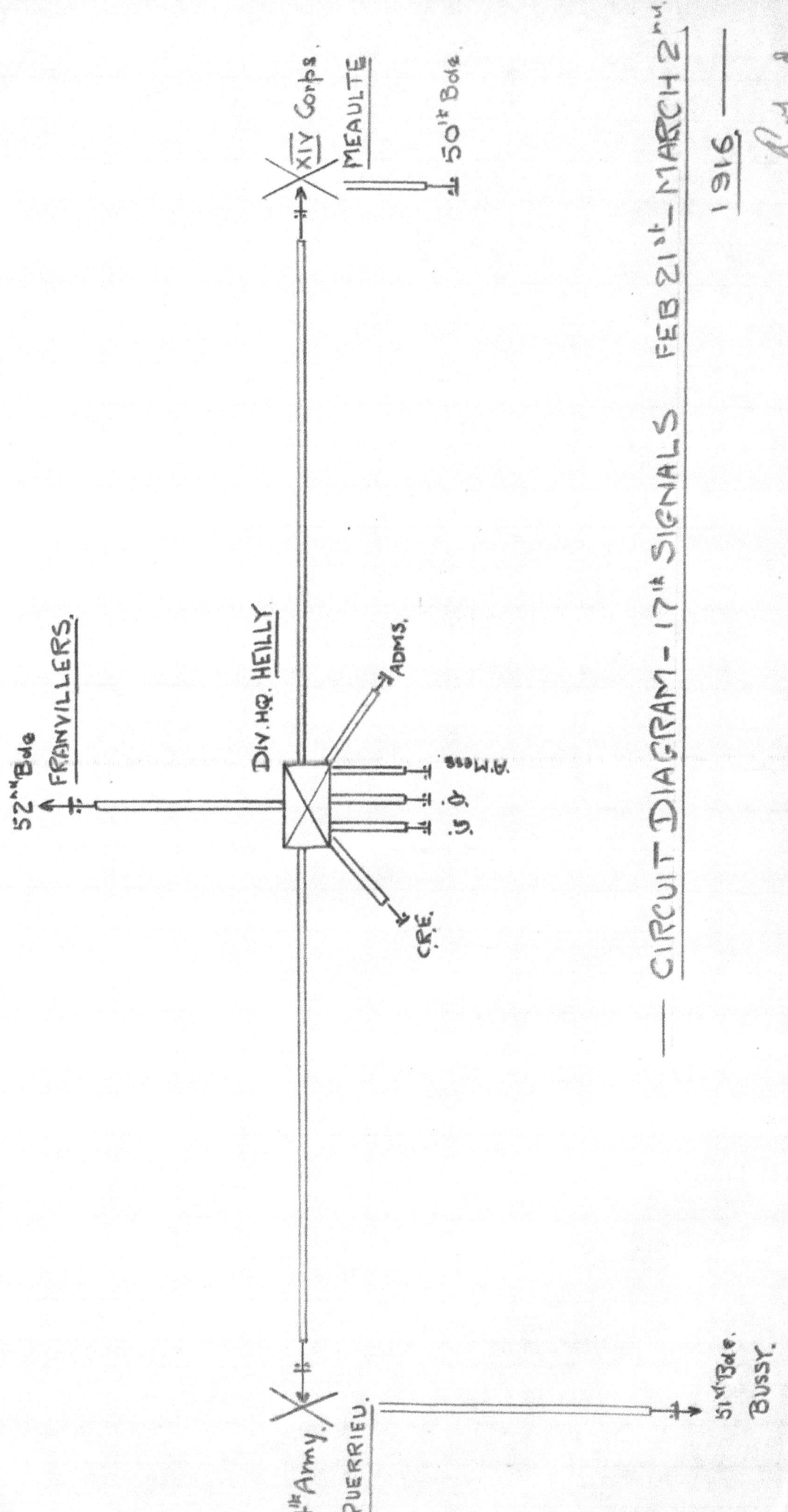

WAR DIARY
or
INTELLIGENCE SUMMARY

Army Form C. 2118

Place	Date	Hour	Summary of Events and Information	Remarks and references to Appendices
Arrow Head Copse	17th		Operating and maintenance work on memory of coys.	A.
	18th		"	A.
	19th		"	A.
	20th		"	A.
	21st		Sun Laid to DODGE WOOD & C.W work set # S.O.S. purposes.	A.
	22nd		Work on memory of Cols. MORAL & HEILLY	A.
	23rd		Officer turned at our H.Qn at 10 a.m. (29th Div. relieve us & Bn hui.)	B.
	24th		Operating and maintenance generally and carrying & checking stores	B.
	25th		recopying & parking.	B.
	26th		"	B.
	27th		Operating, maintenance Recopying & cleaning up. Training	B.
	28th		"	B.

Army Form C. 2118

WAR DIARY
or
INTELLIGENCE SUMMARY

(Erase heading not required.)

N. Div Cyc[?]

Place	Date	Hour	Summary of Events and Information	Remarks and references to Appendices
HEILLY	March 1st		[illegible]	
CONTAY	2nd		[illegible] CONTAY [illegible]	
"	3rd		[illegible]	
"	4th		Operations and [illegible]	
"	5th		[illegible]	
"	6th		[illegible] training [illegible]	
"	7th		[illegible] Bryn [illegible] starting [illegible] Bn [illegible] Ben Staff & Commanders att. [illegible] WARLOY by [illegible]	
"	8th		Transport [illegible] School [illegible]	
"	9th		Riding Schl and [illegible] from [illegible] training [illegible] from SD Det under 40 KA	
"	10th		Transferred on [illegible] YCS Medical School [illegible]	
"	11th		[illegible]	
"	12th		[illegible]	

17th DIVISION

Circuit Diagram of Commns

WILLEMAN

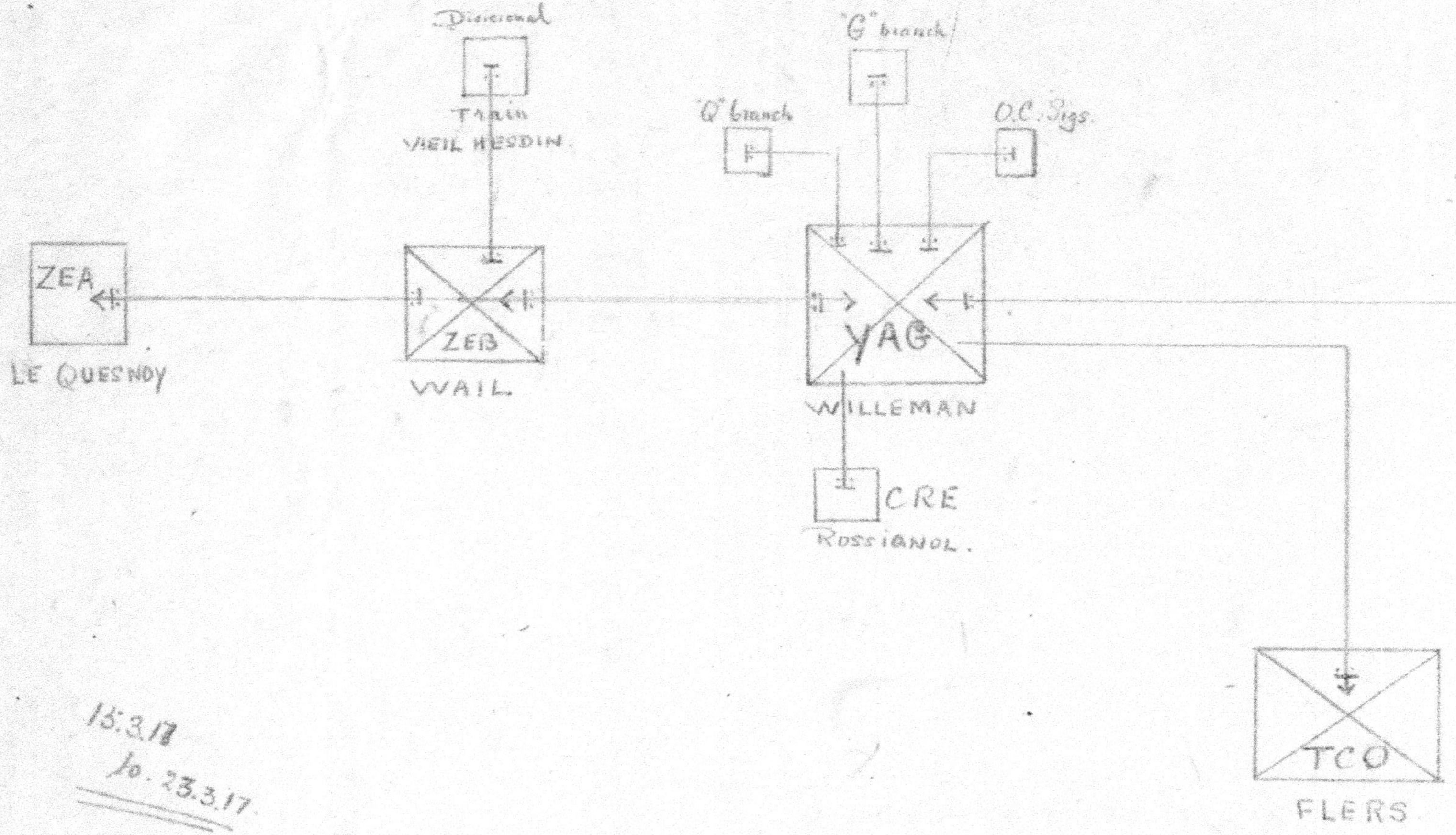
Divisional
Train
VIEIL HESDIN.
"G" branch
"Q" branch
O.C. Sigs.
ZEA
LE QUESNOY
ZEB
WAIL
YAG
WILLEMAN
ZEO
OEUF
CRE
ROSSIGNOL.
TCO
FLERS

15.3.17
to. 23.3.17

Army Form C. 2118

WAR DIARY
or
INTELLIGENCE SUMMARY
(Erase heading not required.)

Instructions regarding War Diaries and Intelligence Summaries are contained in F. S. Regs. Part II. and the Staff Manual respectively. Title Pages will be prepared in manuscript.

Place	Date	Hour	Summary of Events and Information	Remarks and references to Appendices
CONTAY	13th		Pushing F hrs to WILLEMAN. Transmission working better. Several trains arrived Amiens late	I.O.
	14th		Enemy aircraft around Corps H.Qrs & BOURGUIGNON. Train with 15 Am. not arrived	I.O.
WILLEMAN	15th		from 5 WILLEMAN. 30 HQrs arrived	I.O.
			About the same arr. now 12 noon. Regt. reconnoitred to XIX Corps.	
	16th		Rec. [?] 5 WAIL on LE ŒUF to LE [?] 30 [?] Bde	I.O.
	17th		from WAIL & 51st Bde at LE QUESNOY and supplied [?]	I.O.
	18th		Gun range [?] to WAIL Horses taken for Tren Squadron in QS. [?] Regt. to Victors. Good water in [?] Withdraw to position [?] and 2 squads north	I.O.
	19th			I.O.
	20th		Withdrew subunits and 5 VII Corps back on 9 Tanning & dn. amed.	I.O.
	21st		Attacks carried up. Regt. 2nd army to ZULPICHE. Training to a spot on road	I.O.
	22nd		PRUS WILSON ch W. S. order Nbr. 29 Inf. Brigade.	I.O.
LE CAUROY	23rd		Performing to-day. Training and Inst. as usual MOVE to LE CAUROY Arvd 1 Bttn. from by 74 Corps.	I.O.

1875 Wt. W593/826 1,000,000 4/15 J.B.C. & A. A.D.S.S./Forms/C. 2118.

Army Form C. 2118

WAR DIARY
or
INTELLIGENCE SUMMARY
(Erase heading not required.)

Instructions regarding War Diaries and Intelligence Summaries are contained in F.S. Regs., Part II. and the Staff Manual respectively. Title Pages will be prepared in manuscript.

Place	Date	Hour	Summary of Events and Information	Remarks and references to Appendices
LECAUROY	24th		Training being carried out as arranged. [illegible] and Aeroplane formerly	[illegible]
	25th		used to recover [illegible] failure to obtain	[illegible]
	26th		communication Aeroplane [illegible]	[illegible]
	27th			
	28th			
	29th		Coy Strength = 206 OR	
			7 Offrs	
			Total 213	
	30th			
	31st		Two Spare School winners of Coy DAOUR's.	

[signature]
31/5/17 Comdg 17th Sqdn Coy RE

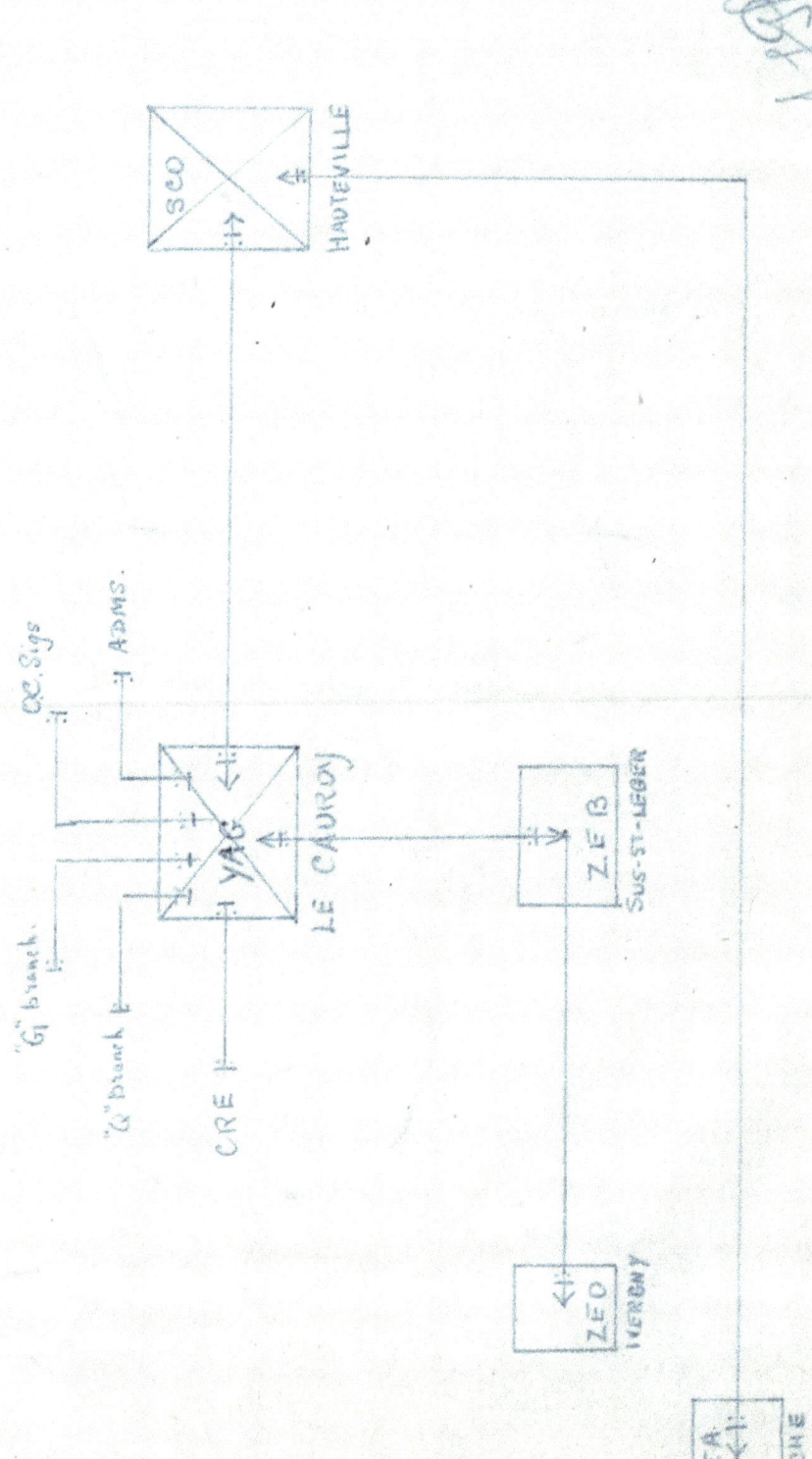

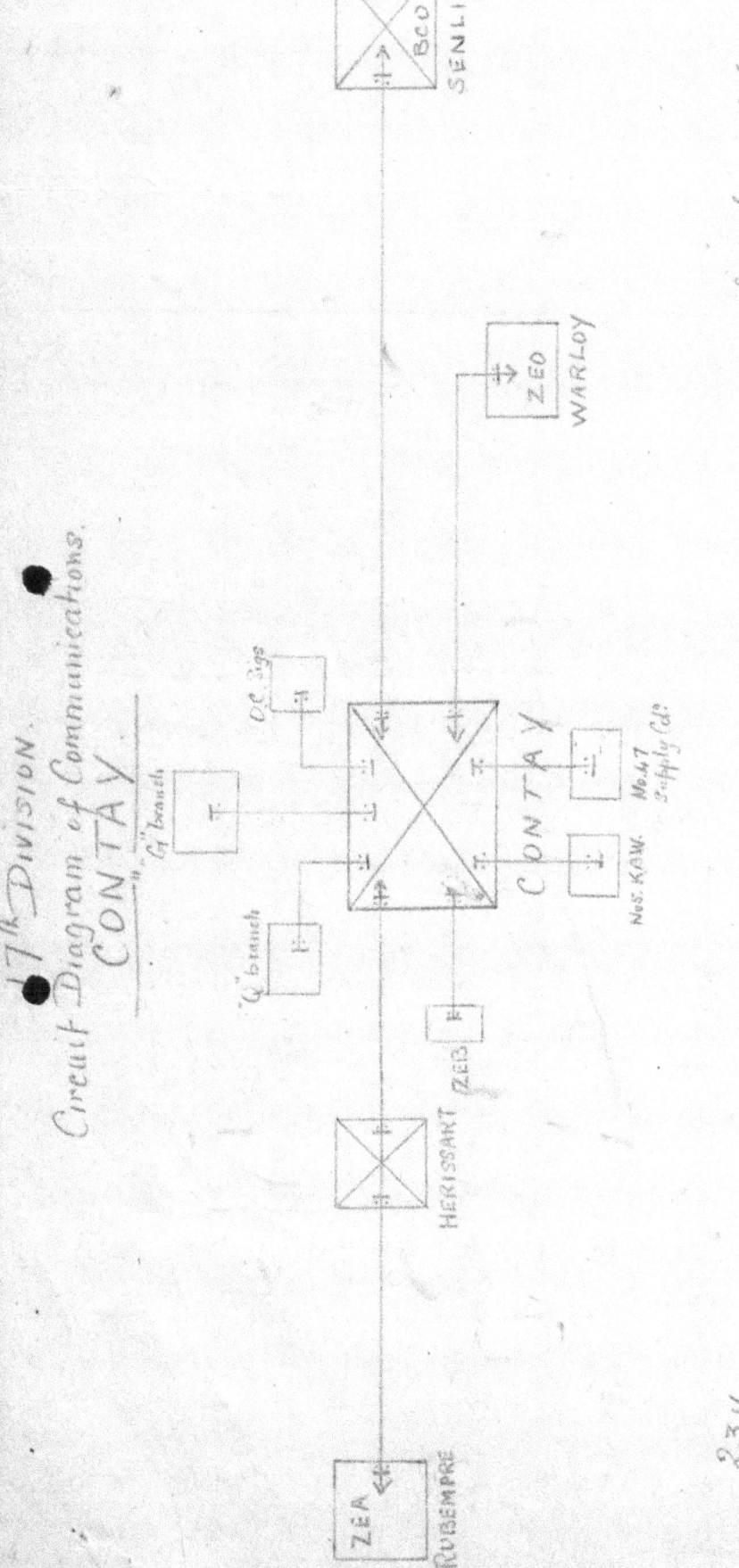

Vol 21

SECRET and CONFIDENTIAL

WAR DIARY

— OF —

17th DIV'N'L SIGNAL Coy RE

VOL 21 — MARCH 1917

WAR DIARY
or
~~INTELLIGENCE SUMMARY~~
(Erase heading not required.)

Army Form C. 2118

— SECRET and CONFIDENTIAL —

— WAR DIARY —

OF

17th DIVN'L SIGNAL COY RE

— VOL. 21 — MARCH 1917 —

Army Form C. 2118

WAR DIARY
or
INTELLIGENCE SUMMARY
(Erase heading not required.)

Instructions regarding War Diaries and Intelligence Summaries are contained in F. S. Regs., Part II. and the Staff Manual respectively. Title Pages will be prepared in manuscript.

Place	Date	Hour	Summary of Events and Information	Remarks and references to Appendices
HEILLY	March 1st		Cleaning up and introductions for the move to CONTAY. A.K. Cable section joined from II Corps.	1st R.
CONTAY	2nd		Struck office at 12 noon. Move to Bédu and locals got out.	2nd R.
"	3rd		Operating and training. Wireless substation (No 31) erected ahead of Bn wrk.	3rd R.
"	4th		Training in riding cable work and generally upkeeping, operating and personnel of this station.	4th R.
"	5th		" " " "	5th R.
"	6th		Continuing training and overhauling stores etc.	6th R.
"	7th		Power Buzzer demonstration F.Bn and Bar Staffs. Bn Communication etc. Eiffel tower pickets	7th R.
"	8th		up and working to WARLOY by power buzzer. Training as above, communications as per diagram.	8th R.
"	9th		Riding, cable and lines buzzer training. Visit of new Signal school (formed in Feb 25th) from 80 Inf and 40 R.A.	9th R.
"	10th		Training as above. G.O.C. visited school and embellished on its appearance and working.	10th R.
"	11th		Church service in heavy rainfall. Further instructions to stations. In write.	11th R.
"	12th		Station training with men opening on at Anthemes. Other training as above.	12th R.

1875 Wt. W593/826 1,000,000 4/15 J.B.C. & A. A.D.S.S./Forms/C. 2118.

17th Division
Circuit Diagram of Communications.
CONTAY

"H" / G branch

OC Sigs

"Q" branch

CONTAY

No.47 Supply Col"

Nos K/3W

HERISSART ZE/3

SENLIS BCO

ZEO WARLOY

ZEA RUBEMPRE

2.3.16. to 15.3.16.

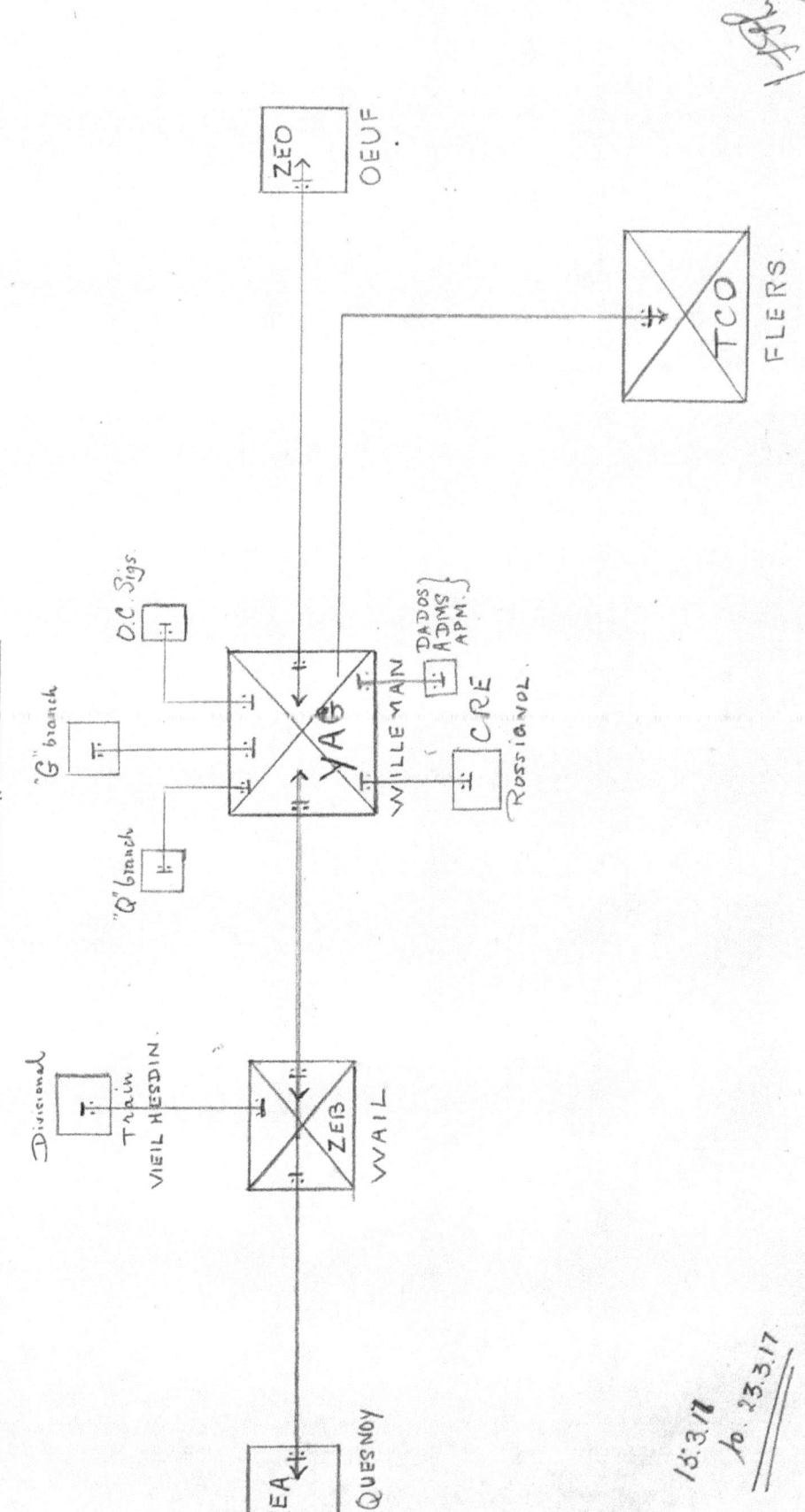

Army Form C. 2118

WAR DIARY
or
INTELLIGENCE SUMMARY
(Erase heading not required.)

Instructions regarding War Diaries and Intelligence Summaries are contained in F.S. Regs., Part II. and the Staff Manual respectively. Title Pages will be prepared in manuscript.

Place	Date	Hour	Summary of Events and Information	Remarks and references to Appendices
CONTAY	13th		Preparing to move to WILLEMAN. Training in riding, cable laying, mounted, horsemanship etc.	
"	14th		Coy marched under Capt Phillips to BOUQUEMAISON. Chief work to officer as usual	
WILLEMAN	15th		" " " from " to WILLEMAN. Hrs HQrs moved direct. Officers opened at new HQrs 12 noon. Lines connected to XIX Corps.	
"	16th		Lines laid to WAIL and OEUF for 50th and 52nd Bdes.	
"	17th		" from WAIL to 5th Bn at LE QUESNOY and completed as per diagram	
"	18th		Power buzzer working to WAIL started a class for Bn Signallers in P.B. and N.C.O's sent to Army for training. Church service in the morning. Football in afternoon.	
"	19th		Training and general work.	
"	20th		Written instruction sent to VI Corps with and of training as usual.	
"	21st		Airable section left Kjerv 2nd Army at ZUTPEENE. Training and work as usual Lt CARUS-WILSON left No 3 section to join 8th Div Signals.	
"	22nd		Preparing for move. Training and work as usual	
LE CAUROY	23rd		Moved to LE CAUROY. Lines has been given by 7th Corps.	

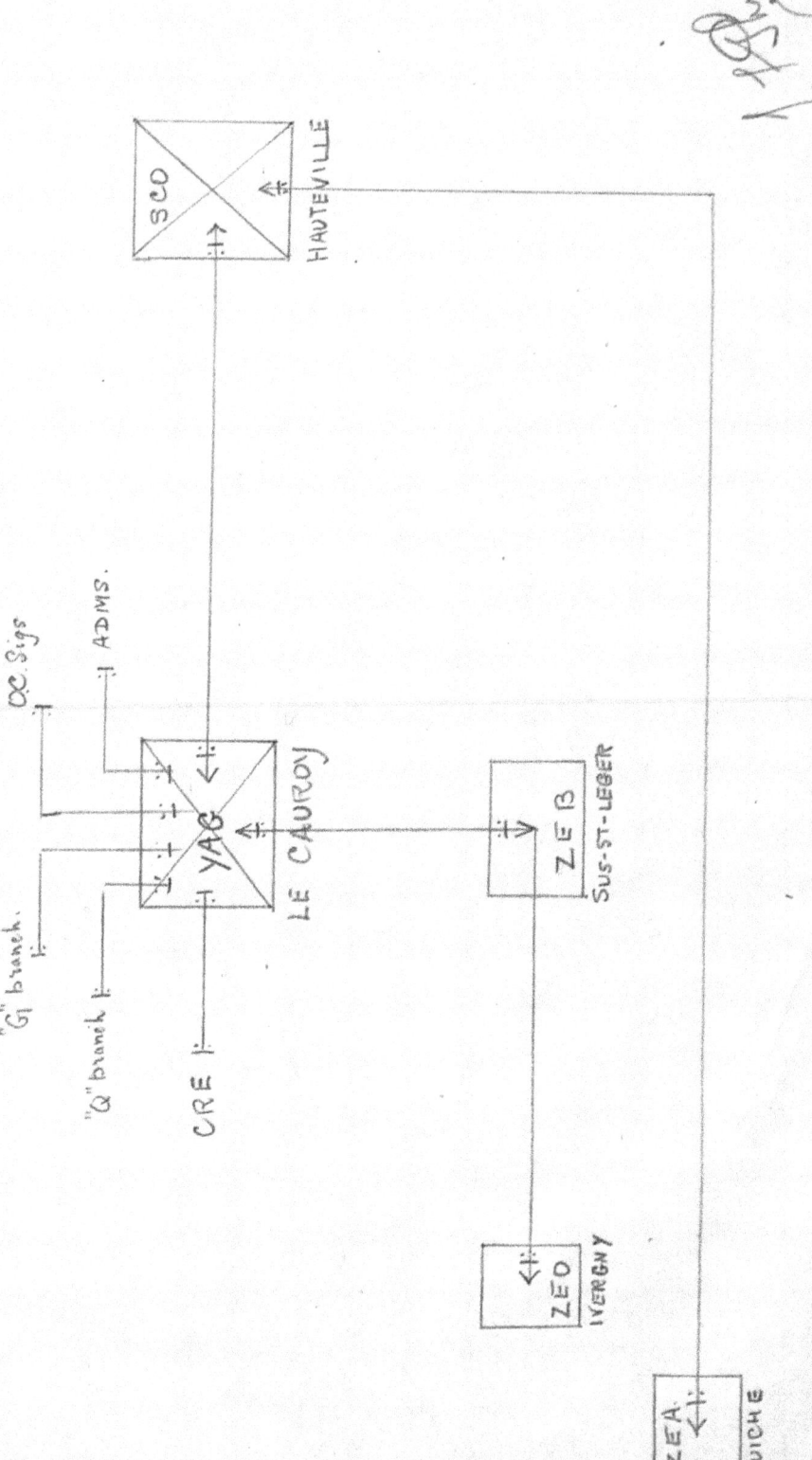

Army Form C. 2118

WAR DIARY
or
INTELLIGENCE SUMMARY
(Erase heading not required.)

Place	Date	Hour	Summary of Events and Information	Remarks and references to Appendices
LECAUROY	24th		Training and work resumed, especially in Acetylene Soundering	
"	25th		Church in morning Football in afternoon.	
"	26th		Intervals in Tourtplane Signalling	
"	27th		"	
"	28th		"	
"	29th		"	
"	30th		"	
"	31st		" tin. Signal & about anoves of from DAOURS.	
			Coy Strength 206 OR	
			7 Offm	
			Total 213	

31/3/17 Cmdg. 17th Signal Coy R.E.

Vol 22

SECRET AND CONFIDENTIAL

WAR DIARY.

17th SIGNAL COY. R.E.

VOL 22 - APRIL 1917.

// SECRET AND CONFIDENTIAL //

// WAR DIARY //

17th SIGNAL COY. R.E.

VOL 22 — APRIL 1917

Army Form C. 2118

WAR DIARY
or
INTELLIGENCE SUMMARY

(Erase heading not required.)

Place	Date	Hour	Summary of Events and Information	Remarks and references to Appendices
LE CAUROY	April 1st		Company training carried on as usual. Cable Carts and limbers overhauled.	
	2nd		do.	
	3rd		do.	
	4th		Company practised a Marching out parade at 10 a.m. Full marching order. Billets cleaned and company arranged in Echelons. One Wireless detachment to 50th and 52nd Brigades. Rationed for two days.	
	5th		Wagons loaded ready for move to HAUTE AVESNES.	
	6th		"A" Echelon office relief to HAUTE AVESNE Sundr. Cpl Denman. "B" " " " " BERNEVILLE under "Chamberlin".	
HAUTE AVESNES	7th		Signal office closed 3 pm LE CAUROY and opened HAUTE AVESNES 5 same time. Stores dumped at LE CAUROY. A.1 and B.3 detachment laid lines to HAUTE AVESNES from HABARCQ (51st Bde) and AGNES (52nd Bde) under Capt Phipps.	

WAR DIARY or INTELLIGENCE SUMMARY

Army Form C. 2118

Place	Date	Hour	Summary of Events and Information	Remarks and references to Appendices
HAUTE-AVESNES	April 9th		Company at HAUTE-AVESNES do	
	9th		Divisional Headquarters closed HAUTE AVESNES at 6 a.m. and opened same time at ARRAS.	
ARRAS	9/10		B.3. Cable detachment under Captain PHIPPS to ARRAS 2 a.m. Division under 50 minutes notice to move. One limber wagon to TILLOY to open Divisional Report Centre by 7 a.m.	
	11th		Working party erected 2 pairs of lines to RAILWAY TRIANGLE and Lieut. LEPPER with his party laid lines to 52nd Bde. Sergt. HANKS laid two pairs of wires to "A" Bac. Ten line exchange installed at RAILWAY TRIANGLE. (51st BDE H.Q).	
	12th		Carrying out above work.	
	13th		Sapper CHAPMAN to 52nd Bde to halved and maintain line to RAILWAY TRIANGLE. Sapper BURROWS to 51st Bde to maintain Division line as far as RAILWAY TRIANGLE.	
	14th			

Army Form C. 2118

WAR DIARY
or
INTELLIGENCE SUMMARY
(Erase heading not required.)

Place	Date	Hour	Summary of Events and Information	Remarks and references to Appendices
ARRAS	April 15		Work on forward lines continued. Two motorcyclists arrived from Depot to replace two casualties.	
	16		Sergt. HANKS and party engaged laying forward lines.	
	17		Sergt. HANKS and party continued work on Airline route to RAILWAY TRIANGLE. Corporal Denman and party enroute to Lt. Laley laying line from 79th Bde. R.F.A. to 78th Bde.	See.
	18		Work on lines continued.	
	19		Sergts. Hanks and Lewis laying lines from FEUCHY to ADVANCED RAILWAY 2 a.m. Cpl Denman & party forwarding on T.A. lines. Three reinforcements arrived from Signal Depot.	
	20		Forwarded lines finished to RAILWAY TRIANGLE. Sergt HUTTON and party to FEUCHY for maintenance	
	21		of armoured line in Canal etc. Cpl Clark and party to Advanced Bde. H.Q. Wireless Station removed from RAILWAY TRIANGLE.	

Army Form C. 2118

WAR DIARY
or
INTELLIGENCE SUMMARY
(Erase heading not required.)

Instructions regarding War Diaries and Intelligence Summaries are contained in F. S. Regs., Part II. and the Staff Manual respectively. Title Pages will be prepared in manuscript.

Place	Date	Hour	Summary of Events and Information	Remarks and references to Appendices
ARRAS	21		to Advanced Base H.Q. Visual party sent to MONCHY.	Sgt. Pearce killed. S/Sgt. Allen wounded
	22		LE-PREUX to work back to Division.	
	23		Prisoners camp put on ringing telephone. Pioneers CLEARY wounded but carried on work until relieved.	
	24		BATTLE of ARRAS raging. Working party and linemen out practically day and night mending and renewing lines. Lines heavily shelled but owing to excellent work on part of linemen communication held.	J18
	25		Advance party of 12st Division arrived. Lines heavily shelled.	
LE CAUROY	26		Relieved by 12st Division at 9 a.m. Office opened same hour at LE CAUROY.	
	27		Resting and training at LE CAUROY.	
	28		do. Cable carts overhauled and cleaned.	

WAR DIARY
INTELLIGENCE SUMMARY
(Erase heading not required.)

Army Form C. 2118

Place	Date	Hour	Summary of Events and Information	Remarks and references to Appendices
LE CAUROY	29		Large Church Parade in morning. S.E. Corner of Chateau. Football match in afternoon.	
	30		Wagons loaded in view of move. Strength of Company 230 O.R. / 8 Officers / 236	

J. Philips Captain.

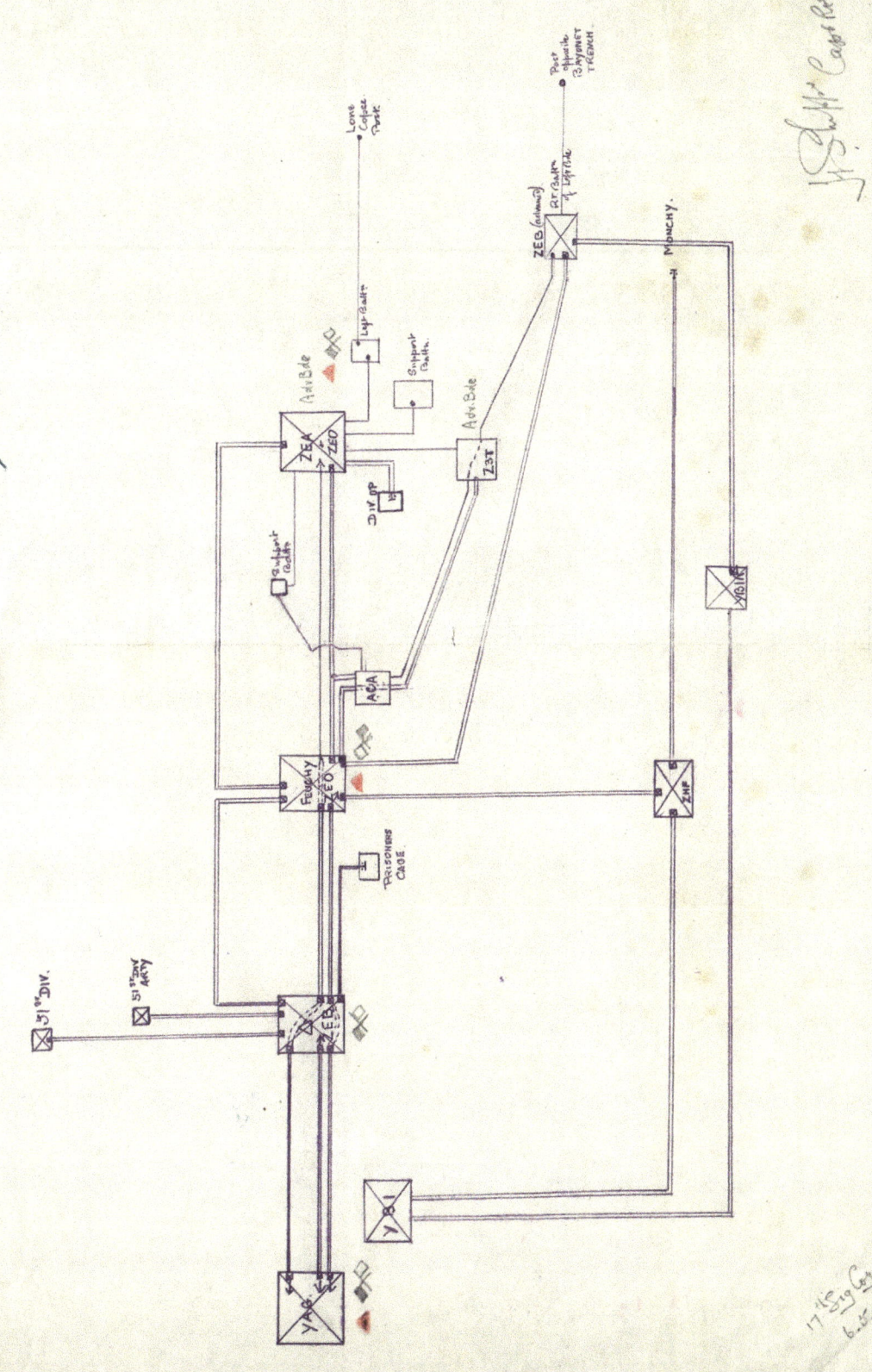

17th Division Signals.

Line Diagram of Communications
April 24th/17

REFERENCE.
△ ...... WIRELESS.
⚑ ...... VISUAL.

17th DIVISION LINES.
APRIL 23rd TO 26th.

Sheet 51.B. North West.
Scale 1/20,000

WAR DIARY
or
INTELLIGENCE SUMMARY

Army Form C. 2118

(Erase heading not required.)

Place	Date	Hour	Summary of Events and Information	Remarks and references to Appendices
LE CAUROY	April 1st		Company training carried on as usual. Call Carts and Limbers overhauled.	
	2nd		do.	
	3rd		do.	
	4th		Company practised a matching order. Billets cleaned and Marching out parade at 10 a.m. Full company arranged in Echelons. One Wireless detachment to 50th and 52nd Brigades. Rationed for two days.	
	5th		Wagons loaded ready for move to HAUTE AVESNES.	
	6th		"A" Echelon office relief to HAUTE AVESNES under 2/Lt Denman. "B" " " " BERNEVILLE " " Chamberlin.	
HAUTE AVESNES	7th		Signal Office closed 3 pm LE CAUROY and opened HAUTE AVESNES same time. Stores dumped at LE CAUROY. A.1 and B.3 detachment laid lines to HAUTE AVESNES from HABARCQ (51st Bde.) and AGNES (52nd Bde) under Capt Phipps.	

Army Form C. 2118

WAR DIARY
or
INTELLIGENCE SUMMARY
(Erase heading not required.)

Instructions regarding War Diaries and Intelligence Summaries are contained in F.S. Regs., Part II. and the Staff Manual respectively. Title Pages will be prepared in manuscript.

Place	Date	Hour	Summary of Events and Information	Remarks and references to Appendices
HAUTE-AVESNES.	April 8th		Company at HAUTE-AVESNES	
	9th		do do	
	10th		Divisional Headquarters closed HAUTE AVESNES at 6 a.m. and opened same time at ARRAS same time. B.3. Cable detachment under Captain PHIPPS to ARRAS 2 a.m. Division under 50 minute notice to move. One limber wagon to TILLOY to open Divisional Report Centre by 7 a.m.	
ARRAS.	11th		Working party erected 2 pairs of lines to RAILWAY TRIANGLE and Lieut LEPPER with his party laid lines to 52nd BDE. Serg.t HANKS laid two pairs of wires to "A" Box. Ten line exchange installed at RAILWAY TRIANGLE (51st BDE H.Q.)	
	12th		Carrying out above work.	
	13th		Sapper CHAPMAN to 52nd Bde. to patrol and maintain line to RAILWAY TRIANGLE. Sapper BURROWS to 51st Bde to maintain Division line as far as RAILWAY TRIANGLE.	
	14th			

Army Form C. 2118

WAR DIARY
or
INTELLIGENCE SUMMARY
(Erase heading not required.)

Place	Date	Hour	Summary of Events and Information	Remarks and references to Appendices
ARRAS	April 15		Work on forward lines continued. From motorcyclists arrived from depot to replace few casualties.	
	16		Sergt HANKS and party engaged laying forward lines.	
	17		Sergt HANKS and party continued work on airline route to RAILWAY TRIANGLE. Corporal Denman and party under Lt Laley laying line from 79th Bde R.F.A to 78th Bde. Work on lines continued.	
	18		Sergts Banks and Lewis laid forward lines at FEUCHY at to ADVANCED R.A.H.Q.	
	19		2 a.m. Cpl Denman & party working on T.A. lines. Three reinforcements arrived from Signal Depot.	
	20		Forward lines followed up and mended where necessary. Forward line finished to RAILWAY TRIANGLE. Sergt HUTTON and party to FEUCHY for maintenance of armoured line in Canal etc. Cpl Clark and party	
	21		to Advanced Bde H.Q. Wireless Station moved from RAILWAY TRIANGLE.	

WAR DIARY
or
INTELLIGENCE SUMMARY

(Erase heading not required.)

Army Form C. 2118

Place	Date	Hour	Summary of Events and Information	Remarks and references to Appendices
ARRAS	21		to Advanced Bde H.Q. Visual party sent to MONCHY LE - PREUX to work back to Division.	Sapper Pearson killed Sapr. ALLEN wounded
	22		Prisoners camp put on ringing telephone. Pioneer CLEARY wounded but carried on work until exhausted.	
	23		BATTLE of ARRAS raging. Working party and linemen out practically day and night mending and renewing lines. Lines heavily shelled but owing to excellent work on part of linemen communication held.	JB
	24th			
	25th		Advance party of 12st Division arrived. Lines heavily shelled.	
LE CAVROY	26th		Relieved by 12st Division at 9. a.m. Office opened same hour at LE CAVROY.	
	27th		Resting and training at LE CAVROY.	
	28th		do. Cable carts overhauled and cleaned.	

WAR DIARY or INTELLIGENCE SUMMARY

Army Form C. 2118

Place	Date	Hour	Summary of Events and Information	Remarks and references to Appendices
LE CAUROY	29		Large Church Parade in morning. S.E. Corner of Chateau. Football match in afternoon.	
	30		Wagons loaded in view of move. Strength of Company 230 O.R. 8 Officers / 236	

J. Philips Capt RE.

SECRET & CONFIDENTIAL

WAR DIARY
— OF —
17th Div'nl Signal Coy RE

Vol 23. — MAY 1917.

WAR DIARY
or
INTELLIGENCE SUMMARY
(Erase heading not required.)

Army Form C. 2118

Place	Date	Hour	Summary of Events and Information	Remarks and references to Appendices
HERMAVILLE	MAY 1st		Arrived at Hermaville expecting relief but took over from 9th Div. took of the scarps, HQrs in the Rookery, Butting. Bews on St Nicholas, Blangy and I had not HQ Mess. established small offices in Arras. Served officers lunch and maintenance. Orderlies as for division.	(i)
	6th			
	7th		Preparations made for moving onto the hill as above. Ordnance parties with us the meantime.	
	9th		Part of 1 Tn over from 9th Div.	
	10th		Relieved 9th Div at Caen. Artillery all forward. Divns by brigades. W.L. started at our puttying through the Riemen Brown cable so as to work newly Telephone and Powerhat cable to 50th and 52nd Bdes in the hill. Work on new forward lines and extending buglers. Served also libations of lines and Stores to as L took over lines & Bses as shown on diagram. Preparation of new HQrs in St Nicholas hrs office and board office closed because Div HQrs joined up Faster at St. Nicholas. Very quiet. Camp and hres very comfortable. Artillery hres manned and busy. Very little limbed (an disposal)	
	11th			
	13th			

Army Form C. 2118

WAR DIARY
or
INTELLIGENCE SUMMARY
(Erase heading not required.)

Place	Date	Hour	Summary of Events and Information	Remarks and references to Appendices
ST NICHOLAS (ARRAS)	14th		Moved into new camp at St. Nicholas. All now busy working out and arranging the program. Very little heard from shelling. Operating and maintenance general on the work.	
	18th			J.S.T.
	19th		Batn HDrs. moved back. Working cutting. Road embanked and Pin and Bax office maintaining bar lines up to Batn HDrs. and to Leaning Bee. The L duty in the hut. L., Capt. J.F. Phipps, Sergt. Penney Lr. and Sqt. machine i dispatches. Operating and maintenance. Preparations made to protection attack on Charlie and Enfilade hinder north of ROEUX. Same as shewn as shewn.	
	20th			
	29th		on diagram. All this took place at night by Inst. Costa and party.	
	30th and 31st		Work as usual. Preparation for landing over L 34.h. On the air to without 40 on 31st at 10am.	J.S.T.

WAR DIARY
or
INTELLIGENCE SUMMARY

Army Form C. 2118

(Erase heading not required.)

Instructions regarding War Diaries and Intelligence Summaries are contained in F.S. Regs., Part II. and the Staff Manual respectively. Title Pages will be prepared in manuscript.

Place	Date	Hour	Summary of Events and Information	Remarks and references to Appendices
			Strength of Company May 1st - 230 men 8 officers.	
			June 1st - 237 " 8 officers.	
			Awards during the month.	
			No A3810 Sergt. Hawke J.L.	
			44666 " Foster C.W.	
			46036 Cpl Bridge A.C.	
			52213 " Cpl Rodgers J.A.	
			63679 A/Cpl Clark A.D. } Military Medals	
			65031 A/Cpl Anderson A	
			44744 Pte Gorham J.S.	
			161871 " Chany T.	
			Officer 17 Injured	
			Capt. J.F. Phipps R.S.	
			No 56723 Sergt. Brimpton T. } Mentioned in	
			No 44666 Sergt. Foster C.W. } Despatches.	

B. Tunny
Maj 17R
Cmdg 17th R. Inniskilling R.

Army Form C. 2118

WAR DIARY
or
~~INTELLIGENCE SUMMARY~~
(Erase heading not required.)

SECRET and CONFIDENTIAL

WAR DIARY

17th Divn'l SIGNAL COMPANY

Vol 23 - MAY 1917

Army Form C. 2118

WAR DIARY
or
INTELLIGENCE SUMMARY
(Erase heading not required.)

Instructions regarding War Diaries and Intelligence Summaries are contained in F. S. Regs., Part II. and the Staff Manual respectively. Title Pages will be prepared in manuscript.

Place	Date	Hour	Summary of Events and Information	Remarks and references to Appendices
HERMAVILLE	MAY 1st		Arrived at Hermaville expecting relief of any kind to take over from 9th Div. North of the Scarpe. HQrs in the Sainbury Gallery. Bns. at St Nicholas, Blangy and Y huts just N of Arras. Established small Office Bras Forward Offr. Reches as per diagram.	
"	6th			[bracket]
"	7th		Preparations have for many weeks been in abeyance towards portion not yet known.	
"	8th		Relief up to date over from 9th Div.	
RAILWAY CUTTING	10th		Relieved 9th Div at 9am. Looking all forward lines by bugga. not stated at once putting through old German buried cable so as to work merely Telephone and powerbuggs with 150th and 52nd Bdes in the line. Work on two forward lines and connecting system pressed on with inortion of keen and Shots so as to test direct lines to Bdes in advance. Preparation of new HQrs in St Nicholas new fire lines and Forward Offrs at St Nicholas very good. Closed because Bri HQrs rained up Cemp and kun very complete. Artillery lines rearranged and have very little trouble (on diagram)	[bracket]
"	11th			
"	13th			

HERMAVILLE

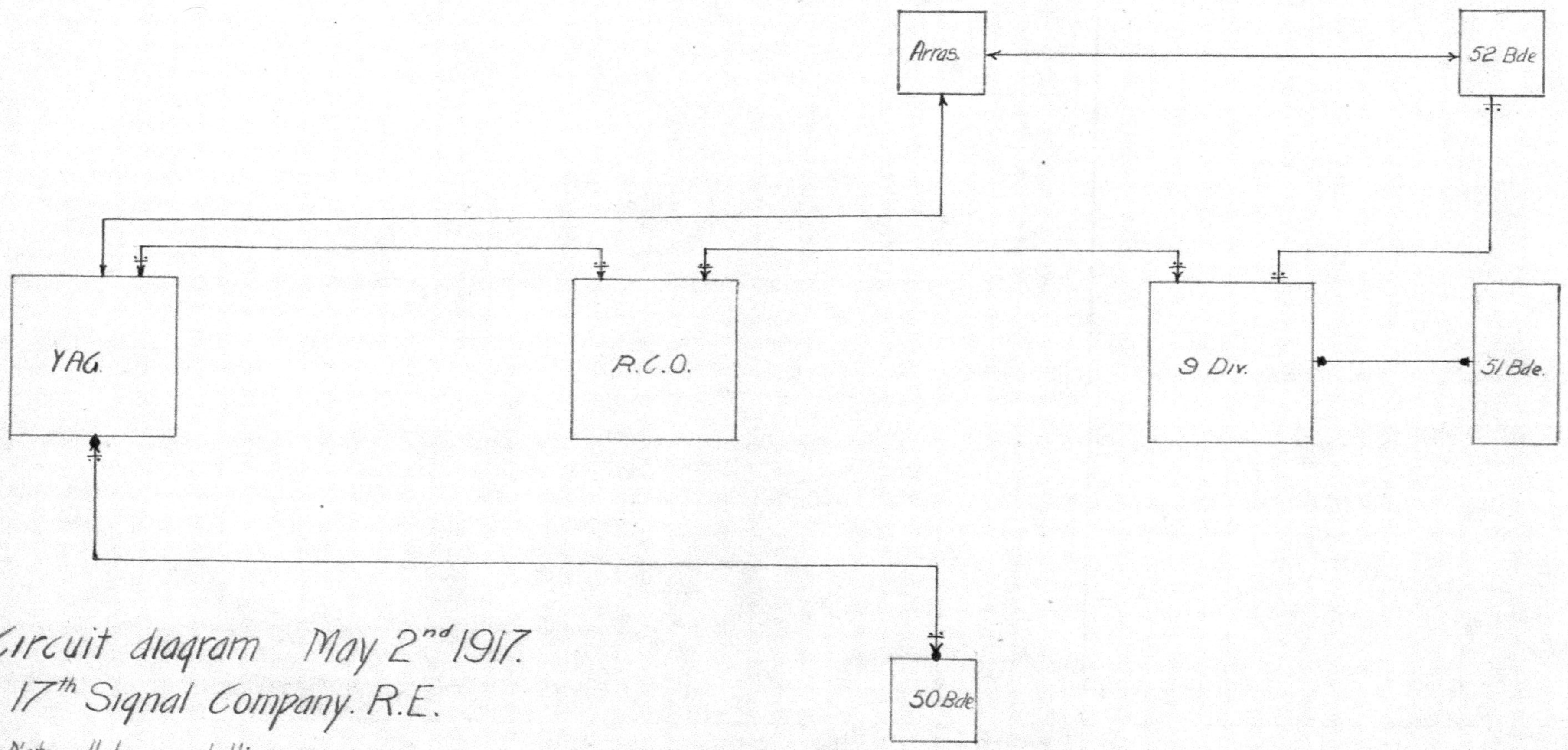

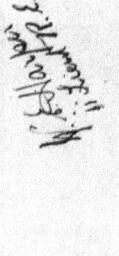

Circuit diagram May 2nd 1917.
17th Signal Company. R.E.

Note. all lines metallic pairs.

W. E. Harper
ii Lieut R.E.

WAR DIARY or INTELLIGENCE SUMMARY

Army Form C. 2118

Place	Date	Hour	Summary of Events and Information	Remarks and references to Appendices
ST NICHOLAS (ARRAS)	15th to 18th		Moved into new camp at St Nicholas. All ranks working well and according to program. Very little heard from Starting & Operating and Maintenance general run the work.	75R.
	19th		Base HQrs moved back to Mondray cutting. Had entrained all Div and Base Offrs transferring Bus lines up to Adv Pos HQrs and to Louvincourt the F. study in the hut. Lt, Capt. F. Phipps, Sergt Binning Lr and Dr. Lr inspected to Lupitoss. Starting and maintenance preparations had for inspective attack on Charli and Guthbut winches North of ROEUX. 3 armoured cars Force as shown on diagram. All this work done at night by Kent, Croll and party.	
	30th and 31st		Work on hand – preparations for Launching ops L. 34th two who are l'adrost to on 31st at 10 am.	75R.

GH 17th DIVISION WIRES
Scale 1:10,000

REFERENCE.
- AIR LINE
- POLED CABLE
- BURIED OPEN GROUND
- POWER BUZZER

DIVISION WIRES.
SCALE 1:10,000.

REFERENCE.
AIRLINE
POLED CABLE
BURIED OR ON GROUND
POWER BUZZER

Fampoux.

WAR DIARY
or
INTELLIGENCE SUMMARY

Army Form C. 2118

(Erase heading not required.)

Place	Date	Hour	Summary of Events and Information	Remarks and references to Appendices
			Strength of Company hay past 230 men 8 officers. June 1st — 237 " 8 officers.	
			Awards During the Month.	
			No. A3810 Sergt. Hawke J.L. 44666 " Fowler C.N. 46036 Cpl. Bridge A.C. 32218 H/Cpl Rodgers J.A. 63679 L/Cpl Shed A.D. 65051 L/Cpl Anderson A 44784 Pr Cochrane J.F. 161871 Pr Cleary J. } Military Medals	
			On 17 April Capt. J.F. Phipps T.F. No 56723 Sergt. Burrough T.C. No 44666 Sergt. Fowler C.N. } Mentioned in Despatches.	

B. Bond
Major R.E.
Cmdg N° Coy R.E.

Vol 24

17th SIGNAL COMPANY R.E.

SECRET AND CONFIDENTIAL

WAR DIARY.

VOL 24 - JUNE 1917.

Army Form C. 2118

WAR DIARY
or
INTELLIGENCE SUMMARY
(Erase heading not required.)

SECRET and CONFIDENTIAL

= WAR DIARY =

17TH DIVN'L SIGNAL COY

VOL 24 — JUNE 1917

Army Form C. 2118

WAR DIARY
or
INTELLIGENCE SUMMARY
(Erase heading not required.)

Instructions regarding War Diaries and Intelligence Summaries are contained in F.S. Regs, Part II. and the Staff Manual respectively. Title Pages will be prepared in manuscript.

Place	Date	Hour	Summary of Events and Information	Remarks and references to Appendices
COUTERELLE	JUNE 1st		Joined up hier to Bus DADOS. Took from 47th DSC. General tidying up and cleaning up.	
	2nd		Shooting and maintenance.	
	3rd		Started two naval stations down of 65 men for 2nd Bns. Training in riding lorry on each side. Usual parade etc.	
	4th		Shooting and maintenance. Training in riding, each side, rifle drill, horse Oxman and harvesy to impenuity general school.	
	5th to 17th		Bn. Signallers were Brigaders under Bde Section School officer for Scheme and naval training. This SC has departure and purchased good results in small arms of methods of instruction and so-ordination.	
	18th		Both as usual. Signal company start — Winter storm concerns	
	19th to 21st		Preparations for taking over. This hui from 34th Bn. This look and training 2nd heat South trads. Lane In	

WAR DIARY
or
INTELLIGENCE SUMMARY

(Erase heading not required.)

Army Form C. 2118

Place	Date	Hour	Summary of Events and Information	Remarks and references to Appendices
ST. NICHOLAS	22nd	6:30	Took over from 34th Divn at noon. Diagram of communications on back. Relieved 89 Div. in charge of fwd. forward communications. Operating and maintenance. 2500 yards of new cable being entrained or buried line by 5 pm. Bow Indn Signed Officer by 6 pm Bows in 71 Renewed Switch line and connections with L. Bri. HQrs. Reorganisation complete except running lines of RA personnel and artillery sub station officers.	

Strength of Company Inne. 107 – 237 ors. 8 offrs.
     "   "   "   Tely. 107– 292 –   8 –

Crossets Anung M_AK.
Nº 43870 Sgt. Hawkins T.
Nº 317044 Sergt Whitehead
Nº 26574 Spr. Holland a

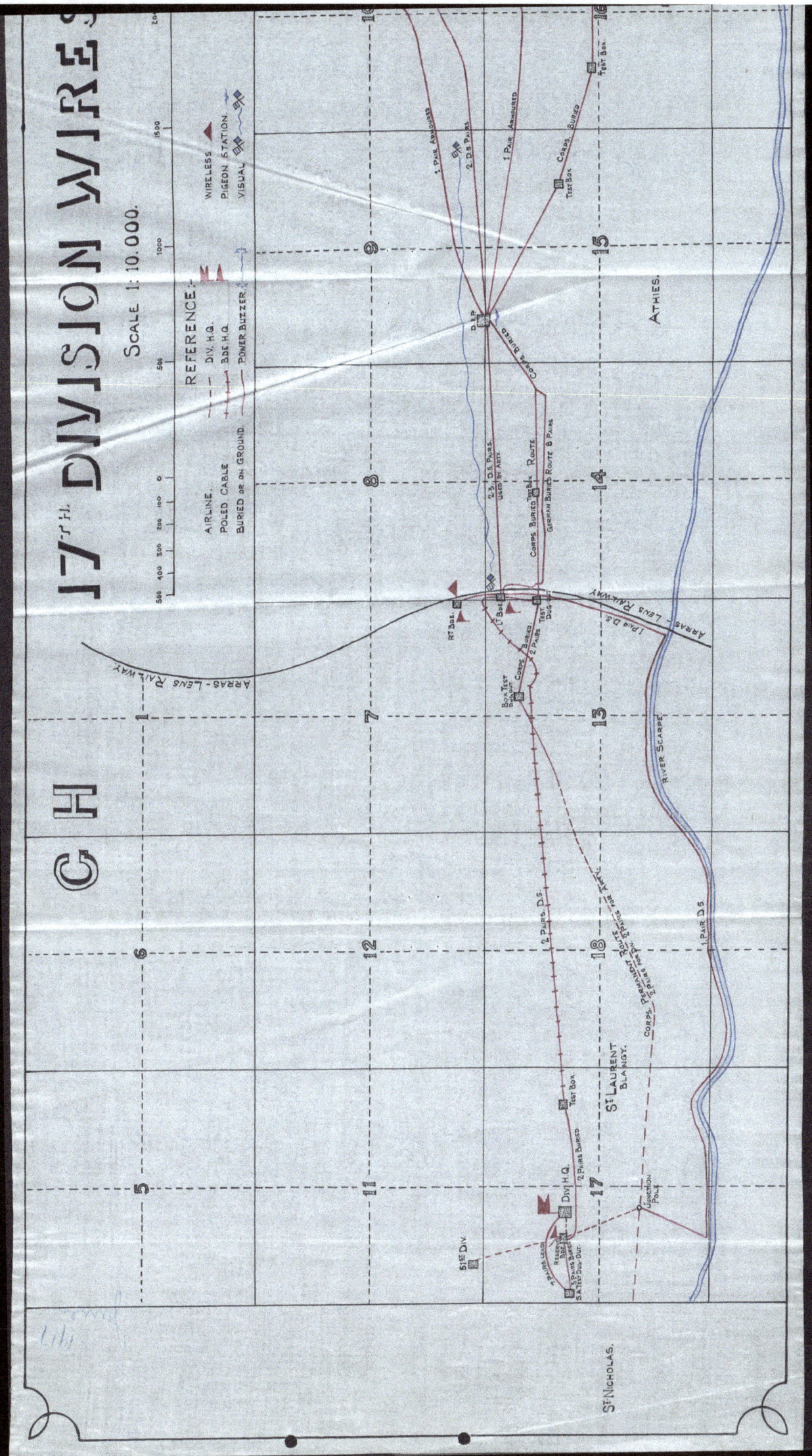

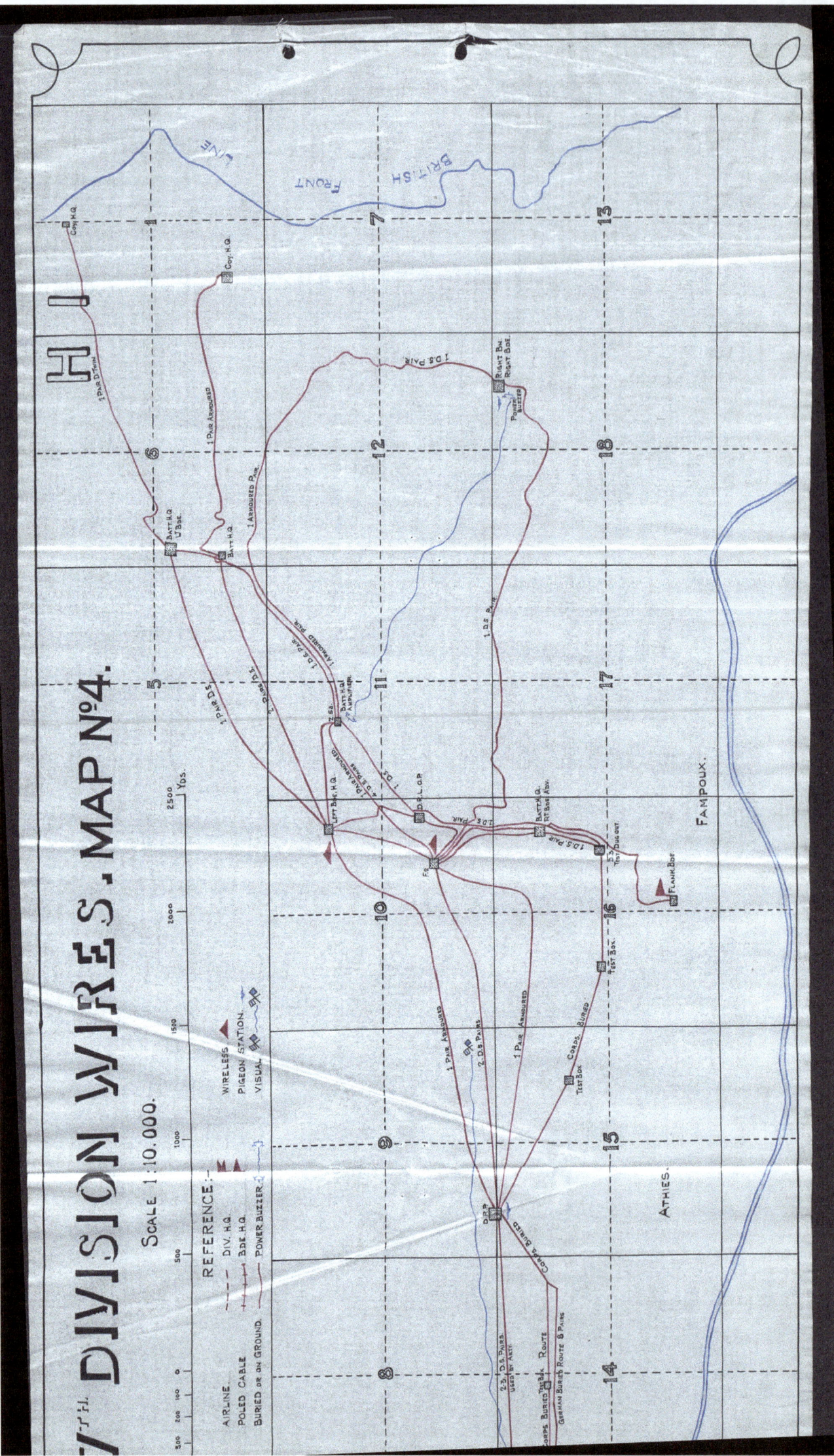

WAR DIARY
or
INTELLIGENCE SUMMARY
(Erase heading not required.)

Army Form C. 2118

Place	Date	Hour	Summary of Events and Information	Remarks and references to Appendices
OUTERSTEENE	JUNE 1st		Joined 71 Batns : Buss DADOS, locab from 47th D.S.C. General tidy up and cleaning up.	
	2nd		Operating and maintenance	
	3rd		Stated new issue + began issue of 65 mm to 71st Bus. Training in MOUUY on a week end, and Saturdays.	
	4th			
	5th		Operating and maintenance. Training in MOUUY entrenchments, musketry & under arms.	
	6th			
	17th		have Octavia am a honey to repairly opened what. Bm. Sowellon and Brigadier arrived. Bus Section Spam officers to Schwan and tried training. There is a nice expenditure and presence of fuel in out of the instructions of nothing of unhing and exercitation	
	18th		had an inward Several one passes spent — to have our means	
	19th			
	&		performance of Lichuy out the 71st bm from 3.4 am. Itis eft and brain as usual. At 11. 2.0° Bm Special School moved to SAVY on an	
	21st		2nd Lieut Fortwick Lewis Bn	

Army Form C. 2118

WAR DIARY
or
INTELLIGENCE SUMMARY
(Erase heading not required.)

Place	Date	Hour	Summary of Events and Information	Remarks and references to Appendices
ST. NICHOLAS	22nd	6.30	Took over from 3rd K. Bn. nr. ALTEN. Belgian Communication on left. Relieve Systhi - unchanged that town & ESPLANADE not in our perimeter. Quietly and unmolested. Left bank entrance - Trenches & houses in 2500 yards of town completely burnt out from Wilfrow had braved Monday by 5th. Bn. Men lived there two miles up to Broca in 7th. Guards search hns and entering not L. Bn's NCOs. Reconnaissance completed except: rumour from J.R.A. personnel and artillery sub-sector officers. Strength of Company Jan. 1st — 237 o.r., 8 officers. Feb 1st — 292 — 8 " Casualties during Month No. 243810 Sgt. Hawker T.B. [killed in action?] No. 317044 Sergt. Whitehead [?] No. 26574 Spr. Hollowed [?]	R.

Army Form C. 2118

WAR DIARY
or
INTELLIGENCE SUMMARY
(Erase heading not required.)

Instructions regarding War Diaries and Intelligence Summaries are contained in F. S. Regs., Part II. and the Staff Manual respectively. Title Pages will be prepared in manuscript.

Place	Date	Hour	Summary of Events and Information	Remarks and references to Appendices
ST NICHOLAS	JULY 1st		Gunnery and recreation. First Class sunk in Port Heer Images women spend	
	2nd		Sunday morning up here. Building Coy. camp and hour drive.	
			On arrival also went station on sea; Bell 1950 Squad (fire am Sargeants Smith	
	3rd		Kerr's (Japan Branch Branch) (somewhere here there from Lefts new-hours)	
	10th		Bell sergeant (This	
			but no above. Also Ben Helen orange tree at Sea 14th at hour antenna went.	
			Glorious Jim Finnian American Known that 16 mornings sun here on Telephone	
			Antennas, 6. 16. 716 A Garden wer named to Purchase of all Telephone	
			1906. (fifty attendee) together with famtain radio office, what coats out	
			be given Sunday form turned by the invasion. Their coats later will	
	16th		han in to the higher 9/16. 10/16.	
	4		General with in interference (however we to live of its form (on arson)	
	20th		Storm sweep from attender colors deep mean) . The inclosed the attck between	

Army Form C. 2118

WAR DIARY
or
INTELLIGENCE SUMMARY
(Erase heading not required.)

Instructions regarding War Diaries and Intelligence Summaries are contained in F. S. Regs., Part II. and the Staff Manual respectively. Title Pages will be prepared in manuscript.

Place	Date	Hour	Summary of Events and Information	Remarks and references to Appendices
St Nicholas	20th (in full)		Officer went out to Pont and of JAMPOUX and to Sir HARRY trench in E (Farriers' area) on tiff culin (on analysis) also 1 power trigger to the Hun on the trench line and contribution at 15 meridian stations. Knox suspending lines from 16 front line developed on an extension LM— Telephone POS filed down Public.	(A)
	21st		On about.	(A)
	22nd		Divl HQrs shelled by 9.45" from Lamp's near avenue and stables. Signal Camp Communications offices lost in transit. Civil inhabitants have arrived and may have surrendered.	
	23rd to 31st		Several work on above. All Bns have been connected to F-RPA Exchange to SBX. Calls by Telephone Tests carried at various enemy day arrange their for intention has approximately 25–28 enemies. GA exchange installed in Farmstead south to Pln. Bns. Heavy and Field Guns; a	(A)

WAR DIARY
or
INTELLIGENCE SUMMARY
(Erase heading not required.)

Army Form C. 2118

Place	Date	Hour	Summary of Events and Information	Remarks and references to Appendices
Spindale	23rd to 31st (incl.)		That Artillery Towers can be taken on by static heavy + field guns from stationed by any O.P. R.A. or D.F. Wireless equipmts have been informed and No. 21 Locator Subsections were transferred to 16 Coy on 24th. Case overture out transfer back to Div. Sigs. Staff officials can be trained. Surveillance communication was noted in round by 7th E.Y.R. Regt in 25th Hunter after sum. Although the Artillery has been experienced in training communication, transport and the Artillery's movements. For 15 out of the Telephone lines had been experienced in training communications have been achieved to have been continued has been achieved to 60% headway covered between fortress reports show a breach of instructions. Gen Staff. 24/7/17 8.1 from 24.4 OR's.	[signature] Cmdr 17th Mtd Sqn

SECRET and CONFIDENTIAL

WAR DIARY

OF

17th DIVNL SIGNAL COY R.E.

VOL 25 — JULY 1917

Army Form C. 2118

WAR DIARY
or
INTELLIGENCE SUMMARY
(Erase heading not required.)

Instructions regarding War Diaries and Intelligence Summaries are contained in F. S. Regs., Part II. and the Staff Manual respectively. Title Pages will be prepared in manuscript.

Place	Date	Hour	Summary of Events and Information	Remarks and references to Appendices
ST NICHOLAS	JULY 1st		Guarding and maintenance of lines. General clearing up area. Building Coy. camp and horse lines.	
	2nd		As above, also well station on his Battn. Signal offrs. in Farrell Smith his (Their head arrived) service in hinder from left main lower to Bde Signal Office.	
	3rd to 10th		Work as above. His Bde HQrs occupied at July 15th. all his mirthway will stationed from human Funer Kner that the miney can have on telephone communications. G. It 7th a meeting was assemed for guidance of all telephone has (copy attached) letter with lineaton with outhost redly could wt be given away toward heard by the enemy. Their cells taken wt has on the lights 8th 15th	
	10th to 20th		General work on maintenance. It came are to hand the fact the enemy steam anoptic attached also of a plan. This includes the outside telegraph.	

1875. Wt. W593/826 1,000,000 4/15 J.B.C. & A. A.D.S.S./Forms/C. 2118.

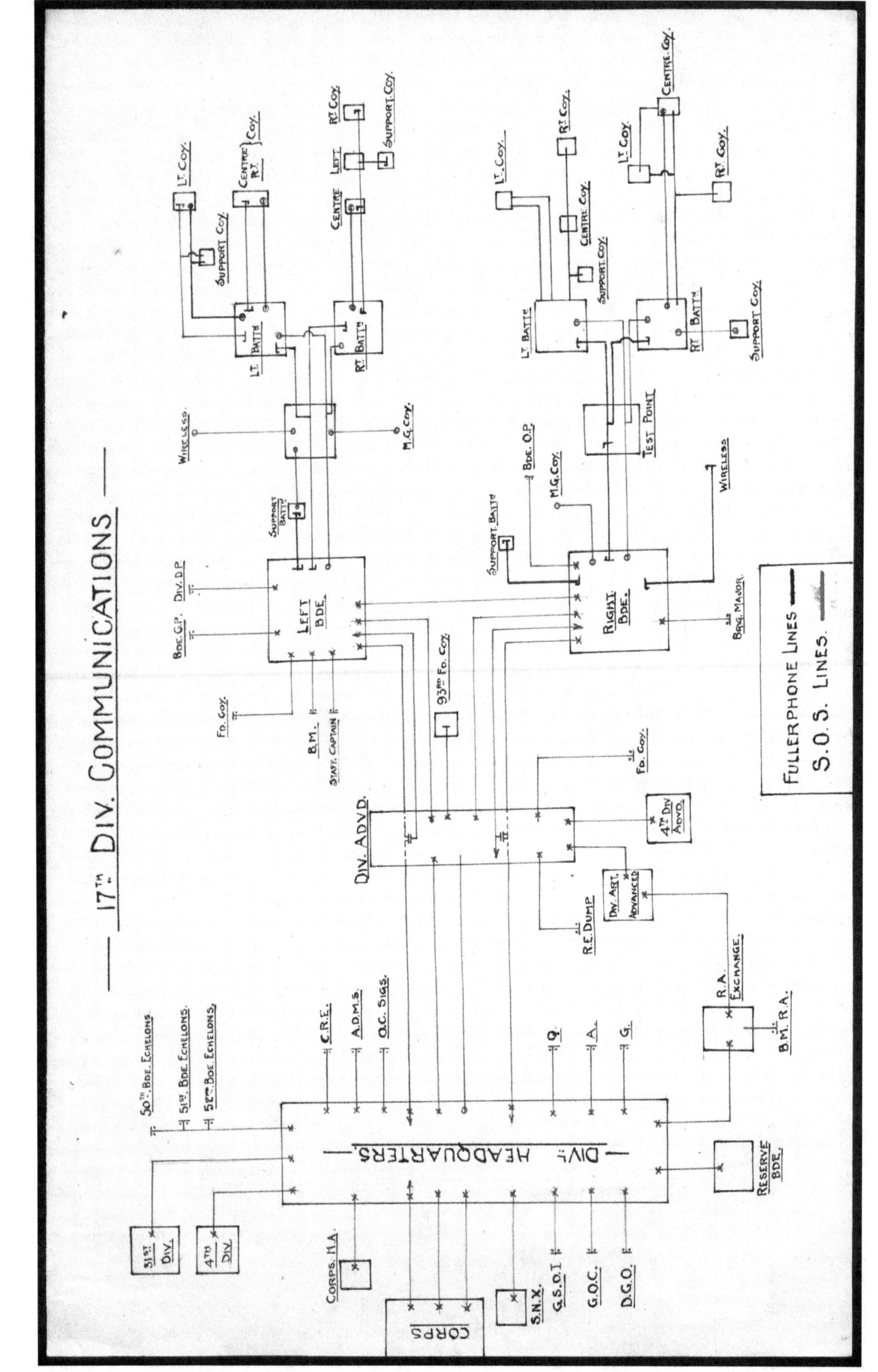

SIGNAL COMMUNICATIONS - 17TH DIVISION.

1. **TELEPHONES.** All Brigades, Battalions and in most cases Company H.Qrs. are connected up by telephone and telegraph lines. Ringing telephone exchanges exist at Divnl. H.Qrs., Advanced Divnl. Signals, in the RAILWAY CUTTING about H.14.A.1.7. and at each Bde H.Qrs. in the line, lines being arranged so that there is a direct telephone line to each Bde H.Qrs., a relay line through the Advanced exchange to each and lateral communication between them. This is accommodated by permanent lines as far as H.13.A. central, forward of which, communication to the Bde. is entirely buried. Telegraph working to the Bdes. is by superimposed sounders on the direct telephone lines, the earths of the sounders being brought back as far as the RAILWAY CUTTING for safety from enemy listening apparatus.

Lines forward of Bde. H.Qrs. as far as Battn. H.Qrs run along the Corps buried system according to the attached diagram. Forward of Battn. H.Qrs Coy's are connected up by trench lines also shown on the attached diagram. The principle has been to discourage as far as possible, conversation forward of Battn. H.Qrs. To this end Fullerphones are installed at every Coy. H.Qrs but Btns. have been allowed to retain their D.III telephones in case of emergency where conversation might be necessary.

2. **ALTERNATIVE MEANS OF COMMUNICATION.**

(a). **POWER BUZZERS AND WIRELESS.** A complete alternative chain of communication is provided by this means. In the Left Sector Power Buzzers are installed at I.1.B.1.7. and I.7.B.8.6. the forward Company H.Qrs. of the two Bns. in the line. These work to an Amplifier situated at the Advanced Bde. Signal Office in HURRUM trench about H.6.C.0.3. A trench wireless set is installed here working back to the Corps Controlling station in ARRAS.

In the Right Sector Power Buzzers are installed at each of the two Bn. H.Qrs at H.18.B.5.8. and H.24.B.8.8. working to an Amplifier at H.18.R.0.0. which in turn is also connected by wireless to the Corps Controlling set.

(b). **VISUAL.** Communication by this means is arranged for between Advanced Divnl. H.Qrs in the RAILWAY CUTTING and Bdes. in the GAVRELLE SWITCH. Forward of this it is practicable to nearly any H.Qrs but is only in use at present for S.O.S. (See para. 4. S.O.S.).

(c). **PIGEONS.** Pigeons are delivered by the Corps Signals on a scale of about 8 per day and are taken up to the trenches at night time so as to be available for use the following day.

(d). **DESPATCH RIDER AND RUNNERS.** This service is normal. D.R's doing three runs per day to the Bdes in the line. The runner service forward of this to Bns. is arranged so that there is a complete chain of communications through to the Bns. from the Divl. H.Qrs and vice versa.

In the left Sector the relay Runner post is established in the SUNKEN ROAD in H.11.A.

In the Right Sector the relay post is at the Wireless H.Qrs in H.18.A.0.0. to which runs are made through FAMPOUX by bicycle thence to Bns. H.Qrs by runner.

3. ARTILLERY COMMUNICATIONS.

The C.R.A., Bdes, Batteries and O.P's are connected everywhere by telephone and as far as possible use is made of the Corps Buried system. An Advanced Arty. Exchange if established in the RAILWAY CUTTING providing relay lines to the Bdes. Trunk lines to central battery positions also connect to this exchange and provide alternative means of communication from Bdes to Batteries. Arty. and Inf. Bdes are also connected up through this exchange.

For the purpose of Liaison with the Infantry, lines connect from battery to the Battn. H.Qrs in the line (see also para. 4.S.O.S.). An O.P. exchange is provided in the GAVRELLE SWITCH in LEMON TRENCH. This accommodates all batteries of the 79th Bde R.F.A. and is also arranged so that it may be used by Observers from the 78th Bde. Arrangements are being made to connect this up with the Divnl. O.P. in HUMBER TRENCH and the heavy Arty. O.P's in the GAVRELLE SWITCH so that fire can be brought on "fleeting targets" seen from time to time by the Divisional Observers.

A diagram of R.A. lines is attached including lines of Heavy T.M.B's.

4. S.O.S.

(a). Provisions for telephonic S.O.S. Calls are made by direct communication between one Company H.Qrs in each Bn. Sector and its covering Arty. Lines from batteries connect via the Corps Main underground route to Bn. H.Qrs where they are brought on to a buzzer exchange manned by an Artillery telephonist. The lines to the Coy H.Qrs is also connected to this exchange and is normally permanently plugged through to the battery line. For distinction all instruments in use on S.O.S. lines are painted red.

(b). VISUAL. S.O.S. calls are also arranged in both sectors. In the right Sector a Lucas Lamp is emplaced outside the Coy H.Qrs at I.14.C.5.8. working direct to the Bde H.Qrs in H.16.D. In the Left Sector this is arranged between Coy H.Qrs in I.1.A.6.4. and the Bde O.P. in LEMON TRENCH close to the Bde H.Qrs. Stations are manned by night.

5. PRECAUTIONS AGAINST ENEMY LISTENING SETS.

Detailed instructions have been issued for the prevention of the use of telephone by all concerned. In addition to this in order to prevent any leakage of information in regard to reliefs or of any relief actually having taken place, Position Calls have been allotted to all H.Qrs connected by telephone and all places in the line where units such as Trench Mortars, Wireless etc. are permanently in occupation.

A copy of these instructions is attached. These are hung up in all Signal Offices together with the large warning notice recently received from the Army.

All message work forward of Bde. H.Qrs is by Fullerphone. All sounder earths moved to 6000 yards behind our front line.

Major R.E.,
Commanding 17th Signal Company, R.E.

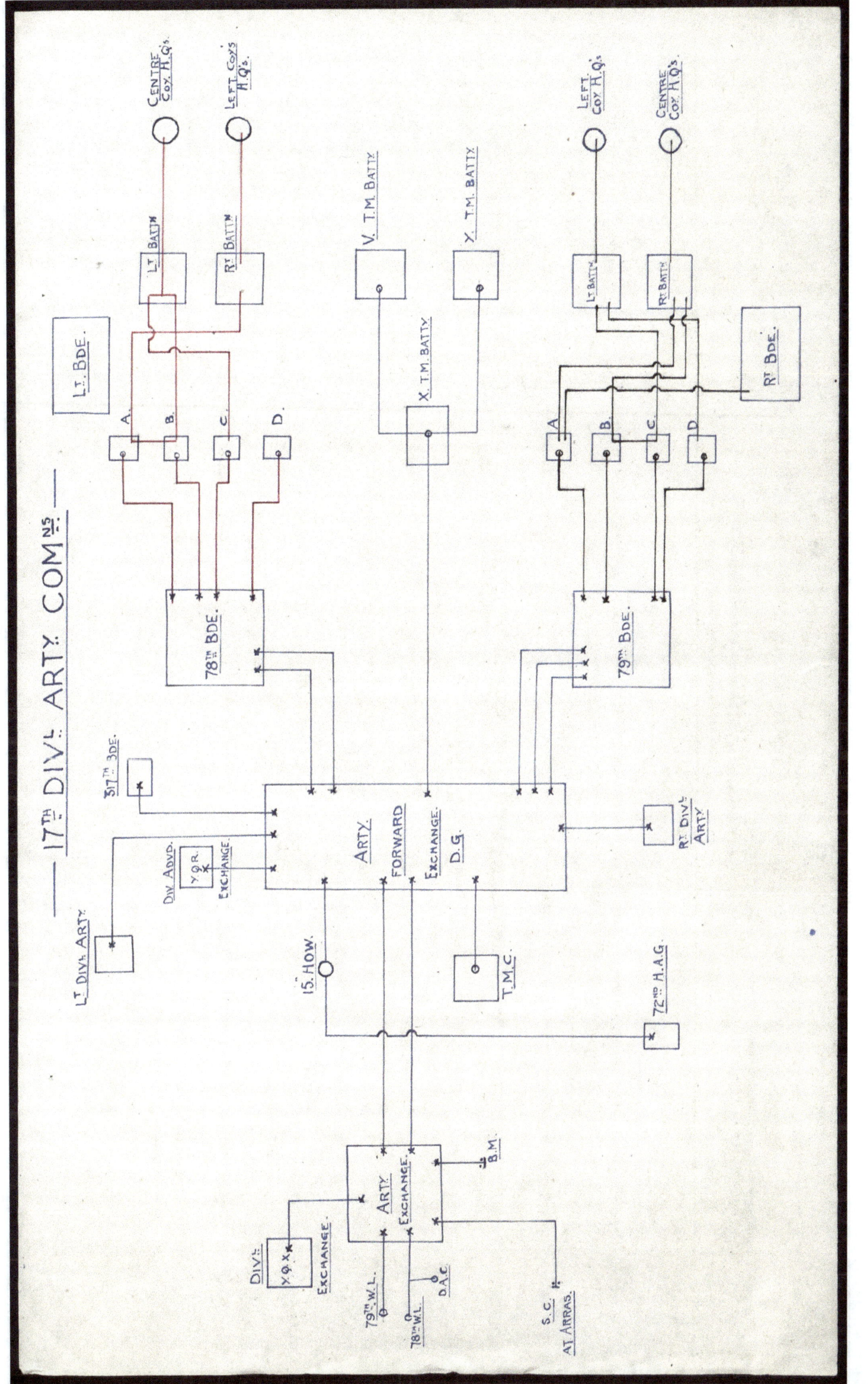

WAR DIARY
or
INTELLIGENCE SUMMARY

(Erase heading not required.)

Army Form C. 2118

Instructions regarding War Diaries and Intelligence Summaries are contained in F.S. Regs., Part II. and the Staff Manual respectively. Title Pages will be prepared in manuscript.

Place	Date	Hour	Summary of Events and Information	Remarks and references to Appendices
St Nicholas	10th-20th (contd)		of wires cut in front and of FAMPOUX and in HURRUM tunnel in the Fosse switch in left sector (see diagram) Also of power buzzers in our line in the front line and amplifiers at 1st wireless stations. Wires signalling back from the front line averaged an alteration 24 hrs. Telephone & SS Stat cams laid.	(1) (2)
	21st		As above	
	22nd		Divl HQrs Shelled by 9.1245 gun. Camp's huvve away and scattered. Some Camp Coun flagged attempture not so unusual. Civilian inhabitants have arrived and play has commenced.	
	23rd to 31st		General work as above. All Bns have been connected to 1st RPH Brickkiln to S.O.S. cable by telephone. Test's carried out every day. Average time for activation has approximately 25-28 seconds. S.R. exchange installed in Favielle switch for Divn, Bdes, Heavy and Field Guns.	(3)

1875 Wt. W593/826 1,000,000 4/15 J.B.C. & A. A.D.S.S./Forms/C. 2118.

CIRCUIT DIAGRAM.
Lines Left Brigade Sector
July 13th 1917.

7.ZEA. — SECRET —

WAR DIARY
or
INTELLIGENCE SUMMARY
(Erase heading not required.)

Army Form C. 2118

Place	Date	Hour	Summary of Events and Information	Remarks and references to Appendices
St Nicholas	23rd to 31st (cont.)		1st Heavy Section- Can be taken on by exist. Horn or field guns from Observatin by any O.P. RA or Inf. Wireless sub sections have been informed. No 21 Wireless Sub Section were transferred to 1st Corps on 24th. One wireless set brought back 1-Din Signals 215. Station can be trained on Stationary Communication was used in circuit by 71st E Yorks R.Sgt. on 28th+29th+ information machine. Dueffler before 1st Army was med. 12 to 25 minutes after zero. Although 1st Shelling has been measured during the month very little traffic has been experienced in hostile communications. Some have had little work and 1st instruction's issued to 1st hor 9 1st Telephone has been ordered to visit machined power. Following report shew 1s broadcast of instructions. Lm. Stanwick 31/7/17. 8 Afrom 246ORS.	

Emery A
LS/Hq..............

Cmdg 17 Army Signal Coy RE

INSTRUCTIONS REGARDING COMMUNICATION BY BUZZER
AND TELEPHONE IN THE DANGER ZONE.

1. ALL INSTRUMENTS WITHIN 3,000 YARDS OF THE FRONT LINE ARE IN THE DANGER ZONE. ANY INSTRUMENT OTHER THAN THE ABOVE, WHEN IN DIRECT COMMUNICATION WITH AN INSTRUMENT IN THE DANGER ZONE, MUST BE REGARDED AS COMING, FOR THE TIME BEING, WITHIN THIS ZONE AS FAR AS THE PRECAUTIONS TO BE TAKEN ARE CONCERNED.

2. All Artillery Units will conform to this order, F.O.O's. being responsible that only those messages necessary for registration and observation are transmitted from O.P's.

3. Special precautions will be taken to avoid any message or conversation passing over the wires, which may give the enemy any clue as to future operations.

    All telephone conversations which may be of the slightest use to the enemy will be in code.

    Communications which are not urgent will be sent by hand. Operation Orders should always be sent by hand if time permits.

    Private conversations are forbidden. It is mainly through such conversations that valuable information reaches the enemy.

    Conversations on the telephone other than those necessary for the technical working of the telephone system will be restricted to officers and to N.C.O's. to whom, for the time being, permission to use the telephone has been given.

    All messages will be signed by an Officer, who will be personally responsible for their contents. Names of Units are not to be mentioned in telephone conversations or messages.

    "Position Calls" should be used in the Address 'To' and 'From' in messages and "Code names" should be used in the text of messages and in telephone conversations. When the "Position Call" is not known to the Station sending a message "Code names" may be used in the addresses.

4. "Position Calls" for all H.Qs. and posts connected by telephone are issued herewith.

5. Signal Offices in direct communication with other Offices in the Danger Zone will not accept for transmission into the Danger Zone, any messages which are not in Code.

6. Any officer, N.C.O. or man who engages in conversation by means of the telephone or buzzer and refers to matters which, if overheard by the enemy, would be to the latters advantage, will be tried by COURT MARTIAL. Severe disciplinary action will be taken with any officer or man discovered by the Amplifier to have infringed these regulations.

P.T.O.

7. When necessary, for tactical reasons, to use the telephone, Code names must be employed and tables of Code Names will be hung up over every telephone.

8. Fullerphones will invariably be used for message work forward of Bde. H.Qs.

9. All telephone lines must be truly metallic. All lines including 'S.O.S.' Lines will be tested every quarter of an hour when not in use.

10. A copy of these instructions will be hung up at every telephone in the Divisional Area.

The following notes are given to overcome the misunderstanding as to what messages are or are not permitted on wires in the danger zone :-

1. PERMITTED over the wire or by any other available means, e.g., Power Buzzer, Visual or Wireless.

    (a) S.O.S.
    (b) Gas.
    (c) Artillery Control messages.
    (d) Calls to R.A. for retaliation.
    (e) Zeppelin.
    (f) Messages in 'B.A.B.' Trench Code.

2. NOT PERMITTED on the wires or by visual, or by Power Buzzer.

    (a) Conversations between Operators (except as regards the working of the line).
    (b) Returns of any sort, especially trench strength, casualties, and ammunition returns.
    (c) Situation and wind reports (except in 'B.A.B.' Code.)
    (d) Messages regarding rations, working parties, courses or leave.
    (e) Any private conversation or messages.
    (f) Any mention of reliefs or projected operations.

Such messages may give away information to the enemy and should be sent by runner.

Messages under sub-heads (b), (c) and (d), may be sent by Fullerphone

It is to the advantage of everyone to keep the Fullerphone in working order and to see that it is used as it saves runners.

3. Short messages should be sent by Wireless where it is installed as this gives practice to the Operators and all messages are coded and decoded by them.

POSITION CALLS.

1. Attached is a complete list of Position Calls for all Headquarters, connected by telephone within the Danger Zone.

2. A small board with the Position Calls marked on it will be placed over the telephone in each Headquarters.

3. Calls will be brought into use from midnight 10th. July.

4. Instructions regarding the use of POSITION CALLS are contained in New Instructions regarding Communication (Para.4) issued herewith.

5. Position Calls are allotted to a PLACE and not to a Unit. When therefore, a Unit changes Headquarters, it will adopt the Position Call allotted to its new position. If one does not exist application to Signals should be made.

6. In case of an advance the usual calls will be reverted to.

POSITION CALLS.

UNIT.	POSITION CALL	MAP LOCATION.
Divisional O.P.	P.49	H.11.c.0.7.

ARTILLERY.

UNIT.	POSITION CALL	MAP LOCATION.
R.A. Headquarters.	DA	
R.A. Advanced Exchange.	DG	
78th. Brigade R.F.A.	P.45	H.7.a.7.8.
'A' Battery.	P.20	H.9.c.8.7.
'B' "	P.21	H.9.b.1.2.
'C' "	P.22	H.9.b.2.4.
'D' "	P.23	H.9.c.4.9.
'D' " Detached Gun.	L.20	
O.P's.		
'A' Battery.	P.29	H.10.d.85.40.
'B' "	L.21.	H.16.b.7.9.
('C' "	P.30	H.16.b.90.75
('C' "	L.22	H.10.a.85.80.
'D' "	L.23.	H.16.b.75.90.
79th. Brigade R.F.A.	P.46	H.8.a.8.4.
'A' Battery.	P.25.	H.10.c.5.7.
'B' "	P.26	H.10.a.3.0.
'C' "	P.27	H.10.a.3.1.
'D' "	P.28.	H.10.c.4.4.
O.P's.		
'A' "	P.31.	H.11.c.15.90
'B' "	P.32.	H.10.d.9.7.
'C' "	P.33.	H.10.b.10.75.
'D' "	P.34	H.10.d.75.30.
Trench Mortars.		
Headquarters.	L.24.	H.13.a.5.0.
'Y' Battery.	G.20.	I.1.b.1.7.
'V' "	G.24.	I.1.b.6.2.
'X' "	G.27.	I.1.a.5.3.
O.P's.	P.47.	I.7.a.5.9.
R.A. Wagon lines call for wagon lines, P.48.		I.7.a.5.6.

ARTILLERY WAGON LINES.

78th. Brigade.

'A' Battery.	Lines P.20	G.3.c.2.5.
'B' "	" P.21.	G.3.c.2.4.
'C' "	" P.22	G.2.d.8.8.
'D' "	" P.23	G.2.b.5.5.

79th. Brigade.

'A' Battery.	" P.25.	L.6.c.4.1.
'B' "	" P.26	L.6.c.5.3.
'C' "	" P.27	L.6.c.2.3.
'D' "	" P.28	L.6.c.8.1.

RIGHT BRIGADE.

Brigade Headquarters.	L.25.	H.16.d.4.5.
Brigade O.P.	L.26.	H.16.b.9.9.
Report Centre for Right Sub-Sector.	L.27	H.18.d.1.2.
Brigade Report Left Sub-Sector.	L.37	H.18.a.1.2.
Wireless	L.38	H.18.a.1.2.
Amplifier.	L.36	H.18.a.1.2.
Right Battalion H.Qs.	L.28	H.24.b.8.9.
Right Company.	L.30	I.14.c.1.3
Centre Company.	L.32	I.14.c.1.7.
Left Company.	L.34	I.14.c.1.9.
Reserve Company.	L.35,	H.18.d.7.1.
Left Battalion Headquarters.	P.35	H.18.b.5.8.
Right Company.	L.29	I.14.a.2.6.
Centre Company	L.33	I.13.d.4.8.
Left Company	P.36	I.7.d.6.4.
Reserve Company.	L.31.	I.13.a.2.2.
Machine Gun Company.	P.37.	H.17.c.2.6.
Support Battalion.	P.38	H.11.a.6.2.
Reserve Battalion.	P.39	H.7.d.8.5.
Company Headquarters) Reserve Battalion.)	L.35	H.16.d.7.7.

LEFT BRIGADE.

Brigade Headquarters.	L.39	H.14.a.0.9.
Brigade O.P.	P.38	H.11.c.1.8.
Brigade Forward Signal Station	G.28	H.5.d.95.20.
Brigade Runner Post.	P.40	H.11.a.6.5.
Wireless.	G.30	H.6.c.2.4.
Amplifier.	P.42.	H.12.b.2.9.
Right Battalion.	P.44.	H.12.b.2.9.
Right Coy.	G.32	I.7.b.8.5.
Centre Company)	G.34	I.7.b.4.3.
Left Company.)		
Reserve Company.	G.36.	I.7.b.1.4.
Left Battalion.	G.37.	H.6.c.2.5.
Right Company.	G.35	I.1.b.1.8.
Centre Company.	G.33	I.1.c.5.5.
Left Company	G.31.	I.1.c.5.5.
Support Company.	G.29	I.1.a.5.4.
Support Battalion.	P.43.	H.11.b.6.8.
Reserve Battalion.	L.40.	G.18.a.9.8.
Machine Gun Company.	P.41.	H.11.b.8.9.
78th. Fld.Co.R.E.	P.49	H.10.b.8.6.

Brigade 'B' Echelons will be addressed Rear (Position Call of Brigade) e.g., Rear L.39 = Left Brigade 'B' Echelon.

POWER BUZZERS.

Right Sector.	Jack - Right.	
	Jill - Left.	
Left Sector.	Darby - Right	
	Joan - Left.	

AMPLIFIERS.
    Big Willie - Right.
    Little Willie - Left.

SCREENING BUZZERS.   Right Sector.   Harry - Right.
    Harriet - Left.
    Left Sector.   Tom - Right
    Dick - Left.

Army Form C. 2118

WAR DIARY
or
INTELLIGENCE SUMMARY

(Erase heading not required.)

Instructions regarding War Diaries and Intelligence Summaries are contained in F. S. Regs., Part II. and the Staff Manual respectively. Title Pages will be prepared in manuscript.

Place	Date	Hour	Summary of Events and Information	Remarks and references to Appendices

1875 Wt. W593/826 1,000,000 4/15 J.B.C. & A. A.D.S.S./Forms/C. 2118.

Army. Form C. 2118

WAR DIARY
or
INTELLIGENCE SUMMARY

(Erase heading not required.)

Instructions regarding War Diaries and Intelligence Summaries are contained in F.S. Regs., Part II. and the Staff Manual respectively. Title Pages will be prepared in manuscript.

Place	Date	Hour	Summary of Events and Information	Remarks and references to Appendices
ST NICHOLAS				
	24th		[illegible handwritten entry]	[illegible]
	25th		[illegible handwritten entry]	[illegible]
	26th		[illegible handwritten entry]	[illegible]
	3rd		[illegible handwritten entry]	[illegible]

1875 Wt. W593/826 1,000,000 4/15 J.B.C. & A. A.D.S.S./Forms/C. 2118.

Vol 26

SECRET and CONFIDENTIAL

WAR DIARY

17TH DIV'N'L SIGNAL COY

VOL. 26.

AUGUST 1917.

Army Form C. 2118.

WAR DIARY
or
INTELLIGENCE SUMMARY.
(Erase heading not required.)

SECRET and CONFIDENTIAL

WAR DIARY

17TH DIVNL SIGNAL COY

AUGUST 1917

VOL 26

WAR DIARY
or
INTELLIGENCE SUMMARY
(Erase heading not required.)

Army Form C. 2118

Place	Date	Hour	Summary of Events and Information	Remarks and references to Appendices
St. Michael	August 1917		Runner Bell was established in ROCHLIN COURT VALLEY. His lines laid & connected.	[initials]
	9th		Hd. qrs. and lines put in order.	[initials]
			Huts and earth latrines for the bn. erected by Mr. Buckton	
	9th to 10th		General work. Trenching and maintenance. Huts in stables and wash camps. Also on road to Divl H.Qrs. Improvements made in arrangement by reinforcing wires with multicore cables. Buried line to Bde HQrs cut by infantry working party in earth home. Then replaced by Thair carried on - the 10th.	[initials]
	11th to 15th		Work on about salvaged 35 miles of cable. General work in testing up to 11-Toren. Hn lines laid from Mr Bees HQrs to its left Bn. Ammunn and D5 limbers down Central Tunnel (see hrs circuit diagram) Test boards put in in all Bn Signal Offices. Several work in improving communication in forward areas.	[initials]
	16th		Work as usual. Kite Signal School closed for a few weeks. 8 others forwarded 1st Class Standard	[initials]

Army Form C. 2118

WAR DIARY or INTELLIGENCE SUMMARY

(Erase heading not required.)

Instructions regarding War Diaries and Intelligence Summaries are contained in F. S. Regs., Part II. and the Staff Manual respectively. Title Pages will be prepared in manuscript.

Place	Date	Hour	Summary of Events and Information	Remarks and references to Appendices
St NICHOLAS	AUG 17th		Operating and maintenance. General work in 14th Corps and improving lines.	
	18th		Test stations in railway cutting improved. Office moving into hut and new comfortable position. Work on 5no portable service at Bois 15bis Signal Office. RE 75th Office reinstated and new restless lamps given. All 14th Corps line has been routed to improve light.	
	20th		Operating and maintenance.	
	21st		" "	
	22nd		" " Radio put on R&B lines and dancing and showing not so as to have a good lines between Pozieres Sentch.	
	23rd		Work as above. Lyt. Campbell employed on survey by lightning	

Army Form C. 2118

WAR DIARY
or
INTELLIGENCE SUMMARY
(Erase heading not required.)

Place	Date	Hour	Summary of Events and Information	Remarks and references to Appendices
ST NICHOLAS	AUG.			
	24th		Bns held ground Tk Bns of right Bde (see diagram).	
	25th		Took a hus an abort. Saltal hors shellis via stemdeing's	
			General work digging cable trench, making roads & Pos/Hqrs and improving lines.	
	26th		Coys of ration Khovers Bns Signal Section and Bn Scouts on Sub-relaying ideas of communication. Power Buzzer an at	
	3rd		Aurflyers and bunker. 500 yards of cable hid at own dump and duck boards Wicker Station constructed at Bn. H.Qrs. Camp evacuated.	

Coy Strength 31/8/17 8 Officers 294 ORs.

[Signatures]
Cmdg 17th Kings (Liverpool) Regt

Vol 27

SECRET and CONFIDENTIAL

WAR DIARY

of

17th Divn'l Signal Coy. R.E.

VOL 27

SEPTEMBER 1917

Army Form C. 2118.

WAR DIARY
or
INTELLIGENCE SUMMARY.
(Erase heading not required)

Instructions regarding War Diaries and Intelligence Summaries are contained in F.S. Regs., Part II. and the Staff Manual respectively. Title pages will be prepared in manuscript.

Place	Date	Hour	Summary of Events and Information	Remarks and references to Appendices
ST NICHOLAS	SEPTEMBER 1st		Checking and maintenance routine in/improvement in the weather.	
	F. &		Firing much better. Class F. work in digging out and boarding C.H.A. twist forward of Tank Dump (M11c Central) as attached diagram. This work was completed on the 18th 1000 yards long and completely dug bank was by Signal personnel. Every Knott ahead of pioneer Bn. at work Materially assisted in General work in forming a work line.	
			A new scheme of lighting H. Bvd Cinema was started every trolie line of the river Scarpe at St-Nicholas Ford and stores the necessary repair of sheeves and chuggers & the river in an h. Staff Kroab G. of Wales and Sgt Sufferend through	75.

(A5093) Wt. W12859/M1293 75,000. 4/17. D. D. & L., Ltd. Forms/C.2118/14.

Place	Date	Hour	Summary of Events and Information	Remarks and references to Appendices
ST NICHOLAS	SEPT 11th & 12th (continued)		At Tambrie the bn marched 25.P and had to dump a Lewis Gun & Cushing Mtl. Going & damage by enemy shellfire LH. Since it was in reply had received its orifard to 30 amps and 110 V. (about 4 P.) After repairing stores and a joint to orifard was reduced to about 90 amps (about 10 P.) This gave sufficient current for the Cinema. The lamps conn- -ected being carbons by a 200 W. Coffer rod a distance of about 450 yards. The Cine being used has given an excellent performance to which cost of this Dott. 12th has also landed most truck of enemy lines. Sha- -lines land 108. 40m and onward from the K. HQ in a out party in front our lines KS through to 12 hour off. Gas aaft. heavy enemy barrage to report is sent forced by infantry -	

WAR DIARY
or
INTELLIGENCE SUMMARY.

Army Form C. 2118.

Place	Date	Hour	Summary of Events and Information	Remarks and references to Appendices
ST NICHOLAS Column "a"	SEPT 9th		and signal scheme before entrained to Salisbury Plain. Determined this left loses naval Corps test time shown orphaia and sand	ab
	10th & 12th		Latrine and communication, Rover Bosen Amplifier and anchor grew. Read Rev. to Turner Key Camie h. nervise same. Starter Sept 3 to 9th 2nd Corps 10th to 15th 3rd Corps 17th to 23rd	
			There were noted attacks by Bn. Signallers on a forward way rapid instruction. Corps under officer change of Lumber other and losses as heard of training and ambrance, but a Staff and how been used. Shelter on standing was nearly complete	v b
	16th		Rare or every hinde superior a low Line and south railway just north of ROEUX. Machine Buns and report known orphaia. Signal advancement completely successful	ab

WAR DIARY / INTELLIGENCE SUMMARY

Army Form C. 2118.

Place	Date	Hour	Summary of Events and Information	Remarks and references to Appendices
ST. NICHOLAS	SEPT 16th (cont)		Telephone communication still found to be not suitable upon which they passed by Grid for satisfactory. Telephones are taken on by a raiding party and the communication back was picked up by Amplifier at Bn. HQrs and S.W. wire was over without any delay. Diagram of arrangement to send attached.	A
	16th & 25th		Officers and Men in trained General work on Camps. Have twice and French lines. Two Lewis found t. 17th Bn Team. Preparations to have an Academy over to Bn. B. Cont. in repair of Issued. Wh. Bn. HQrs. Moved to La CAUROY in 25th Telephone Lines picked up & mothing & Boers at AMBRINES, LUCHEUX and IVERGNY.	B
LA CAUROY	26th & 30th		Several work Standing and hour to Bees & Foor Boys etc. of 2 days duration for Bn. Signallers. Cleaning up and nothing	B

Army Form C. 2118.

WAR DIARY
or
INTELLIGENCE SUMMARY.
(Erase heading not required.)

Place	Date	Hour	Summary of Events and Information	Remarks and references to Appendices
LA CAUROY	SEPT 16th - 30th (Cont)		Preparations & have NOTK woxd hens From Follhi Towing in Pas Kalk drill and given as much time off as possible to football etc. Strength of Coy. Sept 30th. 8 officers 293 ORs ——— 301	B/1

16/17
[signature]
Major R.
CmdG. 19th Bn 1 Lguards Coy Rp

Army Form C. 2118.

WAR DIARY

or

~~INTELLIGENCE SUMMARY~~

(*Erase heading not required.*)

— SECRET and CONFIDENTIAL —

WAR DIARY

OF

17TH DIVN'L SIGNAL COY. R.E.

VOL 27 SEPTEMBER 1917

Army Form C. 2118.

WAR DIARY
INTELLIGENCE SUMMARY
(Erase heading not required.)

Place	Date	Hour	Summary of Events and Information	Remarks and references to Appendices
ST NICHOLAS	SEPTEMBER 1st		Shooting and harrassing fire. Much improvement in the trenches. Enemy much below strength. Coy took a digging out and duck boarding Carlsbad trench forward of Tank Dump (H.11.a.Central) see attached diagram. This took two companies on the 18th. 1000 yards long and completely dug boards by Signal personal. Coy took 60 in general work in forming a water line.	
	2nd		A few returns to boarding of Dart cinema run statted issuing water from F.T.B river scarpe at St-Nicholas lock and sluices. This incorporated system of sluices and supplying the men an even to supply N_tn Co of water, and yet sufficient though	BB 1

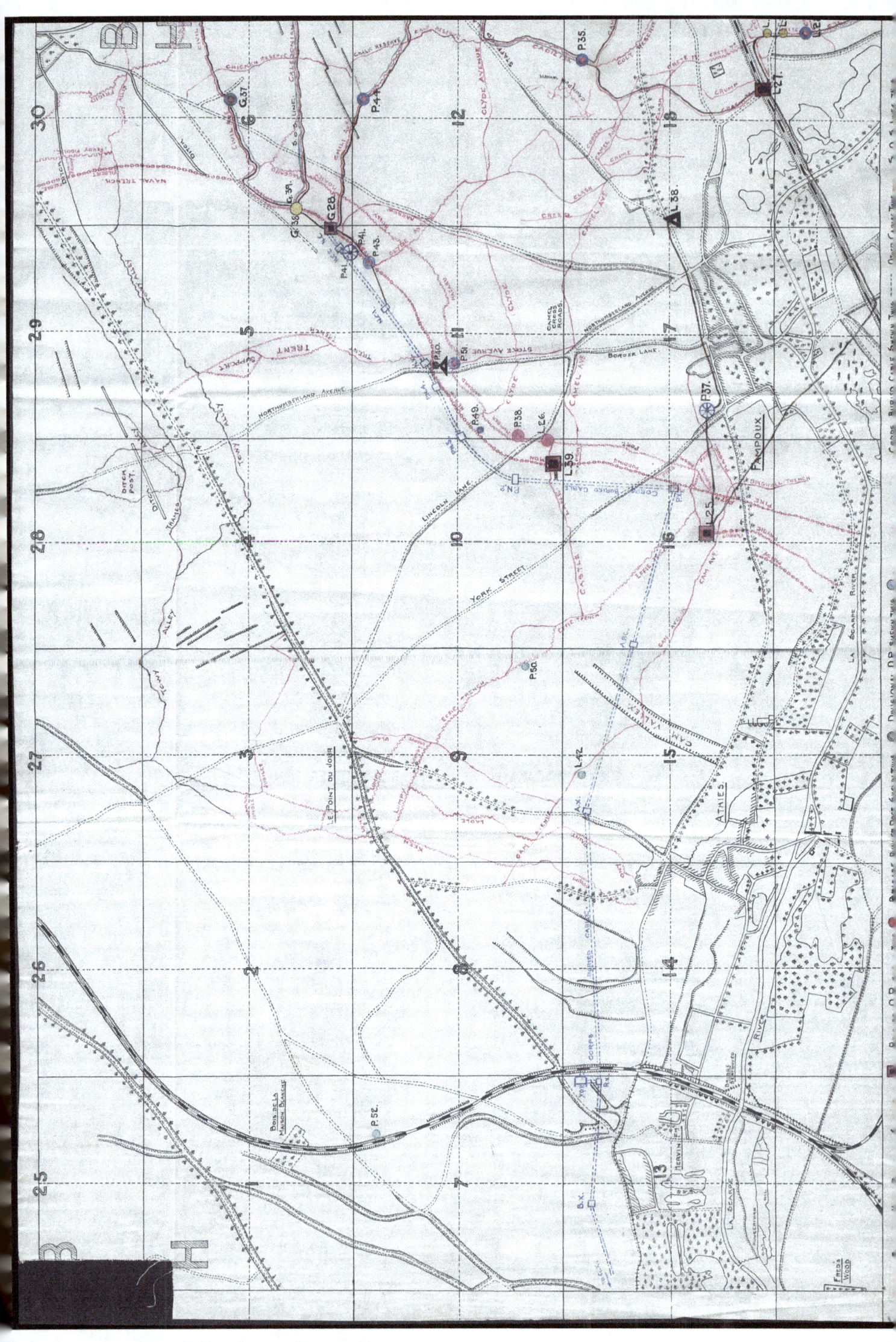

WAR DIARY or INTELLIGENCE SUMMARY

(Erase heading not required.)

Army Form C. 2118.

Place	Date	Hour	Summary of Events and Information	Remarks and references to Appendices
ST NICHOLAS	SEPT 14th 8th W.O. (continued)		To Turbine. This is nominally 25 P. and had to annoy a hostile crushing mill. Being harass by enemy shellfire since it has in role been received its ordent 1st 30 rnds and 110 Y. (about 4 P.) After reporting silence and gas the ordent was increased to abt. 90 rnds. (about 12 P.) This gave sufficient covert for the ememia the Lamps connected being covered by a 200 lbs Gelignite charge a distance of about 250 yards. The Lead being great, has given an excellent opfor limity for attack into rest of this dist. —	
	2nd		12th han dust bin located bst Truck & Everythines E-7a. Twies Lanot. 1st Bn. Athin and forward from Kla F. 40 was dem party in front. Twu lines kpt through to 1½ hrs ago. Bn Ariflie heavy enemy barrage. No reports sent forch by Infantry F.R.	

Army Form C. 2118.

WAR DIARY
or
INTELLIGENCE SUMMARY.
(Erase heading not required.)

Instructions regarding War Diaries and Intelligence Summaries are contained in F. S. Regs., Part II. and the Staff Manual respectively. Title pages will be prepared in manuscript.

Place	Date	Hour	Summary of Events and Information	Remarks and references to Appendices
ST. NICHOLAS Calais.	SEPT 9th		and Signal Palace for the ordinance & Salvage etc. Returning ship high seas wind rough hull here thrown up into the sand	
"	10th		Labour and Communication, River Royal Amphion and Another gone Fred Bell & Twin Hay Danie & Monmore.	
"	13th		Tactics Sept 3rd & 9th 2nd Armt. 1st 6, 10th 3rd Armt 17th 23rd. Men were well attacked by Fr. Squadron on a fwodes way rapid instruction. Ships under officer actions & linker others were taken as usual. Infantry and Cavalry and a but a Rifles and tank lind road. Station on standship was heavy conflict.	
	15th		Rose on enemy who the infantry a lost line and sent Stating part took of FORM Machine Surf and Signal known Collins. Great advance went completely successful	

WAR DIARY

Army Form C. 2118.

Place	Date	Hour	Summary of Events and Information	Remarks and references to Appendices
ST. NICHOLAS.	SEPT 15th (Cont.)		Telephone wire held — but not where upon attack. Try passed by trust & for satisfactory Telephone not taken on by A raising party and the observation that one side of by Amplifier at Bn. HQ. & A.D.S. & was not going without any delay. Diagram of arrangement to Brig. attacked.	A
	16th		Standing and to our France. General work on Camp and trees and Forward lines.	
	25th.		New here long F. 1st Div. Train. Preparation to test and handing over to Corp. Div. with with Brd HQrs. More to La CAUROY in Z.S.F. Telephone first packed up & noting & Acces at AMBRINES, LUCHEUX and IVERGNY.	B
LA CAUROY.	26th to 30th.		General work generally and familiasis to Poor from start of 2 days. duration to Bn. Squadron. Cleaning up and making	C

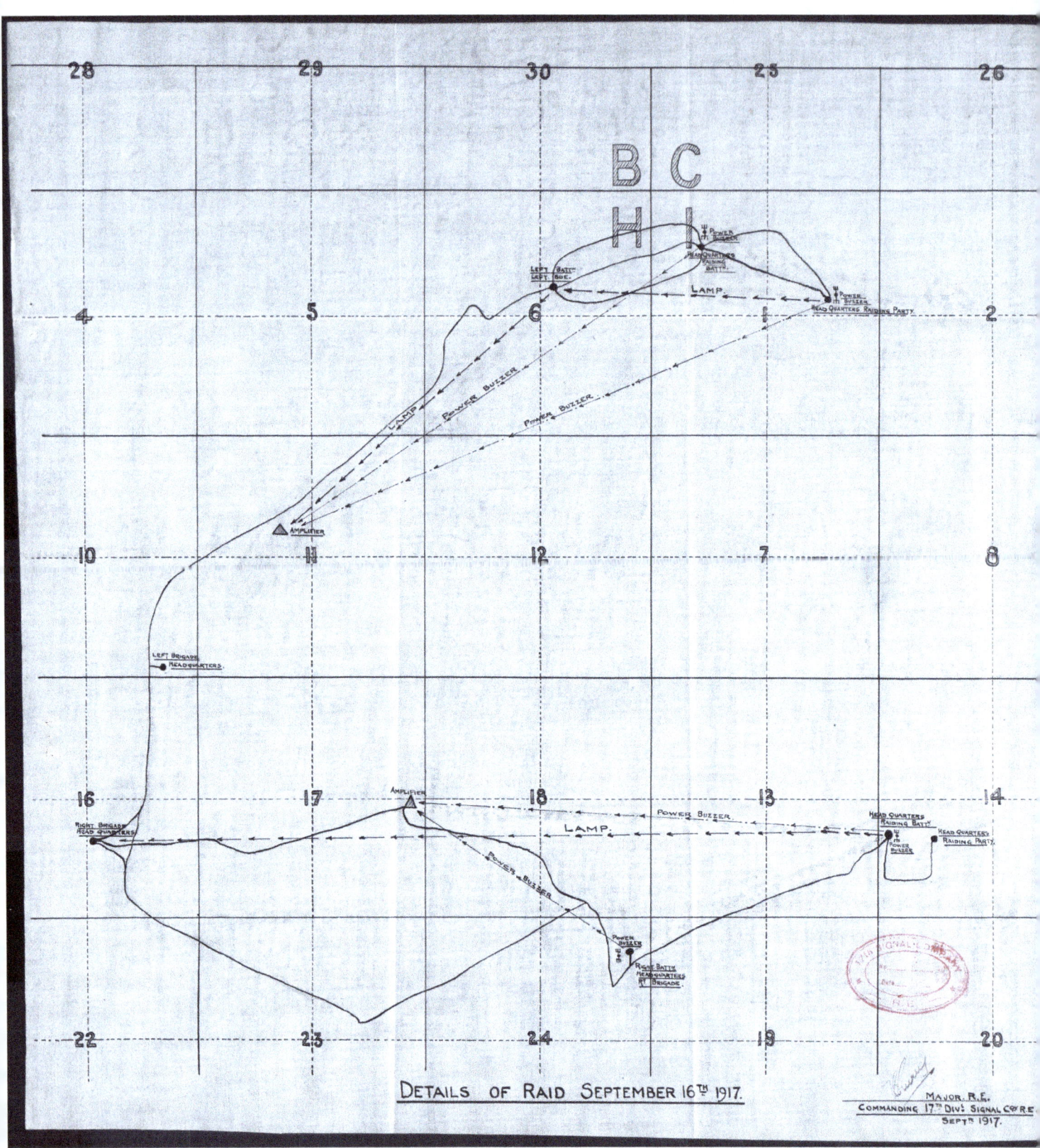

DETAILS OF RAID SEPTEMBER 16TH 1917.

Major. R.E.
Commanding 17th Divl Signal Co RE
Septr 1917.

Army Form C. 2118.

WAR DIARY

(Erase heading not required.)

Place	Date	Hour	Summary of Events and Information	Remarks and references to Appendices
CAUROY	SEPT 26th		preparations to move north wood. hive parts further training in Gas work drill and sports as much time as possible for football etc.	B/1
	30th (cont)		Strength of Coy Offrs 8 ORs 298 Total 306	

16/17

[signatures]
O.C. 19th Bn 1 Signals Coy R.E.

Army Form C. 2118.

WAR DIARY
of
INTELLIGENCE SUMMARY
(Erase heading not required.)

Instructions regarding War Diaries and Intelligence Summaries are contained in F. S. Regs., Part II. and the Staff Manual respectively. Title pages will be prepared in manuscript.

W/W Del

Place	Date	Hour	Summary of Events and Information	Remarks and references to Appendices
Le CAUROY	0st 1st 2 3rd		Gunnery and Reconnaissance from Brigade Squadrons of 53rd Bde Reserve & from Brigade working. Preparations of moving into area of Corps and collecting Reserve Yeres. Advance party with Sqnd Officer Adm and riding left for PROVEN on the 3rd	1st
PROVEN	4th 5th to 10th		Closed Head Quarters at La CAUROY and found at Proven at 10am. Unit moved by train from MONDICOURT to PROVEN. Cleaning and improving camps in PROVEN Area. Unit and all camps in a very sticky state owing to very bad weather and great danger from light winds and bombing. Several Inspections. Friday 6th. K-Law. Overhauling Telephones and wireless stored Ensures to be looked closely at.	1st
ELVERDINGHE	11th		Moved into the Forest Funny HOULTHOUST FOREST, with Batt H.Q. at Elverdinghe. One Bat to the line at AU BONGITE relieved 29th Bn. and made a very comfortable relief. Systm learnt as 2nd Army noted	

Army Form C. 2118.

WAR DIARY
or
INTELLIGENCE SUMMARY.

(Erase heading not required.)

Instructions regarding War Diaries and Intelligence Summaries are contained in F. S. Regs. Part II. and the Staff Manual respectively. Title pages will be prepared in manuscript.

Place	Date	Hour	Summary of Events and Information	Remarks and references to Appendices
ELVERDINGHE	OCT 12th		Wind on front still from E between Cruery and Aubers St au hop. This very bad Kept the. The ground to south bogged and it is therefore impossible. Heavy. Carry & evacuate Tropp and bury still for its WP for the 3 Bdes which continued attacking throughout. a & Coupel instatation ment to Bdes. Sent officer reporting which of communication found.	A
	13th		Attacked at 5.15 am on the left found much to corporation with French on our left and 18th Bde. in on right. To possess all our objectives but 18th Bde were held up. Communication amongst Pigeons have done very well and brought in good reports from the commander, wires to infantry Brigades. 87th Bde 57th Buckstan Reserves out. at The Oak from in hot yet available. Take hover the GS Tangle in charge of W/T at Battery Rd from hour the totally attacked 1200 wages shells with rainy 2 when enemy heavy 1-3	A

Army Form C. 2118.

WAR DIARY
or
INTELLIGENCE SUMMARY.
(Erase heading not required.)

Place	Date	Hour	Summary of Events and Information	Remarks and references to Appendices
ELVERDINGHE	Oct 14th		Lieut WHYE and 12 men from 57th Bn taken prisoner and not away to hospital. Bn relieved by 50th Bn.	
	to		Any officers moved to very heavy shelling and many Bn runners are being knocked out. Chas Taylor died of his wounds early morning 14th and was buried at Proven from his Field Amb. 10th Yorks. lost	
	17th		Nuttin wounded 17th hit at LANGEMARCK. First reinforcing him Bec'HQ. heavily shelled high. of 16th with gas shells and all suffering shock from gas. Being relieved by 55th Bn. Moved to PROVEN. Finished his at 10 a.m.	
PROVEN	18th		57th Bn rests entirely. Progress made gradually. Very cheery. Reinforcements arriving from Depot. Very good about Julian Post - not highly favoured.	
	to			
	20th		Lost in showing up after action Casualties in action from 11-17, 27 Men 190th. (INCE killed, 1 Man 2 off wounded 3 off to 135th Brigade.)	

Instructions regarding War Diaries and Intelligence Summaries are contained in F. S. Regs., Part II. and the Staff Manual respectively. Title pages will be prepared in manuscript.

WAR DIARY

Army Form C. 2118.

Place	Date	Hour	Summary of Events and Information	Remarks and references to Appendices
ZUTKERQUE	21st to 31st		Reorganising Platoons and Sections. Ellis' improving into Sections and Training in Musk, with and Bayonet. Men have trained to fire flying on a Guard against work by Sections. Recreation as much as possible by home running and Football. One Bus left at 7th hour on 14 h/o noon. Men interferon with training and have done a very good work down. Three Casualties during trench. 2 Officers took leave. WHYE W.J. MILITARY CROSS. 31704 Sergt. WHITEHEAD A. DCM. 485948 4/Cpl MORRIS J. M.M. 71316 Pte. WEBB P.L. M.M. Strength of Company 31/10/17 8 offrs / 256 O.Rs / 294	

Vol 28

SECRET AND CONFIDENTIAL

WAR DIARY

17th DIVNL SIGNAL COY. R.E.

VOL 28 - OCTOBER 1917.

WAR DIARY

SECRET and CONFIDENTIAL

WAR DIARY

OF

17TH DIVN'L SIGNAL COY R.E.

VOL 28 — OCTOBER 1917

Commanding 17th Signal Coy, R.E.

WAR DIARY or INTELLIGENCE SUMMARY

Army Form C. 2118.

Place	Date	Hour	Summary of Events and Information	Remarks and references to Appendices
LeCAUROY	Oct 1st to 3rd		Shooting and maintenance Power Buggy. Speech of 32nd Bn Forces to Divs Brigs working. Preparations of moving hut over of attempt practised near YPRES. Advance party with Signal Officer Stores and relief left for PROVEN on the 3rd	
PROVEN	4th		Closed Head Quarters at LeCAUROY and opened at PROVEN. Coy moved by train from MONDECOURT to PROVEN.	
	5th to 10th		Cleaning and improving camps in PROVEN. Have tried and all camps in a very wild state owing to very wet weather and great damage from high winds and bombing. Several Preparation Journeys with Buses. Overhauling Telephones and Wireless Stores. Several to Gas School struck etc.	
ELVERDINGHE	11th		Moved with the Fair Forces HOULTHOUST FOREST, took Divs H.Qrs at Elverdinghe. Our Bus is the hut at AU BONGITE relieved 29th Divn and have a very comfortable Hdq. Sythis removed no Tanking near	

WAR DIARY / INTELLIGENCE SUMMARY

Army Form C. 2118.

Place	Date	Hour	Summary of Events and Information	Remarks and references to Appendices
ELVERDINGHE	OCT. 12th		Intus on Guard duties from Essex Farm to Malcolm Tramway and Cambridge on map. Line very bad & deep thro'. The ground is soaked & roads breed and it is terrible throughout Khaki Camp to excessive traffic and heavy shell fire also buffaloes from the K.Hoofs through continuously. Attacking troops and Camps distribution round & this Brind officers dispatching hutments of Communication Forward.	A.1
	13th		Attacks at 5.15 am on the left Corps front and in conjunction with French on our left and 18th Corps on our right. It seemed all our objectives had 18th Corps were held up. Communication messages pigeon hand dove very well and brought in good reports. From the Commanders, Wilkins & coming Jameson Bty 57th Buffalo Inf- Keresord oll. at The eak. Farm & NA Jul-enclos. Intis heard No0 C/o Taufer in charge of W/T at Boesinghe Rood Farm has been badly instructed. 1200 Messages dealt with during 24 hours ending midnight 12-13.	A.1

Army Form C. 2118.

WAR DIARY
or
INTELLIGENCE SUMMARY
(Erase heading not required.)

Instructions regarding War Diaries and Intelligence Summaries are contained in F. S. Regs., Part II. and the Staff Manual respectively. Title pages will be prepared in manuscript.

Place	Date	Hour	Summary of Events and Information	Remarks and references to Appendices
ELVERDINGHE	Oct. 14th		Wind N.N.E and 12 men from 5th Bn Station gassed and at enemy H. Infantd. Bn relieved by 5th Bn Scots on 14th night. Communication forward still very difficult owing to very heavy shelling and many Bn. runners are being knocked out. Cpl Taylor died of his wounds early morning 14th and was buried at Broeul Farm by hour Tunj. 10.W.Yorks hurt.	
	17th		Matthew wounded 17th hit at LANGEMARCK. Relief infantry been Scottish heavily shelled hgt of 15th with gas shells and all afternoon 17th from gas. Bttn relieved by 55th Bn. Moved to PROVEN France hit at 10am.	ST
PROVEN	18th to 20th		5th Bn rested intently, paraded and gradually going away. Reinforcements arriving from Bybl. Overgrown clothing Jones hut hit highly trained. Coll on cleaning up after action. Casualties in action from 11-17 2 Officers 19 OR (Incs killed, 1 officer 20 OR wounded Skept; 15th. annexed)	B

(A7092) W. W12399/M1293 75,000. 11/17. D.D. & L., Ltd. Forms/C.2118/11.

Army Form C. 2118.

WAR DIARY

~~INTELLIGENCE SUMMARY.~~

(Erase heading not required.)

Instructions regarding War Diaries and Intelligence Summaries are contained in F. S. Regs., Part II. and the Staff Manual respectively. Title pages will be prepared in manuscript.

Place	Date	Hour	Summary of Events and Information	Remarks and references to Appendices
ZUTKERQUE	21st to 31st		Providing Stables and Punching huts improving into spaces and Tramway extended, central and Coy lines [?]. Work has hence to [?] flying and Ground signal work by skeleton [?] as much as permits by hrs racing and football. Gas Box left 47th Div. on 14 trips answer[?]. Much rain has interferred with training and road [?] but camels during [?]. 2 Officers Joint Lieut WHYE W.G. MILITARY CROSS 31704 Sgt. WHITEHEAD A. D.C.M. 180418 Cpl. MORRIS J. M.M. 71316 Spr. WEBB M. M.M. Strength of Company 31/9/17 8 offrs. 286 brs. ——— 294	

Commanding 17th Signal Coy. R.E.

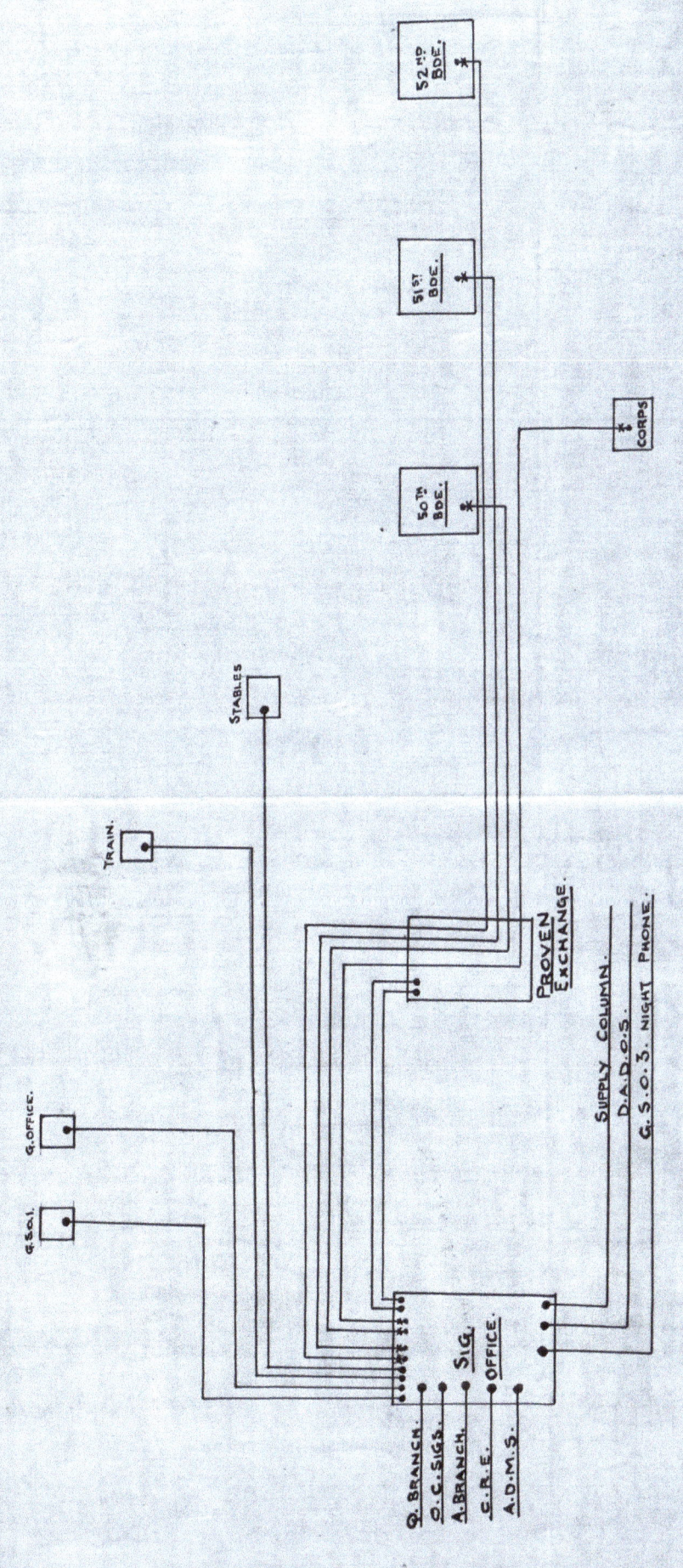

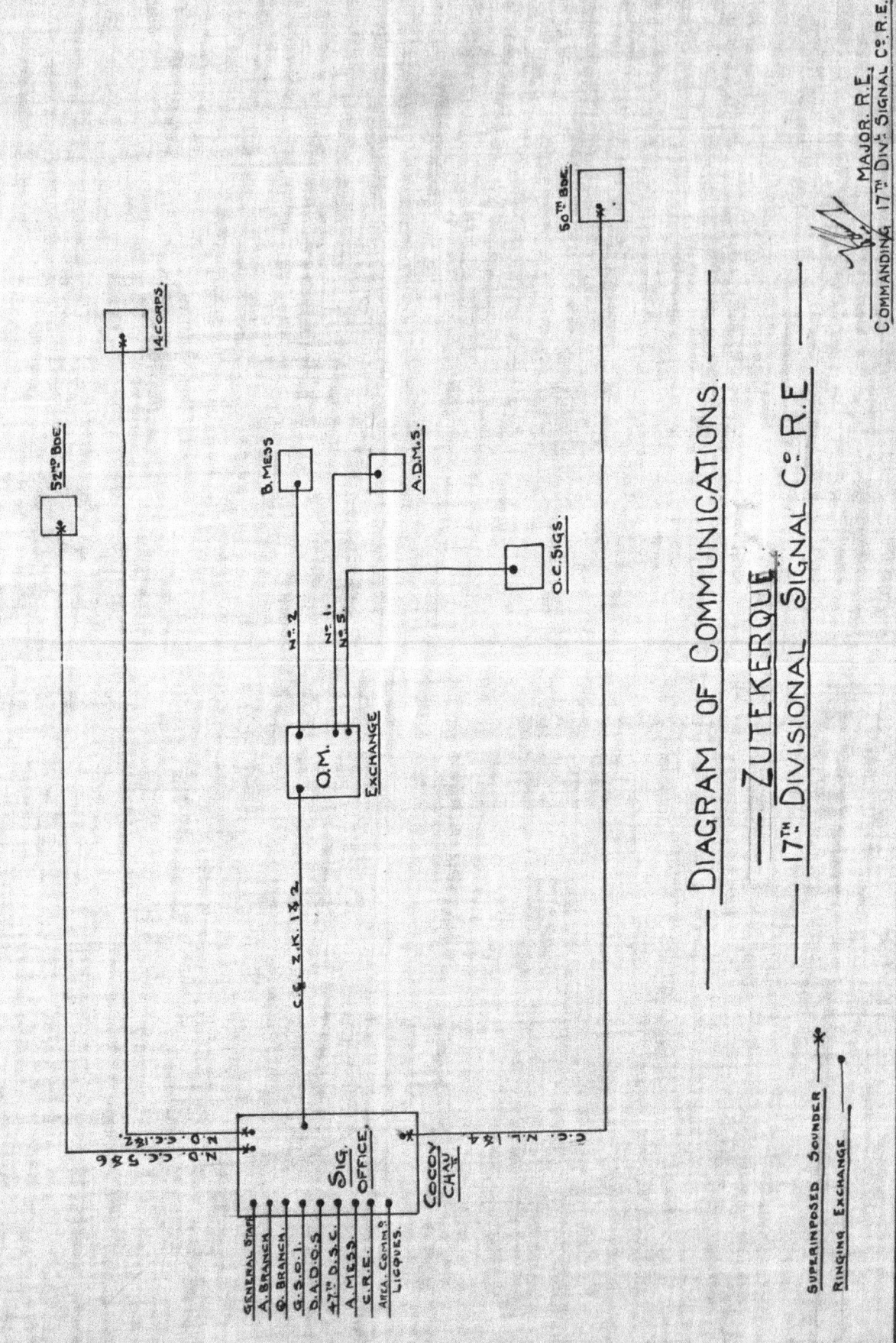

ROUTE DIAGRAM

17TH DIVISIONAL R.E. SIGNAL COMPANY.

ELVERDINGHE

MAP. REF. Nos.
SHEET 20. S.W.
" 28. N.W.
" 20. S.E.
" 28. N.E.

PERMANENT ROUTE SHEWN THUS ———
GROUND LINES SHEWN THUS – – – –
BURIED CABLES SHEWN THUS ·—·—·

MAJOR R.E.
COMMANDING 17TH DIVL SIGNAL Co R.E.
11TH TO 17TH OCTOBER 1917.

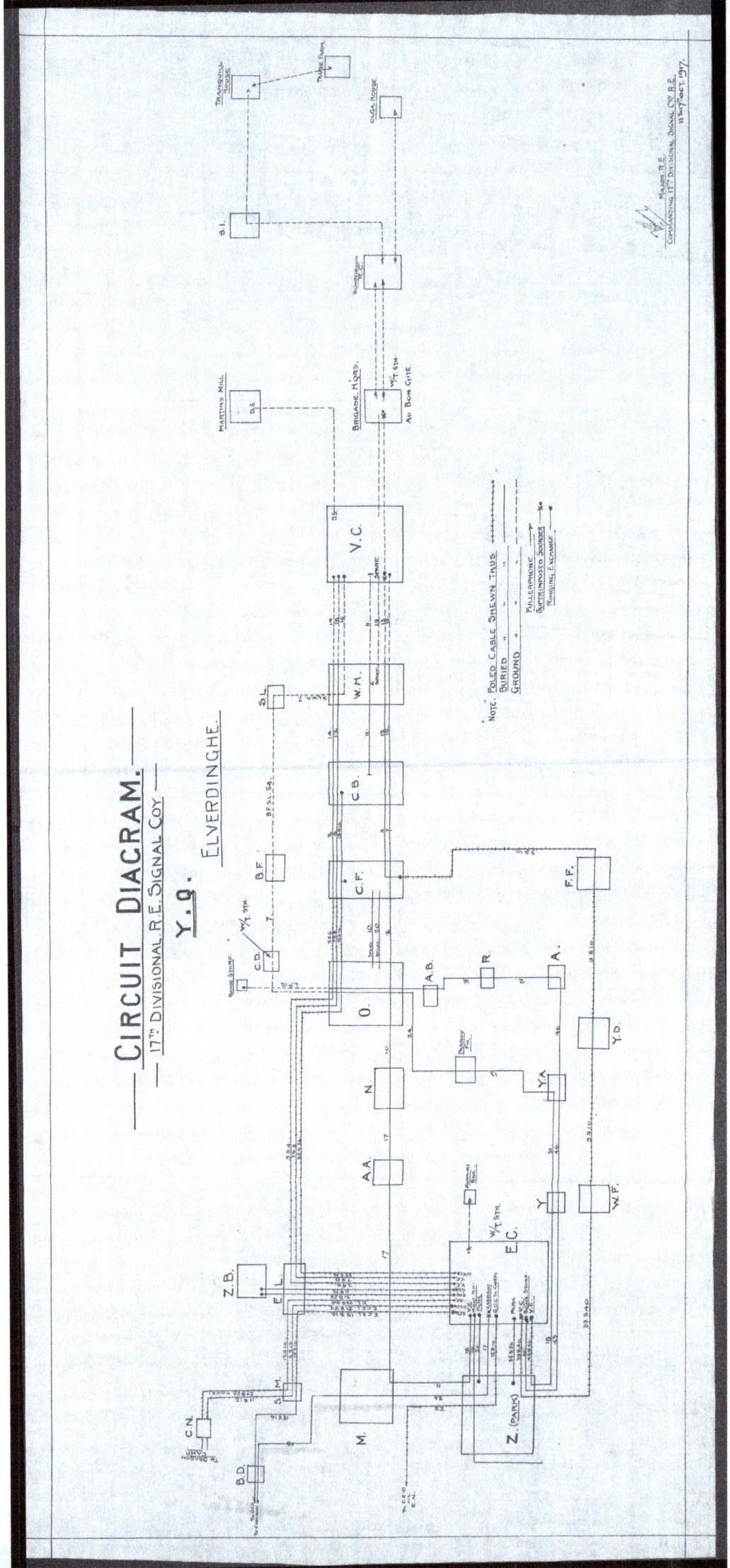

SECRET.

OFFENSIVE OPERATIONS.
G.S. INSTRUCTIONS No. 4
SIGNALS AND COMMUNICATIONS.

1. Communication will be by telephone, telegraph, runners, wireless, pigeons, visual, Power Buzzer and Amplifier and Contact Aeroplanes.

2. TELEGRAPH AND TELEPHONES.

    (a). Location of H.Qrs.

    Divnl. H.Qrs.   ELVERDINGHE CHATEAU.

    Adv. Bde H.Qrs.   MARTINS MILL. U.22.c.Central.

    Adv. Divnl. Signals. VULCANS FARM. U.27.c.4.6.

    The general line of advance will be along the railway and Units will notify position of their H.Qrs, as soon as established, to the next higher formation.

    (b). BURIED CABLE runs from LUNAVILLE FARM to WOOD HOUSE passing through CHASSEUR FARM (B.12.d.8.9) and THACHED HOUSE serving R.A. and Inf. Bdes. This will be pushed forward as circumstances permit. Bns. are connected at present by lines overground. A diagram is attached.

    (c). DURING AN ADVANCE Power Buzzers will be taken forward and established at the Adv. Bn. H.Qrs. Working to Amplifier stns. at Adv. Bde. H.Qrs. These stns. will connect by wireless to the Corps Directing Stn. in BOESINGHE, telephone to Bde. H.Qrs. and if possible be reinforced by visual. As soon as Bn. H.Qrs. are definitely established they will be connected by wire from Adv. Bde. H.Qrs. Forward of Bn. communication will be by runner or as in para. 8. if circumstances permit. See diagrams attached.

    (d). STANDING INSTRUCTIONS REGARDING THE USE OF TELEPHONE will be adhered to. The restrictions placed on the use of the FULLERPHONE are withdrawn.
        Conversations on telephones will be between Officers only. They must be brief. The order of "Priority" will normally be from front to rear. When delay is occurring in "Priority" telephone messages the Signal Offr. will obtain instructions from the G.S. or Bde Major. See XIV Corps No.G.46/1. attached.

    (e). Material assistance will be given to Bdes. If Bns. cooperate with them in laying telephone lines between Bns. and Bde, i.e., by lines laid back from Bns. H.Qrs to Bde.

3. LIAISON BETWEEN R.A. AND INFANTRY.

    So far as possible R.A. Bdes. will be directly connected to Infantry Bdes. and Bns. in the line.

4. RUNNERS AND DESPATCH RIDERS.

    All D.R.L.S. forward is normal to Bdes. except in wet weather when it will be relayed at (Adv. Divnl. Signals) VULCANS FARM. Bdes will provide 3 runners each at Adv. relay posts for carrying up these despatches to their H.Qrs. Instructions as to time and place of reporting will be issued later.

Similar arrangements will be made for despatch service to Bns. and runs so timed that there is a complete chain of runs through from Divn. to Bns. and vice versa with the least possible delay at H.Qrs and relay Posts.

5. WIRELESS. Stations will be under Divnl. control and established at the Amplifier stns. (Adv. Bde H.Qrs). They will work as in para. 2.(c) and also provide inter-communication between Bdes and to flanks as permitted by Corps Directing Stn.

6. PIGEONS. will be available on a scale of 6 per Bn. (of two bdes). Assault baskets to contain 1 bird will be issued later together with special message books and clips. If numbers permit pigeons will also be issued to R.A. F.O.O's.

The lofts are at VOXVRIE FARM which will be directly connected to Divnl. H.Qrs. If a pigeoneer becomes a casualty, his birds should be immediately released by his comrades when the basket in which they are found has obviously been abandoned.

7. VISUAL. Lucas Daylight Signal Lamps will be used for all visual Signalling but flags should be kept at all stns. for use in the event of the lamps being destroyed. With actual assaulting troop a number of small roll up flappers should be carried and indication as to success or otherwise sent back by using a prearranged code.

Two signallers per Bn. will be provided at Divnl. H.Qrs. from Bde. Depots for visual work in back areas. These will be called for later.

The central Divnl. Visual Stn. will be established at VULCAN CROSSING working to AU BON GITE, MARTIN'S MILL and LANGEMARCH CHURCH. From the latter communication should be possible to almost any point forward.

In order to avoid being seen by the enemy, all messages sent back should be DD DD and acknowledged forward by three dots, the message being repeated until this answer is given.

8. POWER BUZZER AND AMPLIFIER.

These will be under Bde. Control. Power Buzzers will be carried forward with Bn. H.Qrs. and used as in para. 2(c). until such time as sound telephone communication has been established when they will be sent forward for communication back from Coy. H.Qrs. or strong posts. A code for S.O.S. will be devised by Bde Signal Offr. when this is done. Diagrams are attached.

The recently organised Bn. Power Buzzer squads will be used for working Power Buzzers in the line reliefs being arranged by the Bde. Signal Officer.

9. GENERAL.

As far as possible all ranks should understand TANK signals and Signal personnel should endeavour to find out and inform their H.Qrs of the positions of flanking units H.Qrs. with the idea of establishing Liaison.

10. PRECAUTIONS AGAINST ENEMY LISTENING SETS.

(1). In newly captured territory a careful reconnaisance should be made to locate any German cables, buried or otherwise. Trench Mortar emplacements, O.P's, Battery emplacements, and dugouts used as H.Qrs should be searched for cables. The reconnaisance should be made by special parties of Signallers detailed for the purpose.

(2). Every cable must be regarded as a possible German listening line which may pick up our conversation and signals within a wide radius so long as it is continuous into the German line.

(3). When a German cable is found, it should be cut as far forward as possible. The wire itself should be cut off short close to the insulation, which should then be pulled forward so as to cover up the end of the wire. The ends should be bent upwards so that they do not touch the ground or one another. The point at which the cut is made should be plainly marked and reported at once to the Signal officer of the formation.

The Signal Officer will report it to the A.D. Signals of the Corps and his own General Staff.

....

SECRET.

EXTRACT XIV Corps G.46/1.

Attention is again directed to the use of telephones in the forward area.

Telephones will not be used in front of Bn. H.Qrs. Fullerphones only may be used.

The only exception is in the case of F.O.O's who will be careful not to say anything that would be of the slightest value to the enemy.

The telephones at Bn. H.Qrs. will be used by responsible officers and then only to speak to the flanks or rear when all restrictions as to the use of the telephone in the danger zone will be adhered to.

8th October, 1917.

Lt.Col., G.S.,
17th Division.

STAGE 2. CONSOLIDATION OF ADVANCED POSITION

FORECAST DIAGRAM
17TH DIVISIONAL COY. R.E. SIGNALS

······ OVERLAND LINES.
----- BURIED LINES.
+++++ RAILWAY.

STAGE I. IMMEDIATELY AFTER ADVANCE.

SECRET AND CONFIDENTIAL

WAR DIARY

of

17TH DIVISIONAL SIGNAL Co, R.E.

November 1917.

VOL. 29.

[signature]
Commanding 17th Signal Coy. R.E.

WAR DIARY
or
INTELLIGENCE SUMMARY.

Army Form C. 2113.

(Erase heading not required.)

Place	Date	Hour	Summary of Events and Information	Remarks and references to Appendices

			Total Casualties during the work:-
			
			      Officers O.R's
			 Killed Coy attached — 2
			                                   1
			 Wounded Coy attached 1 7
			               Total 1 11 Grand Total 12
			
			 Rewards for gallantry in the Field:-
			
			 Military Medal Nº 64839 Sapper A.D YOUNG.
			
			 Strength of Company 30/11/17 8 Officers
			                                           286 O.Rs
			                                         294 Total	

Army Form C. 2118.

WAR DIARY
or
~~INTELLIGENCE SUMMARY~~
(Erase heading not required.)

Instructions regarding War Diaries and Intelligence Summaries are contained in F.S. Regs., Part II. and the Staff Manual respectively. Title pages will be prepared in manuscript.

Place	Date	Hour	Summary of Events and Information	Remarks and references to Appendices
ZUTKERQUE	OCT 1st to 6th		Bn in training area. Shooting and maintenance of plies. General overhauling and cleaning up all wagons, Stores Telephones etc. Football on work afternoons and inspn NCOs and men 57th Coy granted daily leave to CALAIS. Advance party of relief of 57th Bn to R.hue sent off	[IS?]
PROVEN	7th		Advance party of J Coy moved by road to BOYCHEUTRE en rnt to PROVEN. Several parades & they ova from 67 Div Linren and Stores part of from tra 57 Div HQrs & HD W.T. S/S BG and DC ae line diagrain attached.	[IS?]
WELSH FARM ELVERDINGHE	8th		Relief of 57th Bn complt'd at 10am near HQrs as shwn on HQrs at CANAL BANK. B24695 (See diagram) Transport uncouvered hes PROVEN. Unit at Standings as accomodation forward is very poor	[IS?]

WAR DIARY / INTELLIGENCE SUMMARY

Army Form C. 2118.

Place	Date	Hour	Summary of Events and Information	Remarks and references to Appendices
WATSCHAPPOCK ELVER DINGHE	9th Oct		Flash area heavily shelled and line maintenance very difficult. Recent work on tidying up and operating lines. Office out table. Organization for issuing of stores and rations. Corps Kitchen started at Recn HQr.	
	14th		Fr serving party & Engineers in Forward stations. Line Breaks very today. Fr line at Stray Farm. Bn. Ph. etc.	
	14th		Advanced HQrs closed and relay DR Office Pk opens & Brest circuits. Line forward of Bn. HQrs being en-safety forsten.	
	15th		New hostile station faken at Double Cotts. Lucas lamps stations established and working well.	
	16th		Buried cable put in fm WT to SF. burying very difficult but on average of 3'0" in distance and result. Banked up 3'6" high about the Prires.	
	25.		Length of Bury about 1200 yards. In Frower Trib 1600 Canadian 1 OR killed 7 E.York & Lanc Regt.	

Place	Date	Hour	Summary of Events and Information	Remarks and references to Appendices
WELSH FARM EVERDINGHE	16th		knowing line support. Shew enviously low turnout in forward phone lines. This has been the case since the commencement of operations at CAMBRAI. lines were becoming so difficult to maintain that they had been abandoned and work entirely done by forward lamps, visual and Runner. Pigeons distance 1- 2½ m. Per m.p.h. live for day. That set. They were 1- being bred. It often became difficult to get average time from Bn. HQr. to Div. HQr. is about 35 minutes.	
	26th		Several sorts of operators and hams have taken Voice and telephone lines instruments very well. Advanced Signal School of 120 R.E. are at	
	30th		small establishment on 29th at MERCKEGHEM under 2nd/Lieut CASTLE. No men 9th Coy have reported sick owing to the lice.	

Army Form C. 2118.

WAR DIARY
INTELLIGENCE SUMMARY
(Erase heading not required.)

Place	Date	Hour	Summary of Events and Information	Remarks and references to Appendices
WEISHPARMOCT ELVER DINGILE	9th		Hostile area heavily shelled and line Neuruth once very difficult. Received with a very up and cheerly hour at Offr on fire.	
	6.		Organisation for crushing of Stores and rations. Boys Kitchen started	
	14th		at Rue HQn for sending Soup & beverages to become in Forward Stations	
			Line relief very slow.	
	14th		Advanced HQn closed had Stray Farm Bn Bn Rlv etc. Open for trial units. Line Exchange and relay DR Office left forward of Beersheba being on scantily	158
	15th		Wireless Station forward at Dorbl CMS. Lucas Lamp Stations established and working well.	158
	16th		Buried Cable Laid in Fn WT to SF proving very difficult but a average of 3'6" bn obtained and about Burning at 3'6" high about the ground level. Length of Buried about 1200 yards in Green Fields.	158
	6.			
	20.		1 OR Killed 7E Kells.(turn Rgt. 1600 Casualties)	158

Army Form C. 2113.

WAR DIARY
or
INTELLIGENCE SUMMARY.

SECRET and CONFIDENTIAL

WAR DIARY
of
17TH DIVN'L SIGNAL Co. R.E.

VOL 29   NOVEMBER 1917

Army Form C. 2118.

WAR DIARY
or
INTELLIGENCE SUMMARY.
(Erase heading not required.)

Place	Date	Hour	Summary of Events and Information	Remarks and references to Appendices

Total Casualties during the month.

	Officers	O.R.'s
Killed in action	—	2
Wounded in action	1	7
Total	1	11	Grand Total 12

Rewards for gallantry in the Field.

Military Medal No 64839 Sapper A.D. YOUNG.

Strength of Company 30/11/17   8 officers
                                286 O.R's
                                ———
                                294 Total

WAR DIARY
INTELLIGENCE SUMMARY
(Erase heading not required.)

Army Form C. 2118.

Place	Date	Hour	Summary of Events and Information	Remarks and references to Appendices
WELSH FARM	16th		Morning Burg report shows enemy has turned in forward zone but this has been the case since the commencement of operations at CAMBRAI.	
ELVERDINGHE	25th (cont)		Huts were brewing so sufficient to maintain that they had been attended and not entirely done by Lucas Bros. Timber and Pimina. Regiment instructed to 2 per Bn milk due per day. There are being used to bring down the afternoon situation report. Average time from Bn HQrs to Bde HQrs is about 35 minutes.	[S]
	26th		Several took in operation and maintain latest artillery army work. Provisional Special School of 120 Offenca of Squadron established on 29th at MACHEGHEM under 2/Lieut. CASTLE he hun 9/R Cy have reported back since evening and the huts.	[S]
	30th			

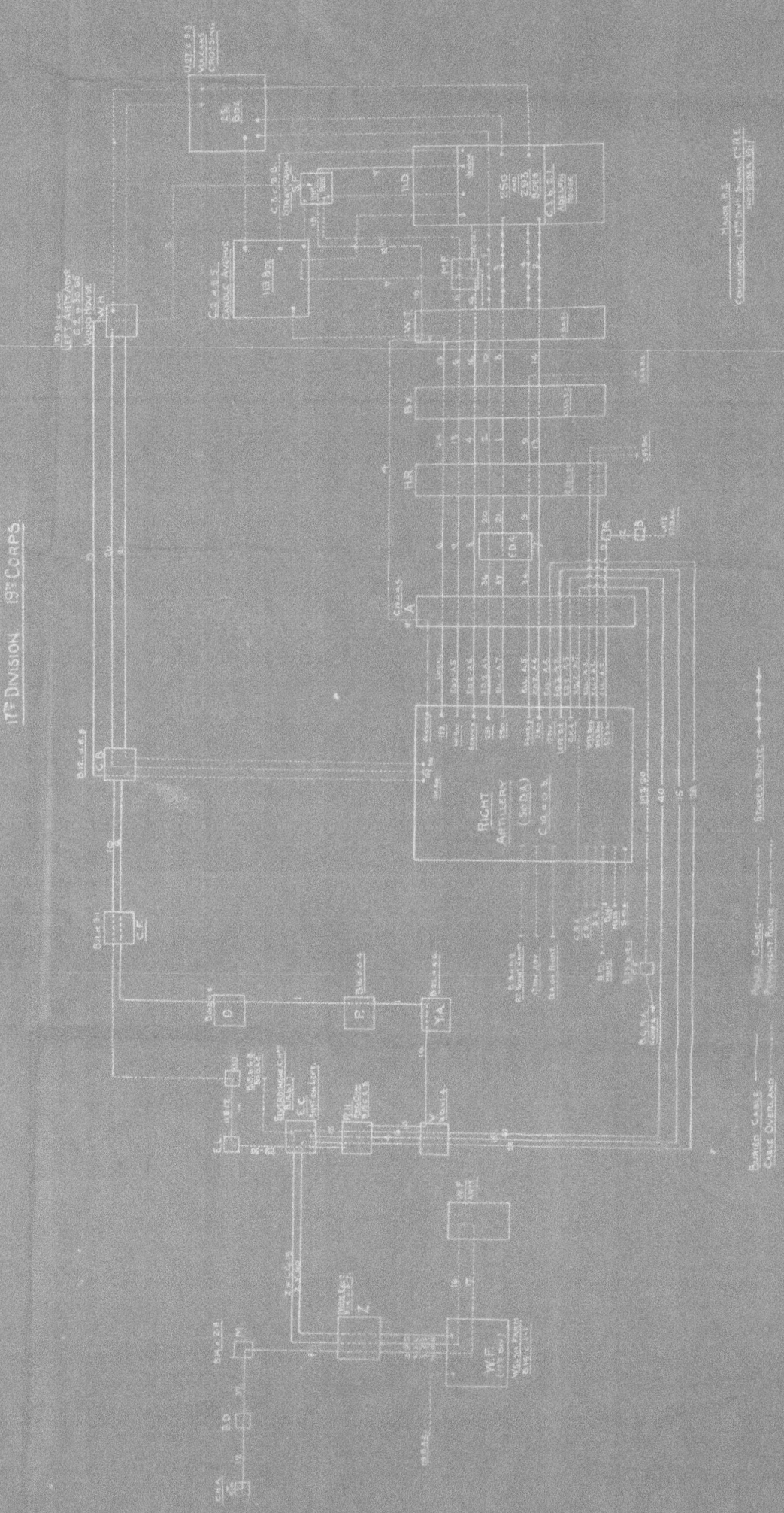

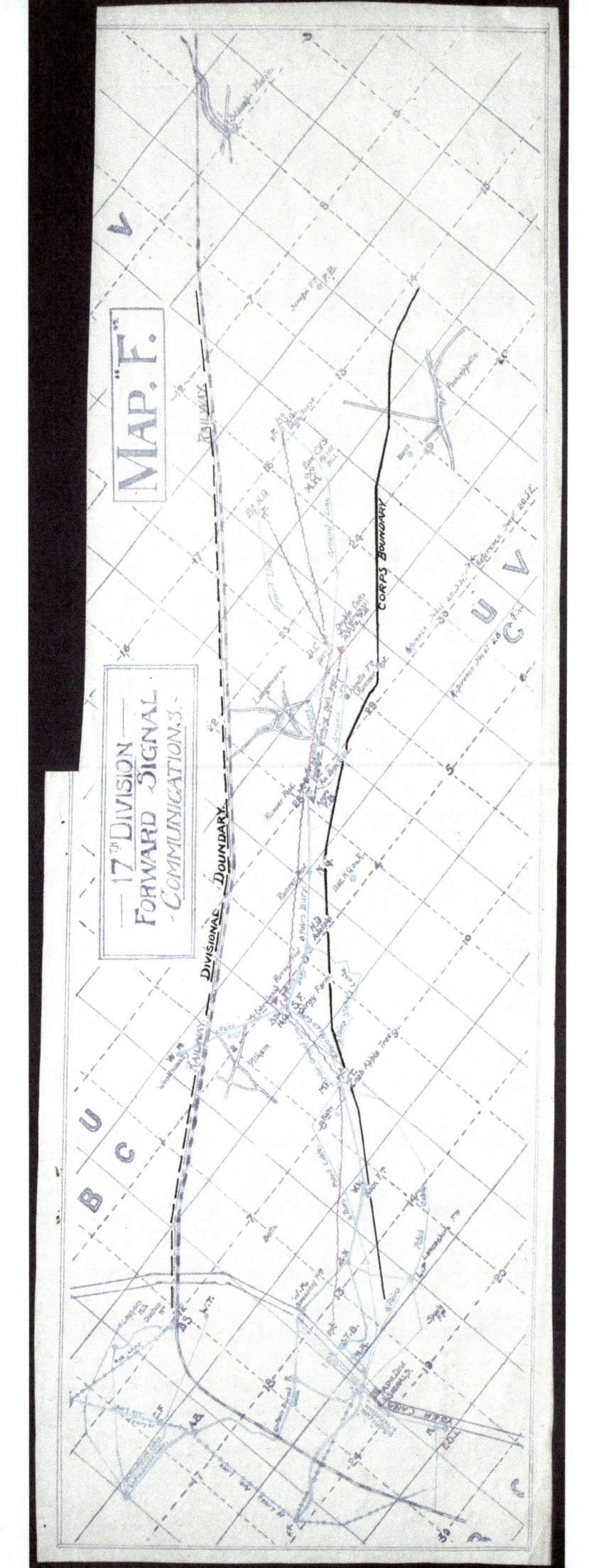

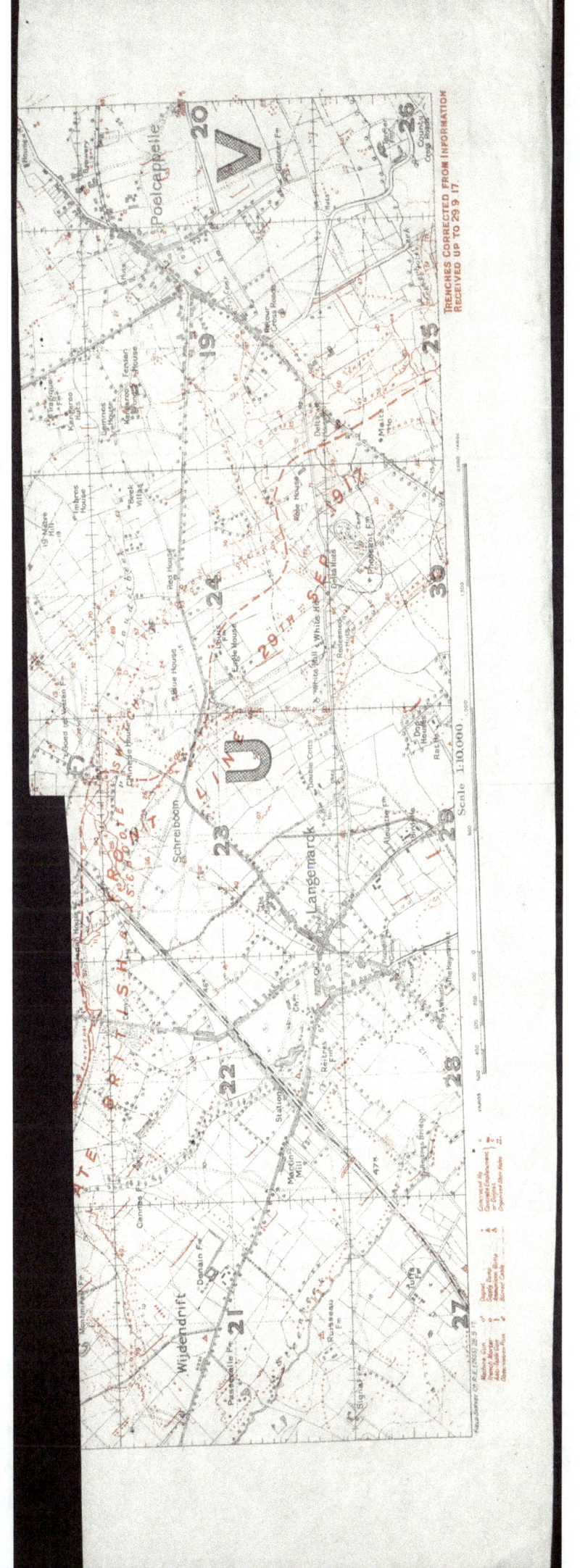

Army Form C. 2118.

WAR DIARY
or
INTELLIGENCE SUMMARY.
(Erase heading not required.)

Instructions regarding War Diaries and Intelligence Summaries are contained in F. S. Regs., Part II. and the Staff Manual respectively. Title pages will be prepared in manuscript.

Place	Date	Hour	Summary of Events and Information	Remarks and references to Appendices
ZUTKERQUE	OCT. 1st to 6th		Bn in training area. Grooming and maintenance of Mules. General overhauling and cleaning up of all wagons, Stores Telephones etc. Drill Bull on most afternoons and most next and new 57th Coy granted daily leave to CALAIS. Advance party for entry of 57th Bn to Whise sent off.	1SS
PROVEN	7th		Remainder portion of Coy moved by road to BLYCHEURE en route to PROVEN. Several infantries to taking over from 57 Bn Limbers and GSGs sent up from sea 57 Bn HQn. & H.D. N.T. SF. BG. and DC. See line diagram attached.	6SS
WELSH FARM ELVERDINGHE	8th		Relief of 57th Bn completed at 10am. New HQn as shown Ark HQn at CANAL BANK B.24b95(see diagram). Transport remained has PROVEN. Infact Stauships as accommodation forward was very poor.	1SS

Army Form C. 2118.

WAR DIARY
or
INTELLIGENCE SUMMARY.
(Erase heading not required.)

SECRET and CONFIDENTIAL

WAR DIARY

OF

17TH DIVN'L SIGNAL COY R.E.

VOL 29 NOVEMBER 1917

17th. Division.
G. 246
21st. November. 1917.

50th. Inf. Bde.
51st. Inf. Bde.
52nd. Inf. Bde.
C.R.A.(Right Arty)
C.R.E.
A.D.M.S.
D.A.D.V.S.
17th. Div. Tn.
================

D. R. L. S.

Many cases of misuse of the D.R.L.Service have recently been brought to light and attention is called to G.R.O.1138. This order must be complied with.

In addition much time is being wasted in the registration of unimportant correspondence.

Only correspondence marked with a large 'R' is now registered in Signal Offices. It has been noticed that many important and secret packages do not bear this registration sign.

Normally all packages are treated in the same way but in time of pressure those not marked with an 'R' may be sent via the Postal Service.

It is notified that unless a package is registered no responsibility can be accepted for its safety and the practice of sending important and secret correspondence unregistered must be discontinued.

Attention is directed to K.R. para 1861 with reference to secret and confidential correspondence which will be strictly complied with.

P.B. O'Connor
Maj for
Lieut.-Col., G.S.,
17th. Division.

Copies to :-
  Signals.
  Div.Dep.Bn.
  Camp Commandant.
  'Q'

R.E.Base Records.
17th Divn 'Q'.

C.R.113.
28th November, 1917.

......

RETURN OF OFFICERS - 17TH SIGNAL COY.R.E.

Major W.E.Gurry R.E.(T.C.).Commanding 17th Signal Coy,R.E.
(T)

Capt.J.M.May,7th Bn.W.Yorks. 2nd in Command.

Capt G.T.Labey R.E.(T.C.). 1/c.,Artillery Signals.

2/Lt. E.Whitley-Baker R.E.(T.C.). No.1.Section.

2/LT.H.G.Castle R.E.(T.C.). No.1. Section.

2/Lt J.P.Marshall R.E.(T.C.). No.2.Section.
(TC)

Lieut. A.R.M.Perring, 11th R.Sussex Regt. No.3.Section.
(TC)

Lieut. D.C.Dunlop, 3rd Buffs. No.4.Section.

CASUALTIES DURING MONTH.

Capt J.F.Phipps R.E. to 5th Corps Signal School 7/11/17.

2/Lt C.F.Taylor, Q.O.R.G.Y. wounded in action and evacuated 20/11/17.

REINFORCEMENTS ETC.

Capt. J.M.May,7th BN,W.Yorks Regt. to 17th Signal Coy,R.E.,
vice Capt J.F.Phipps R.E.3/11/17.

Lt.A.R.M.Perring,11th BN.R.Sussex Regt. XX 10/11/17.

TEMPORARILY ATTACHED.
(TC)

2/Lt G.A.Twigg, 10th Bn.W.Yorks Regt. i/c Wireless.

2/Lt H.Pennock R.E.(T.C.). temporarily attached from 19th Corps Signal Coy.R.E.

Major R.E.,
Commanding 17th Signal Coy,R.E.

C.R.90.

20th November, 1917.

REPORT ACCORDING TO XIX CORPS NO.G.61/1/1.

SIGNALS AND COMMUNICATIONS.

1. TELEPHONE LINES. forward of Bde. H.Qrs. have been almost entirely replaced but are still so difficult to maintain and so costly in linemen that their use is hardly justified. A successful working scheme by alternative means has been devised and is in use. In order to improve telephone and telegraph to STRAY FARM, lines are being buried between MARSOUIN and STRAY FARMS. A trench has been dug to an average depth of 3 feet and it is now proposed to lay the cable and bank up 3 or 4 feet high.

2. VISUAL working front to back is in use from Bn. H.Qrs. to Bde via DOUBLE COTTS and AU BON GITE. No new stations have been established except at the new Bn.H.Qrs in LOUIS FARM.

3. WIRELESS is working successfully between DOUBLE COTTS, Bn.H.Qrs and STRAY FARM.

4. POWER BUZZERS AND AMPLIFIERS have been installed at DOUBLE COTTS AND AU BON GITE to bridge the area over which it is almost impossible to maintain lines.

G
A.D. Sig.

C.R.104.
23rd November, 1917.

REPORT ACCORDING TO XIX CORPS No.G.61/1/1.

1. TELEPHONE LINES. New bury from MARSOUIN FARM to STRAY FARM. Cable completely laid and trench half filled and banked up. Work proceeding on jointing and testing out.

2. VISUAL. No new stations. Aiming posts have been put up for aligning LUCAS LAMPS at night.

3. WIRELESS. Positions unchanged. New set put in at DOUBLE COTTS.

Major R.E.,
Commanding 17th Signal Coy,R.E.

C.R.118.
30th November, 1917.

'G'.,
17th Division.
.....

REPORT ACCORDING TO XIX CORPS No.G.61/1/1.

1. TELEPHONE LINES.

New bury from MARSOUIN FARM to STRAY FARM completed and working.

2. VISUAL.

Direct communication established between Left Battalion at U.18.c.3.7. and Bde. H.Qrs at STRAY FARM: also from DOUBLE COTTS to STRAY FARM. AU BON GITE now only manned for Visual as a stand by.

No new stations.

3. WIRELESS.

Positions unchanged.

Major R.E.,
Commanding 17th Signal Coy, R.E.

SECRET AND CONFIDENTIAL.

WAR DIARY

OF

17th DIVISIONAL SIGNAL COMPANY. R.E.

DECEMBER 1917.

VOL 30.

Army Form C. 2118.

WAR DIARY
or
INTELLIGENCE SUMMARY.
(Erase heading not required.)

Instructions regarding War Diaries and Intelligence Summaries are contained in F. S. Regs., Part II. and the Staff Manual respectively. Title pages will be prepared in manuscript.

Place	Date	Hour	Summary of Events and Information	Remarks and references to Appendices
IN THE FIELD	1		Enemy in view twice French watch. Enemy NO NCO. NV Officer topped with rifle up sandbagging & revetting huts at rear Hqrs.	
	2		NCO to NCO. NV Officer ordered to leave some sandbagging. Sandbagging & revetting of rear Hqrs. improved.	
	3		R. 8.30 am Cynas called & talk about forward line in anticipation of taking over part of our sector. He asked me to take over command of Drill Signal School at MERCK ENGHIEN. 12 Dinner. Cynas here. LtCompany from 3" Divy Coy. Enemy here from 3.30am to 7.30am. Moved Camp. Spent 8.30am thro to forward area 8.30am. R. 5.8 am Signals came to spend most on forward communication. Signal mayflyer did not work by 83. The Bus met 3rd recct. revets. Mes from field cable work telephone & new easy with good results.	

WAR DIARY
INTELLIGENCE SUMMARY

Army Form C. 2118.

Place	Date	Hour	Summary of Events and Information	Remarks and references to Appendices
IN THE FIELD	5		Train from 3rd Div - 17 Div arr. Completed & took in each unit. Liaise etc. Lt. PRIMROSE proceeded to 5th Army Signal School Inspection for voting men in permanent framework. Papers packed ready for MOVE. Harness cleaning etc.	
	6.		P. procceddon MONTH's LEAVE to ENGLAND. Car parti with Lt. Tr:166 & 3/m + 3rd unit lorries driver to RECQUES Area. Transport lorries the BAKER proceeds to OEDEN en route by road to ZUTKERQUE. Relay Race horses , vehicles men & actv. Other Command of Line paraded at 10. ave. to 6.0.3'05. Vehicles men by train to ZUTKERQUE with cycles. Same Coy to OEDEN with more actv. to taken back in SY Div lorry.	
	7.		Before ochum himself over to 3rd Div & receipt therewith Transport from OEDEN to ZEDEZEELE vie GRAVELINES ETC.	

WAR DIARY
or
INTELLIGENCE SUMMARY

(Erase heading not required.)

Army Form C. 2118.

Instructions regarding War Diaries and Intelligence Summaries are contained in F. S. Regs., Part II. and the Staff Manual respectively. Title pages will be prepared in manuscript.

Place	Date	Hour	Summary of Events and Information	Remarks and references to Appendices
IN THE FLD	8	Sept.	Brink HQrs arrived at NESLE-HAME 10 AM. Reported at Corps HdQrs. Bivouacs at 8 PM. Rear party of Company moved up by bus with transport arriving 12:15 about 4 PM. On 9th very heavy firing heard to N.E. Dets. proceeding to R. after arrival were J. Rankin with C.O.'s car. Time 6:30 my time.	
	9	Sun.	9 Ln Trs 166 proceeded to temp. bivouac SIGNY SIGNETS. 12 Ln PIONEER Regt from there under B. Coming past at 3 PM. Company full strength. Orders received given for movement tomorrow. Troops going up to Res. Brigade bivouac tomorrow.	
	10	Mon	Full company parade 9.30 AM. Force service. 1 went to PEROLEGUE to Lt. Col. 5th Division CRE. He had no news attachments for our RE. Returned home to 5th Division and commenced to arrange the move to PERONNE tomorrow. No orders yet. 1/6 N TERRIT FORCE Coy R.E. Staff Sc.	

WAR DIARY or INTELLIGENCE SUMMARY

Army Form C. 2118.

Place	Date	Hour	Summary of Events and Information	Remarks and references to Appendices
In the F.D	11 Tues.	9.15 am	Company Parade 9.15 am. All ranks taken, shown at ranges Shooting to Estlecque not 2 Div ration. Mr Baker out a bit through from Vacoucque & 33rd Division. Those known.	
		11.15am	Telephone casual conversation. B saying that there was rumour that the Division is to entertain fatigues toning at 12 No orders. Scheme all went thro very gay. Cet sent to 7 Divis Signal School for pt Costerley - Mercier. Item. Very heavy rain with all chits from Estlecque.	
	12		Mr. Botrel proceeded in Lone, Cal. S Calais retiring for participation to feast into Beginners ausplices. Parade 9. am. One proprietor's will.	
	13.	7.08	Lt Rometre returned Mr. G Company from Estlecque Col. with Capt Dawes & George RGA permisa & sit I shot shirts out of Rode of the Comme..... (illegible)	
		11am	(illegible handwritten text)	

WAR DIARY
INTELLIGENCE SUMMARY
(Erase heading not required.)

Army Form C. 2118.

Place	Date	Hour	Summary of Events and Information	Remarks and references to Appendices
In The Field	13 anth		SOS is sent to HQ 2 Brigade asking to send up SAA to LSS at two officers & perk of OR & got the ammunition sent up for B Coy. Telephonic communication everything was to zero knocked up getting away all OR appearing in getting away Zero 12 noon. P.E.L. Coy moved over twig to LSs 6.30 trench 57 met with station at the M.G. 31 or twig to 57 met with station at LSS 10 left 10.30 pm in car. 1 Division Company left LSSpioneers HC. 5 PM Office closes Scene chateau reported worth at pinute off and moving. 6 am MOHS transport LSSpioneers 16 LH. arriving at LSSeous passing through arrived DsHsT=9sT=T 1.30pm. Brief Tpr arrived 3.30pm. Officer Period. Mustpass Supplementers	

Place	Date	Hour	Summary of Events and Information	Remarks and references to Appendices
	14		S.S. Bn. Company attended prescribed parade from Bosune.	
BOSBURNE		11.30pm	31st Bn. arrived. Sgt. of "B" Coy arrived	
		6 E.C.O.	C.7 Bn. and O. of the Camp Sedro Woodley from Bodrum. O.K. members to the Camp service order. Capt. & O.C. instruments attended to supply the furniture so as to leave nothing to from to-morrow.	
	15			
	16	9.15pm	Full company parade. Hour service etc. Instructions under orders to be ready to move at a moment's notice.	
			Reports received to say they should.	
			C. raised 5? Due stiff on a little difference, everything mentioned in attended "B"; officers wing upset. 10.30pm C. approve on his new white as in right duty. C. cried spirit, temp up 850. Specimens endured. Very considered condition. Previous nothing further. Previous service. Nervous in hubery severe.	

WAR DIARY
or
INTELLIGENCE SUMMARY

Army Form C. 2118.

Place	Date	Hour	Summary of Events and Information	Remarks and references to Appendices
	17.		Very heavy fall of snow during night. Usual parade 9.15 am. Coy fight drawn up. Captain Cox went to C.O.E report at 5.10pm returned 6.30pm. Monuments repaired. More snow fell. Very cold. Nothing further to report.	
	18.		O. i/c the Costas went over 5.50 Di address for conference then to army tre cache over in relief of 9 to Div. British Force dezeure inspected. Usual parade. Usual service France.	
	19.		Usual parade. Company parade as usual. O. i/c their course in embarkt. Company course in YMCA hut DONNET LE GRAND apply organised by St GEORGES. Quite a success. Usual cinema. Pour men encouraged Sidney James Slater marries, nothing further to Report.	
	20.		O. i/c the Costas visits Ypres trenches. Fr Fall Doe 13.40. to supero who is a young rate to inspect much knowledge of men killed at Paul Corbur. Pr many on return. Will Scott Pgt.	

WAR DIARY
or
INTELLIGENCE SUMMARY.

(Erase heading not required.)

Army Form C. 2118.

Place	Date	Hour	Summary of Events and Information	Remarks and references to Appendices
	21		9.15 am Parade. Rifle exercise & drill. 3 hr Coy with AA Parts. Limber and 5 Ty Dr 1.45 pm Company Day Parade. Officers Lecture. Horse exercise & bayonet exercise. Capt Killeen Gi Mtor taught up for relief of Horse transport Parties & Piquets received. Goods for DEL of Horses afternoon announced 875s & Lighthorses & 3in Coves & Yeomanry also.	
	22		9.15 am Parade. 2 No Light Draw Hor Guesting Recruits 1/c. 2.45 pm Parade for presentation of VMs to 5/50 Yeomanry Reg on AMB 88. Report in evening again.	
	23		Company marches off 9.15 am under CSM at 10 horses together in stables. Off Coy away by 9 am Reserving in clothing ect. intended Rft Return at 2 pm Coy. Office turned Y.M.P.s & Mess buildings & sent Back Bills Coy turned over & Returned Return & changed over all working parties & two Refugees & An Officer from Base Building. Lt. QR/NORP	

Army Form C. 2118.

WAR DIARY
or
INTELLIGENCE SUMMARY.
(Erase heading not required.)

Place	Date	Hour	Summary of Events and Information	Remarks and references to Appendices
	24		V. F. 9th COSTA reconnoitre purposed trench route FLESQUIERES — HAVRINCOURT etc. visited 2 Bdes. Rd. signals much into an advancing strife & reconstruction parties for entering. Div Sub staff reconn. Heavy enemy barrage but our men carried on forming Mal Bde trans duty but n/t necessy tell resources — PRESCOTT Bde. 5th Bde staff more from Pd BRITISH LINE to BEAUCOURT. Lt SYKES & 2/Lt FENN report for temporary attachment. XMAS DAY City Road Camp. Div orders for trans to principal and Div comdr of the reconnce. Divl rendering party on Corps parts to Divisions with Repair & Supplemen.	
	26		Trans pud through relief to. Div memo 174d. 5th Bde trips tour. Q.M. Ord surrendering Divl P. & Fuel Camp RE to the Incoming 95 RE Coy in Grand Ravine. RE trans dumps at DUYOUCOURT.	

WAR DIARY
or
INTELLIGENCE SUMMARY

(Erase heading not required.)

Army Form C. 2118.

Instructions regarding War Diaries and Intelligence Summaries are contained in F.S. Regs., Part II. and the Staff Manual respectively. Title pages will be prepared in manuscript.

Place	Date	Hour	Summary of Events and Information	Remarks and references to Appendices
	26th Thurs.		NEW LISTER 3 KILOMET SEL at arrive from ATHERALE arrangements made to put down Sec. m at TRESCAULT. Corps maintenance train try had. Contacts or permanents.	
	27 Fri		Work in cars be continued, indurrance made to restore the Retirement train. & Cable for twin town up Sunshine in nearly all temperances.	
	28 Sat		Bi, it Sykes TERY Tanks to meet L.C. Division Coy for RWY. India resumable again. Letter from Bno Bone to suspend twin while ones on Ground. twin suspended. Trucks still on Corps train. chiefs from Staff of Corps remain. 8th CORPS proceeded on Leave.	
	30th Sun.		Rainy all day. 9/10 Border withdrawn from Leav. More twin traine Coys twin try had arrived. There was outburst. Heavy attack on G3 on front. twin tram forward. Corps Conference at 2.C. STON. preparations made for twin when action from front taken over.	

(A7092) Wt. W12896/M1293 75,000 6/17. D.D. & L., Ltd. Forms/Carr864.

Army Form C. 2118.

WAR DIARY
or
INTELLIGENCE SUMMARY.
(Erase heading not required.)

Instructions regarding War Diaries and Intelligence Summaries are contained in F. S. Regs., Part II. and the Staff Manual respectively. Title pages will be prepared in manuscript.

Place	Date	Hour	Summary of Events and Information	Remarks and references to Appendices
	31st Mar		Buried cable D5 laid Flesselles 7th Div HQ whilst was partly running south through Tarqui was relaid slight crew. accident with Car in execution. Head again tried to Flesquieres but did not succeeded to do great. Exchange at DR now working onto the 4/T communication network established between On Hd at Flesquieres DR at present GDB HPMO working well in that Div area. New permanent lines traced out between with GD5 in reserve.	

9 Thro 255 SQ.

Khrushchay Capt
Commanding 17th Signal Coy. R.E.

SECRET AND CONFIDENTIAL

WAR DIARY

OF

17TH DIVL. SIGNAL COY. R.E.

JANUARY 1918.

VOL 31.

Army Form C. 2118.

WAR DIARY
OF
INTELLIGENCE SUMMARY.
(Erase heading not required.)

Instructions regarding War Diaries and Intelligence Summaries are contained in F.S. Regs., Part II. and the Staff Manual respectively. Title pages will be prepared in manuscript.

IN THE FIELD

Place	Date	Hour	Summary of Events and Information	Remarks and references to Appendices
	Jan 1			
	2			
	3			

Place	Date	Hour	Summary of Events and Information	Remarks and references to Appendices
	Jan 4			

Army Form C. 2118.

WAR DIARY
or
INTELLIGENCE SUMMARY.
(Erase heading not required.)

Instructions regarding War Diaries and Intelligence Summaries are contained in F. S. Regs., Part II. and the Staff Manual respectively. Title pages will be prepared in manuscript.

Place	Date	Hour	Summary of Events and Information	Remarks and references to Appendices
	7	10 pm	3" Inf Bde relieved the 141 Bde of 47 D. 1st Inf Bde to Mazingarbe 2nd Inf Bde to Bully Les Mines 3rd Inf Bde to Sailly Labourse. O.B. — 90 + 91 cancelled. Report of 3rd Div Arty arrangements O.B. Returns from Divisions for transport accommodation O.O. 70 N=	
	8	to 7/23	Heavy rain N/T all attention at Brigades & 1st Division H.Q. Orders published to cancel O.O. 70 Gives arrangements re move by bus. R. of Reinforcements to be recommended after 7 Days.	
	9	Wed	Excellent statement of Men at Duty states the most unfavourable condition re refurbishing Sciatica was prevalent.
— Diary phrased
3 Trans to office complete with list — 3º Inf Bde with 15 offs NCO reported to 95	

(40091) Wt.W9090 M.293 750,000 9/17 D. D. & L. Ltd. Forms/C2118/24.

WAR DIARY
or
INTELLIGENCE SUMMARY.
(Erase heading not required.)

Army Form C. 2118.

*Instructions regarding War Diaries and Intelligence Summaries are contained in F. S. Regs., Part II. and the Staff Manual respectively. Title pages will be prepared in manuscript.

Place	Date	Hour	Summary of Events and Information	Remarks and references to Appendices
	13.	Sun	Various parties out in forward area collecting cable. Harness inspected. 1 working party going to relief in line. Lines traced & patrolled. 1 C.S.M. proceeds on LEAVE.	
	14 15 16 17		Work on forward lines proceeded with. New lines from Bdes forward laid & some of the old lines picked up. Work in trenches carried on in spite of inclement weather. Cable laid to about 500 yds up Portsmouth Lane. Visual communication from front line Bns to central transmitter back to Bde working OK. F.O.O. Officer consulted with regards to doing out & test points on buried cable route. 6.45 am Stables parade for [illegible]. Company [illegible]. Lines maintained & repaired during stormy weather. Car returns from Boulogne after repair.	
	18		Trench for buried cable [illegible]. Cable reeled up & Bde lines overhauled & repaired. Rain, roads in very bad condition.	

Army Form C. 2118.

WAR DIARY
or
INTELLIGENCE SUMMARY.
(Erase heading not required.)

Instructions regarding War Diaries and Intelligence Summaries are contained in F. S. Regs., Part II. and the Staff Manual respectively. Title pages will be prepared in manuscript.

Place	Date	Hour	Summary of Events and Information	Remarks and references to Appendices
IN THE FIELD	Jan 1		OC:U Hd Field asmn. 7/H Irish chased cattle & relief up from @ hotpoint 8747 Two Two pack Two to Dirt Dump via 19 item good & event. Pt of H Sykes Not Round enemy line from St 5 Buett2 reported very qt.	
	2		Lrumun m/c rel. El. Event enr/m to St Bx of Inter Sloss round. One pack Tr; to Beet in event in fans cattle normal YTres Beet went attacked. Returning from Lens to Remiere returnd Signal Octo to enemy cullen bonney Trake harry.	
	3		Irumun m/c art to pulse out of S" Bx of Inty Cattle from YTR5s Beet went to received in SS Should reed from @ test pt & Barbue to Bufance? pt cattle noise no new shot took tornnho continues.	

Army Form C. 2118.

WAR DIARY
or
INTELLIGENCE SUMMARY.
(Erase heading not required.)

Place	Date	Hour	Summary of Events and Information	Remarks and references to Appendices
	Jan 4		4/th Cable tested in ① - Finish leaving up to Bde. Diagram Dumo continued. OB & 19 return to Bde Section brought in. Lines to 57 & 17 Bde working. After a semi-permanent route brought down by motor lorry further tests to be put up to morrow.	
	5		F. 16 Supp Bde. Liaison between 57 & 53 Brist & arrange lines for 53. When necessary to Stonewall Castor Turner Bas to Ypse. Party set to repair semi-permanent route SN - Bde Cable tested up to Neuville & guinoire.	
	6		Wire cable tested up. OB & H obstructed in from Fleurbaix. Trouble in driven in of 74 Trench. Work on line tested & repaired. Fires continuing. B. Cureio & 77th assembled near Bde tested 07 & 8 near all assembled line SN 58 at 7.30	

WAR DIARY
or
INTELLIGENCE SUMMARY

(Erase heading not required.)

Army Form C. 2118.

Place	Date	Hour	Summary of Events and Information	Remarks and references to Appendices
	7	MN	57 Inf Bde relieved by 141 Bde of 47 Div to Hazincourt. 52 Inf Bde Hd Qrs from Tancourt to Corée Bank. QBs – 9th MD station reports to 57 Bde drive. H. Murphy. O/C S/Rs reports from Hargicourt to B007043.	
	8	Tues	Stationary. N/7 at disposal at Br HQ. 8 its actor. 5000 buried wire & gas reach. 8500 numbered markers reserve wire. New communication with drive. R. & Britannic trenches & communication A/F Sykes to 4/7 Div.	
	9	Wed	Extreme stationary attacks to Bde across & Hargicourt. Bund orderlies to Bde ranks & reproduction in town on 8th Bn complete orders sent up by 57 & 52 Bdes with rest in forward area. DD S/L Collin in afternoon.	

WAR DIARY
or
INTELLIGENCE SUMMARY.
(Erase heading not required.)

Army Form C. 2118.

Place	Date	Hour	Summary of Events and Information	Remarks and references to Appendices
	10 Thurs		Great excitement. Boche probably attack. 50" Bn moved up from from [?] to Pinon [?] to S.H. Sec. H/T reinforced at 5 Fort Garré. O.C. T.M's working at cable picked up. They state Germans trench still continued. Offrs & working parts of Prince Patricia's cable, did not return up to Pincoat. Wired line prev Strong. Wire from On Major George St. to corner R Lentre Cable repair in	
	11		Weather cold, but still thaw. Working parts of 3rd from 4 coys. 50" Bn report at 7.30. At 8.30 am. P. working on Pens trench. French stated from Pruith's to Portsdown trench ground where trench not complete. No 10-12 noon 1.30 to P finished, & Line & 9's to coy. Cattle a trois armoured lorries, their train CB & fleur trench [?] another reinforcement from 5th to Queestrig.	
	12		50" Bn report at 7.30 am. O.C. 573's the coy [?]	

Army Form C. 2118.

WAR DIARY
or
INTELLIGENCE SUMMARY.
(Erase heading not required.)

Instructions regarding War Diaries and Intelligence Summaries are contained in F. S. Regs., Part II. and the Staff Manual respectively. Title pages will be prepared in manuscript.

Place	Date	Hour	Summary of Events and Information	Remarks and references to Appendices
	13.	Sun.	Parties ferried out to Steamers collecting cable. Harbour officials informing parties now stuck in 2 m³ into dock & retrieved. C.S.O. proceeded in Liffey.	
	14.		Work on shore and on proceeded with. New crew from Gare forward train & crew officers picked up. Forth & Bury arrived on parade.	
	15.		Picking up return cable laid to shore so you up Dartmouth Lane. Naval communication from Erie Bro to central transmitter test office.	
	16.			
	17.		Jersey F.S. F & S.O. officer conducted attempts to carry out & tie points on burial cable laid to Unsuan cloth forme on shore company navigates too maintained & repaired during stormy weather. Cartwrighting from Dartmouth after repair.	
	18.		Search for broken cable proceeded with. Cable picked up & Bale torn & refuelled & repaired. Term made as any end condition.	

Army Form C. 2118.

WAR DIARY
or
INTELLIGENCE SUMMARY.
(Erase heading not required.)

Instructions regarding War Diaries and Intelligence Summaries are contained in F. S. Regs., Part II. and the Staff Manual respectively. Title pages will be prepared in manuscript.

Place	Date	Hour	Summary of Events and Information	Remarks and references to Appendices
	19		Shaw exit continued, trains becoming impassable. Corps training cable scheme proceeded with in addition to D.V.N.I. scheme.	
	20		Trench board work. D.V.N.I. Senior School. 25-30mm returned for further instruction.	
	21		Finished instruction. Central reserve dugout proceeded with. T.S.T. Scheme Corps Strategy completed.	
	22		Carried cable to radio proceeded with. Geopoint's put in.	
	23		Corps Shooting. Royal met Revt. Rev to reprose training at D to D.V.N.I. S.G.S.O.4. had the honour to lunch with the Divisional Commander and the Brigade Major, also had tea with the R.E. Major from the 17th Brigade.	
	24		Never received action information regularly sincerely	

Army Form C. 2118.

WAR DIARY
or
INTELLIGENCE SUMMARY.
(Erase heading not required.)

Instructions regarding War Diaries and Intelligence Summaries are contained in F. S. Regs., Part II. and the Staff Manual respectively. Title pages will be prepared in manuscript.

Place	Date	Hour	Summary of Events and Information	Remarks and references to Appendices
	25		Cattles reached us Each day. Working parties on Bee Berry, but new improvements from the Bns to left. 8th not relieving to 4th Bns. Weather still last. All companies Strong also found out now to Divide platoons. Now in our strong organisations as for Divs. took time make up.	
	26		Scheme. By bombing such weapons & Aircraft. Hun Brig & 43 Divs cut section killed on course front. Reliefs from today all as say. Aid Bn Berry forward his Companions from Barns + Balmoral etc.	
	27		B. to south. 117 August October organised for week. ... to Sharpin to So IB. to tile our Hd after referral Tho at Hague ... ... Tho at Hague. The Bureau. Hd Tenn. Hd Tres.	

Army Form C. 2118.

WAR DIARY
or
INTELLIGENCE SUMMARY.

(Erase heading not required.)

Instructions regarding War Diaries and Intelligence Summaries are contained in F. S. Regs., Part II. and the Staff Manual respectively. Title pages will be prepared in manuscript.

Place	Date	Hour	Summary of Events and Information	Remarks and references to Appendices
	24 Cont.		Weather clear & moonlight, greatest of bombing activity further & front.	
	28		Weather mild. all buries proceeded with nothing further to report.	
	29		Inter Brigade bury completed from R Bn HQrs to Tyne Cot. 3 ldr. points now completed in 50D1 120D Bde. Corps bury completed to Freenies [illegible] road. 3 points ready for junctions. Moonlight & frequent bombing.	
	30		Work on buried cable routes proceeded with, owing to visibility party in open had to bury and not work. Weather good quiet night. Cpl. Tabor & 20 signals proceeded on leave.	
	31		15 O.R.s also proceeded on leave. Weather mild, all work proceeded with nothing further of importance to report.	

Commanding 17th Signal Coy, R.E.
1/2/18.

Army Form C. 2118.

Instructions regarding War Diaries and Intelligence Summaries are contained in F. S. Regs., Part II. and the Staff Manual respectively. Title pages will be prepared in manuscript.

WAR DIARY
or
INTELLIGENCE SUMMARY.
(Erase heading not required.)

Place	Date	Hour	Summary of Events and Information	Remarks and references to Appendices
[illegible]	1		All work on buried cable routes proceeded with.	
			Main [illegible] Road cut & cable laid, road bridged over by sleepers. [illegible] beyond the road	
	2		[illegible] at night, all main permanent routes down [illegible]	
			Poles falling in all directions.	
			[illegible]	
			permanent [illegible]	
			9.30 pm [illegible]	
			all traffic [illegible]	
			All working O.K. by [illegible]	
			Buried cable route between [illegible] completed.	
			[illegible]	
			[illegible] to [illegible] Signal School	

Army Form C. 2118.

WAR DIARY
or
INTELLIGENCE SUMMARY.
(Erase heading not required.)

Instructions regarding War Diaries and Intelligence Summaries are contained in F.S. Regs., Part II. and the Staff Manual respectively. Title pages will be prepared in manuscript.

Place	Date	Hour	Summary of Events and Information	Remarks and references to Appendices
Fell	7th		Fete no new in lines with covers. All fits they could no TK	
"	8th		I m L nation Divinal thangaton all not on heave with works proceed with Rowing under all the day Whenlion ding out stated with fit going the	
"	9th			
"	10th		A longs working party in, working one human work to day to with any difficult only to track any late light ale to use weather fair	
"	11		All off personne right taking to justice preserve welcome appear confuter afford to maintain precaution in some in out in morning that in time to accident non internal at at tigarty to take care is surrise hickory from again from 5 any to sunbyphane at large that cultura Norman offence times up of preparation	
"	12			
"	13			
"	14			

WAR DIARY
or
INTELLIGENCE SUMMARY.
(Erase heading not required.)

Army Form C. 2118.

Instructions regarding War Diaries and Intelligence Summaries are contained in F. S. Regs., Part II. and the Staff Manual respectively. Title pages will be prepared in manuscript.

Place	Date	Hour	Summary of Events and Information	Remarks and references to Appendices
Fri	Feb 15		Weather clear & frosty. Both sides cutting wires in positions. No enemy further shelled.	
	16		Weather good. Nothing clear & new. Enemy very tempting. Shelled Boston B 57 7 B M L Q 20.16 & Hopwood	
	17		Nothing much to report except lights between 61-7 & Z at Bois O. Stag Trench & some cable Pte Stb 40 Pay Corp Harrow guard dog no 3pfs 2/4th Penn [FS?] 53 1st [?] on No Standard & M I School B & G drill.	
	18		No enemy fire. Weather cold & very few BE attached to Coy reconnoitred groups pictures the enemy position to report.	

Instructions regarding War Diaries and Intelligence Summaries are contained in F. S. Regs., Part II. and the Staff Manual respectively. Title pages will be prepared in manuscript.

WAR DIARY
or
INTELLIGENCE SUMMARY.
(Erase heading not required.)

Army Form C. 2118.

Place	Date	Hour	Summary of Events and Information	Remarks and references to Appendices
[illegible]	19		Working party on Spoil Heap [illegible] [illegible]. 1 NCO & [illegible] men to Bertincourt to prepare HQ [illegible]. Capt [illegible] now [illegible] to [illegible] [illegible] [illegible] [illegible] [illegible]. Weather still very good [illegible] but cold	
	20		Working party for Spoil Heap [illegible] of [illegible]. [illegible] [illegible] in Slag Alley. [illegible] by [illegible] [illegible] working hard enough. Working party [illegible] until 5.45 pm when [illegible] [illegible] by Coy Comdr. Working [illegible] of [illegible] [illegible]. Weather [illegible] [illegible] but holding out.	
	21		Weather good & clear. Working party of [illegible] on [illegible] [illegible] and [illegible] [illegible] [illegible]. Capt [illegible] also [illegible]	
	22		All work on [illegible] until [illegible] with New Headquarters at Bertincourt going on [illegible]. Capt [illegible] [illegible] on month leave	

(A7092). Wt W12830/M1293 75,000. 1/17. D. D. & L., Ltd. Forms/C.2118/14.

WAR DIARY
or
INTELLIGENCE SUMMARY.

Place	Date	Hour	Summary of Events and Information	Remarks and references to Appendices
[illegible]	23		All were [illegible] and [illegible] at [illegible] Headquarters at Bethencourt. Army [illegible] and [illegible] settle in town.	
	24		Move to new Headquarters at Bethencourt. New office about next to army [illegible]. Unable [illegible] also noticed as 5 = points.	
	25		No [illegible] had [illegible] Spent that day in Capt [illegible] [illegible] [illegible] [illegible] [illegible] No [illegible] [illegible] to Spent that [illegible] but [illegible] [illegible] [illegible] up to the [illegible]. I the [illegible] that late Army being however not very [illegible] are [illegible] in Bethencourt [illegible] as [illegible] in [illegible] [illegible]. Bad [illegible].	
	26		Party of 50 men or [illegible] that [illegible] now begun being made out by Army [illegible] and Laws + [illegible] [illegible] to Brigades [illegible] regulated [illegible] from [illegible] other [illegible] B [illegible] a new [illegible] and [illegible] and new [illegible] [illegible] another few	

WAR DIARY
of
INTELLIGENCE SUMMARY.
(Erase heading not required.)

Army Form C. 2118.

Instructions regarding War Diaries and Intelligence Summaries are contained in F. S. Regs., Part II. and the Staff Manual respectively. Title pages will be prepared in manuscript.

Place	Date	Hour	Summary of Events and Information	Remarks and references to Appendices
Ju-	27		Cold, dark & dull. Half men detailed to care of horses, working party of 50 or so. Spent time in lifting dry providing to sent for any long marches and resting in huts. Nothing to Record.	
	28		Bruise cold & dull. Half on field and new ones) for full use. Left Headquarters at h. Bois Hueppuston Potanteau under Capt Lea Prescott with now BERTIN 40305, who got involved in other muddles with Signal office keep unused papers being sent in clearing them over in Restaurant. Such strongth of 2/7/16. Officers 9 O.R. 272 Total 281	

Graut Lt
Major
In

Vol 32

17th Signal Coy, Royal Engineers.

WAR DIARY.

Vol: 32.

February 1918.

Secret & Confidential

WAR DIARY
INTELLIGENCE SUMMARY
(Erase heading not required.)

Army Form C. 2118.

Place	Date	Hour	Summary of Events and Information	Remarks and references to Appendices
F.E.	1		All work in forest cable proceeded with from HERNIES Road cut & cable laid. Road trieed on by SLEEPERS. Enemy now come & go beyond the tree.	
	2		Heavy frost at night, all main permanent works down. ALL to everybody kept @ Co at P.STEEN. @D.R.s taking in all direction. Inside DG took to SO to aerie country. Permanent Tournean Pt. & the two pre through about 9.30 am. in Terme. Cliff musicians Pont rebite all traffic stopped & with our gradewear all working DR by night-fall. OVERHEAD route between Baba thence to Y & Baba complete. Lt OSTOBY returns from N/F export school absowhe Lt OSTOBY to joins Signal School.	

Army Form C. 2118.

WAR DIARY
INTELLIGENCE SUMMARY.
(Erase heading not required.)

Instructions regarding War Diaries and Intelligence Summaries are contained in F.S. Regs., Part II. and the Staff Manual respectively. Title pages will be prepared in manuscript.

Place	Date	Hour	Summary of Events and Information	Remarks and references to Appendices
Sm	3		Weather fine & mild. Trio on new nits. Sale Busy taking up	
			Division D8 Hq. and trench & replace armoured wire	
			in previous position round Bn. Hq. nos. Trio run	
			also on Bny wires.	
			Trench Stores for cables from permanent Bn.	
	4		entrance to Bry. ok. 3 to 6 men working only.	
			Corps DIrnt. Trios still going strong.	
	5		Weather mild & fine. Nothing further to report.	
			Bn. Lieut. allotment as for the Company during	
			the month. All wire forward with	
			cable pens across Hoomies road Trench filled in	
			Bry. now duty through in service wires between two	
	6		new towns at D.Trk. Signal School started.	
			C.S.M. to Octrode for 4 to 10 days.	

Nil. anything further to report.

Army Form C. 2118.

WAR DIARY
or
INTELLIGENCE SUMMARY
(Erase heading not required.)

Place	Date	Hour	Summary of Events and Information	Remarks and references to Appendices
Feb	7th		Fatigue men on lines and covers. Cable job being carried on etc.	
"	8th		C. in C. visited Divisional Headquarters. Cable work on forward cable routes previous nth. Raining nearly all the day.	
"	9th		Wireless dug-out started. Cable job going OK.	
"	10th		Cd large working party 200, working on Aruine route to clay dugouts. Work very difficult owing to trenches being water logged due to recent rain. Weather fine.	
	11		All not provided with working kit. Maintenance report. Further gunner cable clothing to forward positions more or not may have to be moved to horsemen. Wired at to horsemen.	
	12			
	13		Cable down in trenches leading from Hyrne Wood to dug out. Working party cut Scape Trench. Callcen moved. Plans to trench up by Hyperatus	
	14			

Army Form C. 2118.

WAR DIARY
or
INTELLIGENCE SUMMARY
(Erase heading not required.)

Instructions regarding War Diaries and Intelligence Summaries are contained in F. S. Regs., Part II. and the Staff Manual respectively. Title pages will be prepared in manuscript.

Place	Date	Hour	Summary of Events and Information	Remarks and references to Appendices
Ypres	26/2/15		Weather clear & frosty. Both batteries entrenched in progress. Nothing further to report.	
	16		Weather good, night's clear & not much shrapnel from enemy. No. Battle to 57/1.D. nei ut SECEN& is hostile	
	17		Morning bright & see on ground during between 6 & 7 & 1/2 hrs fire in SLAG ALLEY & several cases of SSO's tack fell clear. Harass, several day we on testing 2/Lt FENN 6. 53/1.D. nei to Dunlop to M/T 2/Lt SERVILLE	
	5		evening quiet. Weather still very good. Entrenched camp reconstruction nearing, practically finished. Nothing further to report.	

Army Form C. 2118.

WAR DIARY
or
INTELLIGENCE SUMMARY

(Erase heading not required.)

Place	Date	Hour	Summary of Events and Information	Remarks and references to Appendices
January	19		[illegible handwritten entry] 1 NCO & 8 men to Beaucourt to prepare HQ there. Capt Bury now attached to the New Scheme. 5/T/S Cpl Smith. Weather still very good.	
	20		Working party for SD & steel report of BDO. Shots filed. Shifted by SS for 22 mo. dugouts at Stars Alley. Working parties preparing new huts when liberated demounted by Gen Corps. Heavy artillery to New Regs. [illegible] of huts but waiting in the [?]	
	21		Weather good. Clear. Working party & 100 w Shrub Hut and one [illegible] preparing [illegible] Cap. Bury also preparing	
	22		All quiet on front line. Worked with New Headquarters at Beaucourt going on alright. Cap. Bury worked in [illegible]	

Army Form C. 2118.

WAR DIARY
of
INTELLIGENCE SUMMARY.
(Erase heading not required.)

Instructions regarding War Diaries and Intelligence Summaries are contained in F.S. Regs., Part II. and the Staff Manual respectively. Title pages will be prepared in manuscript.

Place	Date	Hour	Summary of Events and Information	Remarks and references to Appendices
Jer:	23		All ranks being passed out. Iron Ck. Mer Headquarters at Belmont being lent out and well in hand.	
	24		Moved to new Headquarters at Belmont. New office Shack without any trestle. Electric light also installed at 3 x points	
	25		No working party on April 14th being Cup Day. Continued next day with two clip steely April 14th being but cable being laid. No working party for April 14th, for cable being laid up to position of the outside trench. Capt. Ivey being "promoted out". Many wounds now H——— in Birkenwood Estes are white in Weather fair. Bad morning.	
	26		Party of 50 men on April 14th kept busy, two bogies being made out being busy front out. Down in permanent rose to Brigade.	
			No "B" hole, main tunnel not detailed out and poke Static. Weather fair. being regulates. Road from Epul after	

WAR DIARY
or
INTELLIGENCE SUMMARY

Army Form C. 2118.

(Erase heading not required.)

Instructions regarding War Diaries and Intelligence Summaries are contained in F. S. Regs., Part II. and the Staff Manual respectively. Title pages will be prepared in manuscript.

Place	Date	Hour	Summary of Events and Information	Remarks and references to Appendices
HQ	27		Cables laid to Spoil Heap and started to ode of trench. Working party of 50 on Spoil Heap being busy providing as much food as being made and resting in spare when in Betinenent.	
	28		Bornies cable to Spoil Heap completed and now ready for pull use. Up buy ready up to Bde Headquarters. Rehensions made to dry house cable namer BERTIN COURT, which when completed will allow memphily cable to Signal Office being removed. Progress being made in clearing stone mans being removed. Meade strong in Betinement.	

Strength of by 28/7/16.
Officers 9
O.R.s 272
Total 281

[signature] Major
Commanding 177th Signal Coy. R.E.

www.ingramcontent.com/pod-product-compliance
Lightning Source LLC
Chambersburg PA
CBHW081427300426
44108CB00016BA/2321